ire I

ENCYCLOPEDIA OF
ELITE FORCES
IN THE SECOND WORLD WAR

ENCYCLOPEDIA OF
ELITE FORCES
IN THE SECOND WORLD WAR

MICHAEL E. HASKEW

Pen &
Sword
MILITARY

This edition first published in 2007 by
Pen & Sword Books Ltd
47 Church Street
Barnsley
South Yorkshire
S70 2AS

ISBN: 978-1-8-441-5577-4

Editorial and design by
Amber Books Ltd
Bradley's Close
74–77 White Lion Street
London N1 9PF
www.amberbooks.co.uk

Project Editor: Michael Spilling
Designer: Jerry Williams
Picture Research: Terry Forshaw

Printed and bound in Dubai

CONTENTS

INTRODUCTION

The concept of elite military forces is nearly as ancient as the military itself. Since the dawn of history, men at arms have distinguished themselves as members of formations that may have been constituted with elite status as a prerequisite or as members of units whose reputation is gained in the crucible of combat. The army of ancient Assyria conquered vast territory and may be considered the first standing army in the world. The military prowess of Sparta was evidenced by the epic stand of its hoplites at Thermopylae. The bodyguard of Persian King Xerxes, known as the Immortals, were sworn to defend the monarch and offer their lives at

British soldiers of the Long Range Desert Group pose in front of their heavily armed Chevrolet trucks in the North African Desert, 1942.

his command. Perhaps no other elite force in history has influenced Western civilization like the legions of Imperial Rome.

DISTINCTIVE CAPABILITIES

The establishment of elite forces was a logical progression during the feudal period and the Middle Ages, both East and West. The epic stand of Roland, protecting the rear of Charlemagne's army will be remembered forever. The Mongol hordes of Genghis Khan struck fear in the capitals of Europe. The samurai, or warrior class, developed in Japan, and King Arthur's legendary Knights of the Roundtable were an elite force steeped in fact, myth and legend.

On land, at sea, and later in the air, combat commands with distinctive capabilities, incredible

An Sd Kfz 232 armoured car from the elite SS division **Hitler Jugend** *passes through rubble in the town of Caen amidst the fighting following the D-Day landings, June 1944.*

as well as for the irregular forces of Francis Marion, who came to be known as the Swamp Fox. The elite shock troops of General Daniel Morgan won the day for the Colonials at Cowpens. The American Civil War produced a number of elite units in both in Northern blue and Confederate grey. Colonel Hiram Berdan's Sharpshooters were renowned for their accuracy with the rifle, while the raiders of Colonel John Singleton Mosby so controlled an area of Northern Virginia that it came to be known as Mosby's Confederacy. The 'foot cavalry' of General Stonewall Jackson and General John Gibbon's famed Iron Brigade opposed one another on the battlefield.

During World War I, elite Prussian units populated the Kaiser's German army, while Baron Manfred von Richthofen's Flying Circus was the scourge of Allied air forces. The German High Seas Fleet and the British Royal Navy were the pride of their respective nations and fought to a tactical draw at the Battle of Jutland.

By 1939, the armed forces of virtually every industrialized nation around the globe included elite units. During the opening hours of World War II, soldiers of Germany's Brandenburger Regiment, wearing Polish uniforms, facilitated their army's advance with clandestine raids on border crossing sites and radio broadcast facilities. Throughout World War II, elite forces were employed by every army, accepting the challenges and the inherent risks of the most dangerous operations. Through courage, stealth, and determination, these units ensured the perpetuation of their kind for military generations to come.

bravery, and recognized *esprit de corps* became symbols of both respect and dread.

During the age of empire, the Great Armada of King Phillip of Spain was destroyed by a relative few, yet intrepid warships of Queen Elizabeth's navy, and England was saved. Sir Francis Drake, the Queen's privateer captain, harassed the Spanish and plundered their gold ships returning from the New World. As Napoleon ravaged the European continent, the Emperor's Imperial Guard established a new standard for excellence among elite troops, while the army of the Duke of Wellington was championed by such famous fighting units as his elite Foot Guards, who defended the Chateau of Hougoumont during the Battle of Waterloo.

The American Revolution was the stage for the marauding British cavalry leader Banastre Tarleton,

UNITS
LAND
The Belgian SAS
The French Foreign Legion
French Special Air Service

AIR
Normandie-Niemen Squadron

BELGIUM AND FRANCE

Their countries overrun by the Nazi aggressors, a large number of fighting men from Belgium and France found their way to Great Britain and enlisted in a variety of units, some retaining the distinction of their national origin, while others became members of the British military. Throughout the war, the soldiers of the SAS, the French Foreign Legion, and the Normandie-Niemen Squadron resisted the enemy and upheld their national honor, contributing significantly to the Allied victory and the liberation of their native lands.

THE BELGIAN SAS

- •FOUNDED: 1942
- •STRENGTH: 120
- •THEATRE: WESTERN EUROPE

In the spring of 1940, France and the Low Countries fell victim to the marauding German *Wehrmacht* following an extended period of inactivity along the Western Front which had become known as the 'Sitzkrieg'. Within a matter of weeks German forces had reached the English Channel, compelled the British Expeditionary Force to evacuate the

Left: An NCO from **13e Démi-Brigade Légion Étrangère** *(13e DBLE), proudly holds the brigade flag atop a truck in the North African desert, 1942.*

European continent at Dunkirk, and taken hundreds of thousands of prisoners. Organized resistance crumbled and the Belgian armed forces effectively ceased to exist.

Although their country was overrun, a large number of Belgian expatriates enlisted in the armed forces of the British Commonwealth, fighting in the air, on land and at sea. Often, these patriotic Belgians became members of standard British units. One exception, however, was the Belgian Independent Parachute Company (BIPC), which was formed at Malvern Wells, Worcester, on 8 May 1942, upon the order of Henry Rolin, the Undersecretary of Defence for the Belgian Government in exile.

Company A, 2nd Battalion Belgian Fusiliers, which consisted of volunteers from North and South America, and a platoon of the 1st Battalion Belgian Fusiliers consolidated with former members of the Belgian armed forces to form the BIPC, and paratroopers won their wings at the Ringway Parachute School in 1942. Further training took place in company with units of the British Special Air Service (SAS) at such locations as Inverlochy Castle in Scotland. By February 1944 the BIPC was formally absorbed into the SAS. Captain Eddy Blondeel, a resident of Ghent and an engineer in peacetime, commanded the unit, which was designated '5 SAS' and numbered about 130 men.

Members of 5 SAS participated in numerous operations behind German lines in the summer of

1944. Belgian SAS troopers often operated in small groups, disrupting enemy supply and communications, gathering intelligence, inflicting casualties and supporting advancing Allied units. In July 1944, during Operations Chaucer, Bunyan and Shakespeare, three teams of six men were dropped into northern France on reconnaissance missions. In August, three groups of 15 soldiers parachuted into the Perche hills in support.

The largest Belgian airborne action of the war occurred in August when 80 troopers parachuted into France east of the Falaise Pocket, from which thousands of retreating German troops were attempting to escape a rapidly closing trap. During Operation Trueform, members of 5 SAS harassed the enemy at every opportunity and kept Allied commanders apprised of the direction of German troop movements.

The Belgian SAS used heavily-armed jeeps that were ideal for quick raiding in the fighting that occured in the low countries in the spring of 1944.

ALLIED AND ORGANIZED

When eight members of 5 SAS parachuted into the Ardennes Forest of France on 15 August and moved across the border into Belgium, they became the first Allied soldiers to enter that country in more than four years. Soon after, a group of 11 soldiers were mistakenly dropped east of the enemy's Westwall defences, becoming the first organized Allied formation to enter Germany in World War II.

Several groups of SAS men fought in the Ardennes with highly mobile Jeeps, which had been parachuted to them. These Jeeps, equipped with Vickers machine guns, facilitated the hit-and-run tactics of the SAS. The Belgians took a heavy toll in the Ardennes, killing approximately 300 Germans and destroying 100 vehicles along with large stores of supplies. Near the Belgian town of Peer, elements of 5 SAS attacked a well protected battery of heavy artillery, destroying numerous guns and killing 52 Germans, with the loss of only a single trooper.

In support of Operation Market-Garden, the

ARMOURED JEEP

The heavily-armed Jeeps used by the SAS were driven into combat during operations involving only ground movement or parachuted to the soldiers during airborne missions. These rugged vehicles were reinforced with steel plating for added protection and armed with twin .30-caliber Vickers or Browning machine guns, or a combination of the two. With all guns in action, a single Jeep could fire up to 5,000 rounds per minute. The Vickers K weapon, originally an aircraft weapon, was well adapted to the hit-and-run tactics of the SAS. In order to carry the necessary fuel, food, and water, eeps were stripped of non-essential parts, including windshields, radiator grill bars, and bumpers. By the summer of 1942, the SAS operated 15 specially equipped jeeps in North Africa.

airborne invasion of the Netherlands in September 1944, the Belgian SAS troopers were dropped at numerous key positions. Before withdrawing in the spring of 1945, these men aided the escape of British airborne troops through German lines and transmitted intelligence on enemy troop dispositions. Another group parachuted into the Netherlands in October and remained there until the following April, training members of the Dutch resistance. One 5 SAS trooper was captured, brutally interrogated, and executed on 10 April.

DESPERATE FIGHTING

In the autumn of 1944, the men of 5 SAS were transferred to a Belgian base and reorganized for a primary mission of reconnaissance. The desperate fighting during the Battle of the Bulge required the unit to deploy in heavily armed Jeeps as a screening force for the right flank of the British 6th Airborne Division, while gathering intelligence and making contact with the left of the hard pressed US Army in the Ardennes.

Following its withdrawal to the Belgian port city of Antwerp, 5 SAS participated in Operation Larkswood in support of Canadian and Polish armoured and infantry units in the Netherlands. The paratroopers met stiff resistance from a German naval unit fighting as infantry at

Oosterhesselen and along the approaches to the town of Winschoten. During the Allied advance into Germany, 5 SAS was involved in bitter clashes with German troops as the Canadians and Poles pushed toward Emden and Wilhelmshaven. Two Belgian troopers were killed in action during the final week of the war.

Immediately after the unconditional surrender of Germany, 5 SAS was designated for counter-intelligence work and aided in efforts to apprehend fugitive leaders of the former Nazi government. The Belgians participated in the capture of Admiral Karl Doenitz, successor to Adolf Hitler, and members of his government at Flensburg. They also arrested Alfred Rosenberg, the leading Nazi philosopher and Reich Minister for Occupied Eastern Territories. A Belgian SAS member was among a group of men who surprised Nazi Foreign Minister Joachim von Ribbentrop, arresting him in his pyjamas in a Hamburg apartment.

From July 1944 to May 1945 the soldiers of 5 SAS constituted the only Belgian unit employed regularly in combat. Casualties suffered during operations in Western Europe totalled 16 killed and 58 wounded.

THE FRENCH FOREIGN LEGION

- •FOUNDED: 1931
- •STRENGTH: 2000
- •THEATRES: NORTH AFRICA, ITALY

Already a legendary fighting force at the outbreak of World War II, the French Foreign Legion was formed more than a century earlier, in the spring of 1831. At first, the nature of global war and the numerous nationalities represented within the ranks of the Legion posed problems for the French Government.

In particular, large numbers of Germans had traditionally served in the Legion, and on the eve of the war as much as 80 per cent of its non-commissioned officers were German. It quickly became apparent that the German intelligence service, the Abwehr, had begun to infiltrate the Legion, spreading Nazi doctrine, coercing and intimidating otherwise loyal German and non-German Legionnaires alike. The French Government dealt with this internal threat in part by dispatching many Germans to desert posts in

At the Battle of Gazala, the Legion played a crucial role in holding the Allied extreme left flank to protect the strategically important port of Tobruk.

North Africa or the Middle East. Elements of the Foreign Legion were also deployed as garrison troops on the Maginot Line, the string of fixed fortifications which stretched along France's border with Germany from the Swiss frontier to Belgium. Foreign Legion units were stationed in numerous locations around the world when the war began, and fighting men from as many as 50 different nations populated new Legion regiments, which were activated in the autumn of 1939.

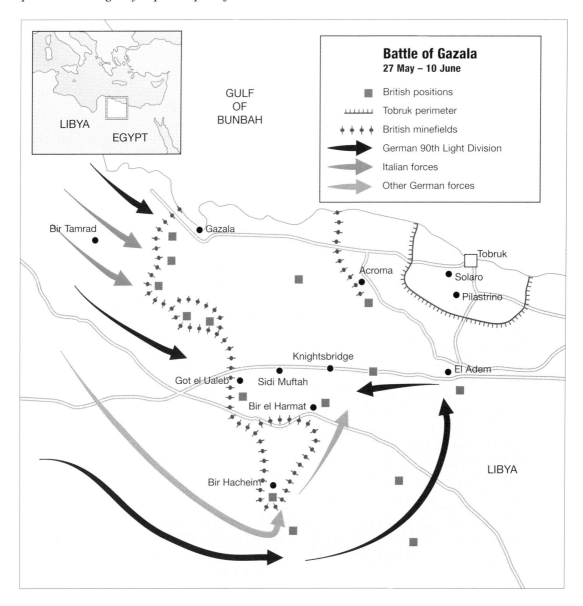

Legionnaires sprint across open desert during the
Battle of Bir Hacheim. The battle was a notable
success for the Legion, cementing the unit's reputation
as part of the Free French Forces in North Africa.

LEGIONNAIRE LEGENDS

The most famous and indeed the best travelled unit
of the French Foreign Legion during World War II
was the *13e Demi-Brigade*, which included a former
Russian prince and the only female Legionnaire,
Susan Travers. Commanded by Lieutenant Colonel
Magrin-Verneret, who was known by his alias as
Montclar, the 13e was originally ordered to Finland
to aid the heroic Finnish armed forces in the struggle
against the Soviet Union, which was an ally of Nazi
Germany in 1940. However, the hard-pressed Finns
were compelled to accept peace terms dictated by the
Soviets before the 13e could deploy.

In May 1940 the 13e was ordered to Norway as
a component of the 1st Light Division under the
command of General Marie Emile Béthouart. Other
units included the French 27th Chasseurs Alpin and
a brigade of expatriate Polish mountain troops. The
primary objective of the 13e was the capture of the
northern port of Narvik, which was held by a
regiment of German mountain troops under
General Eduard Dietl. In a brief but sharp clash at
the end of May the 13e, supported by warships of
the British Royal Navy and aircraft of the Royal Air
Force, succeeded in linking up with the Polish
troops and occupied Narvik after the Germans
evacuated the town.

Meanwhile, the Nazi *blitzkrieg* had been
unleashed on France and the Low Countries.
Defending portions of the Maginot Line, the 11th
Regiment held its position for two weeks in the face
of overwhelming German pressure, and lost more
than 2500 men – 85 per cent of its strength – before
withdrawing to North Africa.

DE GAULLE VERSUS VICHY

With the fall of France a new threat to the existence
of the Legion arose. The German Government
pressured Vichy France to disband the Legion and
allow soldiers from Axis nations and some of those
countries occupied by Axis forces to be released.

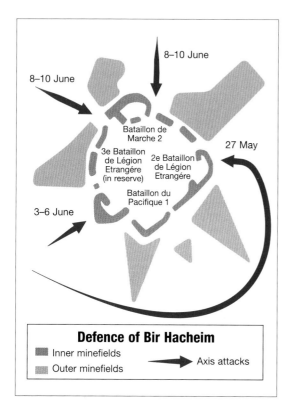

8–10 June

8–10 June

Bataillon de
Marche 2

3e Bataillon
de Légion
Etrangére
(in reserve)

2e Bataillon
de Légion
Etrangére

27 May

Bataillon du
Pacifique 1

3–6 June

Defence of Bir Hacheim

Inner minefields

Outer minefields → Axis attacks

At the Battle of Gazala, Bir Hacheim was the most important position in the defensive line. The men of 13e DBLE held off Axis forces for two weeks before withdrawing after taking heavy casualties. Their brave defence imposed serious delay on Rommel's advance toward Tobruk.

About 1000 German soldiers requested discharges, and the Legion itself fractured into factions either loyal to the puppet Vichy government or to the Free French forces under the command of General Charles de Gaulle. The *13e Demi-Brigade* lost an entire battalion, which was disbanded in Morocco. Other Legion units located in the Middle East, North Africa and French Indochina remained under Vichy control.

In June 1940 the *13e Demi-Brigade* took part in an abortive expedition by de Gaulle to French West Africa in the hope of wresting that colony and its large port of Dakar from Vichy control. The Legionnaires never left their transport ships after it became apparent that the opposing force was loyal

to Vichy and an assault would be doomed to failure. After several months in the Cameroons the *13e Demi-Brigade* once again loaded aboard transport vessels. This time the long voyage ended at Port Sudan, where the brigade was to support British offensive efforts against the Italian Army in Eritrea.

In a difficult fight near the village of Keren several hundred Italian prisoners were captured. Following their victory the soldiers of the 13th were ordered to assault Fort Victor Emanuele, which protected the harbour city of Massawa on the Red Sea. Fighting hand to hand against Italian defenders inside the fort and in the surrounding countryside, the Legionnaires captured their objective. At the end of a spectacular three-month campaign the Italians had been completely ejected from Eritrea.

BATTLE FOR DAMASCUS

In the summer of 1941 the *13e Demi-Brigade* was the nucleus of a French force which was ordered to the Middle East. The area comprising modern Syria and Lebanon, known as the Levant at that time, had been under French mandate since the armistice which ended World War I.

As the German Afrika Korps under Field Marshal Erwin Rommel advanced toward the Egyptian frontier, the Vichy government was obliged to provide assistance. Now, General Henri Dentz commanded a sizable force of Vichy loyalists which included the Legion's 6th Regiment and numbered over 30,000.

Legionnaire fought Legionnaire during a bitter battle for the city of Damascus as the *13e Demi-Brigade* and British Commonwealth forces struggled to end the threat of Vichy assistance should Rommel capture Cairo and seize control of the Suez Canal. Damascus fell on 21 July and many survivors of the 6th Regiment elected to join the 13e.

Some Vichy Legion units briefly opposed Operation Torch, the US Army landings on the beaches at Oran, Algiers and Casablanca in North Africa. A number of these, however, also joined the Allied side and fought the Germans during the final months of the war in North Africa. The *13e Demi-Brigade*, meanwhile, joined the British Eighth Army in pursuit of Rommel following General Bernard Montgomery's stunning victory at El Alamein. By

1944 a number of previously scattered Legion units, including the *13e Demi-Brigade*, were combined into a single regiment which participated in the liberation of Rome and landed at Toulon in southern France. Legionnaires crossed the Rhine River into Germany, with the 13e capturing Colmar on 2 February 1945, and other elements of the regiment taking Stuttgart. By the end of the war this consolidated Legion regiment had advanced eastward across the Danube River and into Austria.

The record of the French Foreign Legion in World War II is nothing short of remarkable, particularly in light of the fact that the legendary unit was, for a time, at war with itself.

Gathered on a street in a German city at the end of World War II, members of the battle hardened French SAS pause for a photograph.

FRENCH SPECIAL AIR SERVICE

- •FOUNDED: 1941
- •STRENGTH: 500
- •THEATRE: WESTERN EUROPE

With its roots in the pre-World War II airborne units of the French Army and the Free French parachute formations organized in North Africa in September 1940, the French Special Air Service was patterned after its British counterpart, actually serving as the 3rd and 4th squadrons of the British SAS brigade.

In September 1941 Captain Georges Bergé, who is acknowledged as the father of the French SAS, persuaded General Charles de Gaulle to permit his

1st Compagnie de Chasseurs Parachutistes to become the 3rd SAS Squadron. Bergé and SAS founder Lieutenant David Stirling cooperated in training and operational efforts. While many of the Frenchmen were already experienced in airborne operations, recruits trained alongside Polish and British soldiers at several locations in Britain, including Largo, near the Firth of Forth in Scotland.

During the summer and autumn of 1942 the French SAS participated in numerous raids behind German lines in North Africa, attacking airfields and supply bases along the Libyan coast of the Mediterranean. Bergé was captured during an airborne action on the island of Crete and held as a prisoner of war at the infamous Colditz Castle in Germany. In December 1942 a second SAS squadron was formed in North Africa. By February 1943 both French squadrons had been relocated to Britain. A March 1943 reorganization resulted in the two French squadrons being designated the 1st and 2nd Air Infantry Battalions. A third air infantry battalion was recruited in the Middle East and North Africa and arrived in Britain at the end of 1943. These units were redesignated the 3rd and 4th SAS Squadrons in January 1944.

D-DAY AND AFTER

The French SAS squadrons contributed to the success of the Normandy landings on 6 June 1944, as troopers of the 4th were dropped into Brittany during the pre-dawn hours of D-Day. Establishing drop zones for the insertion of more airborne troops and contacting members of the Resistance, these SAS men set ambushes, blocked roads and severed enemy communications in a successful effort to prevent German reinforcements from reaching the landing beaches on the Norman coast. At peak strength in Normandy, the French SAS units never numbered more than 450 men; however, small teams known as 'cooney parties' harassed German troop movements and wrought havoc wherever possible.

Standing at attention, an honour guard of the French SAS prepares for inspection. Two French regiments served in the SAS during World War II.

In the weeks following D-Day, troops of the 3rd SAS Squadron parachuted into Brittany to reinforce the 4th Squadron and to support the US Third Army under General George S. Patton during Operation Cobra, the breakout from the Normandy beaches, and the Third Army's subsequent dash across France. At times the French SAS forces used Jeeps armed with machine guns, which were parachuted to them, as they engaged in their hit-and-run tactics.

In one sharp clash at the French village of Sennecey le Grand, Lieutenant Combaud de Roquebrune led four of these Jeeps, guns blazing, in an attack against a superior German force. All four Jeeps were destroyed by fire from German tanks. Today, a monument stands in the town, commemorating the heroism of these SAS men and others, who suffered 65 per cent casualties in combat during the Allied invasion and fighting in the wake of D-Day.

Before returning to Britain the French SAS units participated in the liberation of Paris and engaged German forces during the Battle of the Bulge. In the spring of 1945, Operation Amherst, an airdrop of 700 French SAS paratroopers took place in the Netherlands in support of the 1st Canadian Armoured Corps.

Shortly after the end of the war the French SAS squadrons were absorbed by the French Air Force. Throughout their combat experience the airborne troops of the French SAS lived up to their motto 'Qui Ose Gagne' – 'Who Dares Wins'.

NORMANDIE-NIEMEN SQUADRON

- •FOUNDED: 1942
- •STRENGTH: 96
- •THEATRE: EASTERN FRONT

After the fall of France in the spring of 1940, projecting French influence politically and militarily around the globe became a priority for the Free French Government headed by General Charles de Gaulle. Wherever possible, de Gaulle

THE YAK-3 FIGHTER

The pilots of the Normandie-Niemen Squadron brought 40 Yakovlev Yak-3 fighter planes back to France with them in 1945. Development of the aircraft began in 1941 in an effort to improve on earlier Yakovlev designs. The Yak-3 made its combat debut during the epic Battle of Kursk in the summer of 1943. Its outstanding performance was a shock to the pilots of the *Luftwaffe*. The Yak-3 was capable of a maximum speed of 447 miles per hour and was heavily armed with a 20mm (.8in) cannon and two 12.7mm (.5in) machine guns.

promoted the deployment of French forces in support of the Allied cause.

To that end, in September 1942 de Gaulle authorized the establishment of an all-volunteer squadron of French fighter pilots which would serve on the Eastern Front with the Soviet Red Air Force. Officially known as Groupe de Chasse GC 3 Normandie, the French pilots flew Soviet aircraft during 5240 sorties. They claimed 273 confirmed aerial victories and 36 probables. From March 1943 to the end of World War II, 96 pilots flew with the Normandie-Niemen Squadron, and 42 of them lost their lives.

The first aerial victory by a Normandie-Niemen pilot took place on 5 April 1943, while Commandant Jean Tulasne led the squadron. On 17 July Tulasne was among the first of the French pilots to die in action. Three Normandie-Niemen pilots, Marcel Lefèvre, Marcel Albert, and Roland de la Poype, were awarded the title 'Hero of the Soviet Union'. After serving in France in 1940 and briefly with the British Royal Air Force, Albert transferred to the Normandie-Niemen Squadron in the winter of 1942-43. While commanding a flight of fighters Captain Albert became his country's top scoring ace of World War II with 23 victories. Other aces of the Normandie-Niemen included Captain de la Poype with 17 victories, Lieutenant Jacques André with 16, Commandant Louis Delfino with 16, and Lieutenant Roger Sauvage with 16.

During the war the squadron participated in three major campaigns as the Red Army battled its

Captain Marcel Albert was France's leading fighter ace of World War II with 23 victories. For his service with the Normandie-Niemen Squadron, he was named a Hero of the Soviet Union.

way inexorably westward toward Berlin. Soviet Premier Josef Stalin recognized the heroism of the pilots and their contribution to the coming victory over the Axis by adding the name 'Niemen' to the squadron following the Battle of the Niemen River. In a single day's action in the skies above East Prussia on 16 October 1944 the squadron's pilots shot down 29 German aircraft without sustaining any losses.

On 20 June 1945 the Normandie-Niemen pilots were honoured with a victory parade in Paris. In gratitude for the unit's service Stalin allowed the French Government to take possession of its Yakovlev Yak-3 fighter planes. In the modern French Air Force, 2/30 Squadron, which flies Mirage F-1 aircraft, continues to bear the Normandie-Niemen title.

BRITISH AND COMMONWEALTH FORCES

The armed forces of Great Britain and the Commonwealth nations fought in every theatre, defending the Empire in Europe, the deserts of North Africa, and the Far East. The British and Commonwealth forces employed numerous elite units. Some of these were already reputed to be of elite status. Others gained their enviable reputation during the conflict.

AUSTRALIAN 7TH INFANTRY DIVISION

- •FOUNDED: 1940
- •STRENGTH: 6000
- •THEATRES: NORTH AFRICA, FAR EAST

In February 1940, the Australian 7th Infantry Division was formed from a combination of

Left: Australian 'Diggers' of the 7th Division pose with their Bren Carriers in the Egyptian desert, early 1941.

existing troops of the Australian Army and a number of volunteer recruits. Commanded by Sir John Lavarack, the division originally consisted of two brigades and was assigned to the Second Australian Infantry Force. General George Vasey led the division from October 1942 until his death in a plane crash in 1945, and was followed by General Edward Milford.

Deployed to the Middle East in the autumn of 1940, the majority of the division was committed to the successful campaign against Vichy French forces in Lebanon and Syria. The detached 18th Brigade participated successfully in raising the siege of the vital Libyan port city of Tobruk in the spring of 1941 as Commonwealth forces held out for eight months against repeated pressure from the vaunted German Afrika Korps, commanded by the legendary Field Marshal Erwin Rommel.

After the attack on Pearl Harbor and the eruption of war in the Pacific, the 7th Division was recalled to defend Australia against a potential Japanese invasion. Elements of the 7th Division were deployed to Java in an effort to resist Japanese expansion into the oil-rich Dutch East Indies.

Australian 'Diggers' trudge along the treacherous Kokoda Track in New Guinea as native labourers take a brief rest during their service as bearers.

Eventually, these forces and the Dutch units which fought alongside them were overrun by superior numbers of enemy troops. In New Guinea, the 21st and 25th Brigades fought jungle actions against the Japanese along the Kokoda Track, while portions of the 7th Division, joined by a small contingent of American troops, stopped the advance of Japanese forces on land for the first time in World War II during a savage battle at Milne Bay in the summer of 1942.

Known to many as the Rats of Tobruk, the soldiers of the 7th Division reached Milne Bay on 22 August, and encountered a very different kind of warfare. 'It was a bastard of a place,' remembered Captain Angus Suthers. 'It rained solidly for weeks, and the mud was waist deep in parts – and if you fell, you drowned.'

BRAVERY IN BATTLE

During World War II five members of the 7th Division were awarded the Victoria Cross, the Commonwealth's highest decoration for bravery in combat. These included Lieutenant Roden Cutler, Private Jim Gordon, Private Bruce Kingsbury, Corporal John French, and Private Richard Kelliher. The 28-year-old French, a member of the 2nd Platoon, 9th Infantry Battalion (Queensland), seized the initiative when his unit came under heavy machine-gun fire from three sides at Milne Bay on 4 September 1942. Advancing alone, French knocked out two enemy machine gun positions with grenades. Seriously wounded, he successfully pressed home his attack against the third position. His advancing comrades found French's lifeless body moments later.

Months of bitter fighting in New Guinea followed, particularly at Gona in December, and Buna and Sanananda in January 1943. These engagements were followed by an airlift operation at

Nadzab in the Markham Valley and the subsequently successful operations at Lae and Madang, in the mountains of the Finisterre Range, and at Shaggy Ridge.

At Nadzab on 13 September 1943 Private Kelliher, a 33-year-old Irish-born naturalized citizen of Australia and a member of the 2nd Platoon, 25th Infantry Battalion (Queensland), charged a Japanese machine-gun position and killed several enemy soldiers with a pair of hand grenades. Although the Japanese fire slackened, the position was not silenced. Kelliher picked up a Bren gun and moved forward once more – this time wiping out the enemy soldiers. He then rescued his wounded section leader while under continuous enemy fire. Kelliher's Victoria Cross was auctioned for $2,000 in 1966, three years after his death, and is now on display at the Australian War Memorial in Canberra.

Following a brief respite in Australia, the 7th Infantry Division, which at that time included the 18th, 21st and 25th Infantry Brigades, landed on 7 January 1945 near the town of Balikpapan on the island of Borneo. For six weeks, the Australians steadily advanced against sometimes fanatical Japanese resistance. In the midst of this final campaign, the war ended. The heroic division was disbanded in 1946.

After the war, General William Slim, who led the British Fourteenth Army in Burma, wrote, 'Some of us may forget that of all the Allies it was the Australian soldiers who first broke the spell of the invincibility of the Japanese Army.'

CANADIAN FORCES AT DIEPPE

- •FOUNDED 1942
- •STRENGTH: 6090
- •THEATRE: FRANCE

As early as the spring of 1942, Allied planners were seriously considering a large-scale raid against the coastline of German-occupied Europe. Such a raid would not only bolster morale among the civilian populations in Great Britain and the occupied countries on the continent, but also send a clear message to German commanders that they would be obliged to defend their coast from attack. Soviet Premier Josef Stalin, whose Red Army was fighting for its very existence in the East, was also urgently requesting some offensive action to relieve the pressure on his forces.

A full-scale invasion and a permanent lodgement on the coast of France would not be feasible for some months; however, the success of previous raids and the need to test new tactics for amphibious operations led to the conception of a plan called Operation Rutter. The French coastal city of Dieppe was chosen as the target for the raid. Although it was well defended and imposing cliffs ringed the port, the beach was deemed appropriate for landings and there were several exits nearby. While the planning was well under way it was decided that the Canadian armed forces should play a major role in the event. To date, the Canadians had seen little action. The Ottawa government, the Canadian public and the soldiers themselves had grown decidedly restless.

When General A.G.L. McNaughton, commander of the Canadian First Army, accepted the offer to employ his troops, one armoured and six infantry battalions of the 2nd Division, led by Major-General J.H. 'Ham' Roberts, were selected for the mission. These included the Royal Regiment of

This private from the Australian 7th Division wears the typical khaki drill uniform of British and Commonwealth forces, Syria, 1941.

Upon their return to England from the debacle at Dieppe, Commandos who took part in operations on the flanks of the main landings found little to cheer themselves.

Canada, the South Saskatchewan Regiment, the Queen's Own Cameron Highlanders of Canada, the Royal Hamilton Light Infantry, the Essex Scottish, the Fusiliers Mont-Royal, and the 14th (Calgary) Tank Battalion, each of these among the finest fighting units in the Canadian military.

Joining them were troops of British No. 3, No. 4 and No. 40 Commando along with a contingent of 50 United States Army Rangers. The oldest of the Canadian infantry formations dated back to the

mid-19th century, while others had been formed in the 1930s as war clouds gathered over Europe. Altogether, the attacking force included about 6100 combat troops along with more than 230 naval vessels and hundreds of aircraft from both the Royal Air Force and the Royal Canadian Air Force.

OPERATION JUBILEE

Foul weather at the beginning of July forced the cancellation of Operation Rutter, which had been slated for the 7th. However, Lord Louis Mountbatten, head of Combined Operations, resurrected the plan, renamed it Operation Jubilee, and rescheduled it for 18 August The Dieppe raid was to be prosecuted at five separate points. East of Dieppe at Berneval No.

3 Commando was to neutralize a battery of German artillery, and to the west No. 4 Commando was to silence a battery at Varengeville. The Canadians would make the main assault on the port of Dieppe, as well as landings at Pourville to the west and Puys to the east.

In the pre-dawn hours of 18-19 August, the landing craft and screening warships of Operation Jubilee set off from Newhaven on the southern coast of England. Almost immediately, things began to go wrong. Elements of the landing force stumbled into a German convoy, which included armed escorts, and a sharp fight ensued. A large number of the craft carrying No. 3 Commando were scattered, and only seven of the original 23 reached the landing point.

With the element of surprise lost, No. 3 Commando ran into heavy fire. Most of the men were eventually rounded up and captured. Although

German forces inspect the remains of a Canadian Churchill tank of the Calgary Regiment on the beach at Dieppe following the failure of the raid.

their efforts to destroy the battery at Berneval failed, a small group of commandos succeeded in preventing the German guns from being fully effective, picking off the crews with accurate sniper fire. At Varengeville, No. 4 Commando followed a strafing run by RAF Hurricane fighters, storming the gun emplacements with fixed bayonets and destroying the weapons. Losing 45 men in the process, No. 4 Commando had achieved the greatest success Allied forces would realize on the day.

BEACH CASUALTIES

Meanwhile, the soldiers of the Royal Regiment of Canada hit the beach at Puys at about 5 a.m. The men were mowed down by accurate mortar and machine-gun fire. Scores of soldiers were hit at the water's edge, and by the times survivors could be withdrawn at around 8.30 a.m. the regiment had sustained a horrendous 95 per cent casualties. Its original complement of 554 officers and men had been reduced to only 67.

At Pourville, the South Saskatchewan Regiment fared little better. Followed by the Cameron

Highlanders, the Saskatchewan men landed on the wrong side of the Scie River at 4.50 a.m. As they tried to reorient themselves and cross the river, German small arms and artillery decimated their ranks. By the time the 341 survivors of the attack were evacuated around 10 a.m., 144 were dead and 541 prisoners were left behind.

DISASTER AT DIEPPE

Major-General Roberts, aboard the destroyer HMS *Calpe* offshore, was unable to grasp the situation fully. His vision was obscured by a huge pall of smoke hanging over the beach, and communications were fragmentary at best. Around 5.10 a.m. the doomed main assault on the port of Dieppe went forward with the Essex Scottish on the left and the Royal Hamilton Light Infantry on the right. The 29 Churchill tanks of the Calgary Regiment left their landing craft about 20 minutes later. Ahead of them lay a seawall and a grassy expanse called the esplanade.

Immediately, the Essex Scottish came under fire from their flank and front, failing even to get off the beach. The Royal Hamiltons managed to reach the first floor of Dieppe's large casino, now a fortified strong point. But they could go no further. Fifteen of the Churchills succeeded in climbing the seawall but milled around on the esplanade, bottled up by obstacles and hit by accurate anti-tank fire. Some retreated to the beach, covering the remnants of the landing force.

At 7 a.m. a confused Roberts gave the order to commit his reserves, the Fusiliers Mont-Royal and elements of No. 40 Commando. As he approached the debacle, Lieutenant Colonel Joseph 'Tiger' Phillips recognized that his men were heading into a hopeless situation and he waved most of the boats carrying No. 40 Commando out of harm's way before falling in a hail of bullets. The Fusiliers, 584 strong, sustained 79 per cent casualties within minutes, only 125 of them returning to England.

A general retreat was ordered at 10.50 a.m. and the devastated force evacuated. A total of 1027 Allied soldiers – more than 900 of them Canadian – had been killed, and 2340 were captured. German losses were light at 314 killed and 294 wounded. Two Canadian soldiers earned the Victoria Cross at

Dieppe. Major Charles Ingersoll Merritt of the South Saskatchewan Regiment led attacks on a series of German pillboxes, was wounded twice and taken prisoner. Chaplain John Weir Foote, an honorary captain of the Royal Hamilton Light Infantry, stayed on the battle scarred beach at Dieppe for eight hours, calmly walking among the wounded, providing comfort and reassurance. After boarding a landing craft, Foote changed his mind and returned to the beach. He remained with the wounded until captured by the Germans, and was liberated from a prisoner of war camp in 1945.

BITTER LESSONS

The lessons of Dieppe were bitter, but of great value in the planning for the D-Day invasion two years later. Clearly, a strong pre-invasion bombardment from both air and sea would be necessary to assist any initial landings.

A fortified port city would be nearly impossible to capture by frontal assault. Improvements in technology would be necessary to assist troops in overcoming natural and man-made obstacles. Perhaps of greatest importance, it was acknowledged that better command and control were necessary and that cooperation between the armed services would be crucial in the future.

Although the disaster at Dieppe was a severe blow, the Canadian armed forces participated in large numbers for the remainder of the war in Europe, including the D-Day landings.

CHURCHILL TANKS AT DIEPPE

Their mission to provide heavy fire support for the troops landing on the beach at Dieppe, the 29 Churchills of the 14th Canadian Army Tank Regiment experienced difficulty from the beginning. After rumbling from their landing craft nearly a half hour behind schedule, the tanks were taken under fire almost immediately. Several of them foundered in the loose gravel at the water's edge, while only 15 were able to move beyond a low sea wall. Traversing a grassy area called the esplanade, these were held up by mines and other obstacles, which forced a general retirement to the beach.

THE CHINDITS

- **Founded: 1942**
- **Strength: 3000**
- **Theatre: Burma**

To say that Brigadier Orde Wingate was an eccentric may well be the greatest understatement of World War II. Wingate was reported to have boiled tea using his socks as strainers, entertained subordinates in his quarters while stark naked, and to have carried copies of the Greek classics by Plato and Homer into combat areas. However, Wingate was also known as a daring and innovative leader of men who had proven himself in combat before World War II.

A confirmed Zionist and the son of Puritan parents, Wingate had successfully led counter-insurgency units, called special night squads, against marauding bands of armed Arabs who terrorized Jewish inhabitants of Palestine and sabotaged oil pipelines. In 1940 he had led Gideon Force on several operations against the Italians in Ethiopia. When he put forward the idea of inserting small groups of soldiers behind Japanese lines in the Burmese jungle to conduct extended operations against rear areas, and further asserted that the men could be resupplied by air, some senior commanders endorsed the idea. Chief among these was General Sir Archibald Wavell, commander of British forces in India.

In late 1942, Wingate was authorized to assemble a force of approximately 3000 men to conduct these operations. Adopting the name 'Chindits', a corruption of the Burmese word 'chinthé' which describes a mythical lion, the officially designated 77 Indian Infantry Brigade embarked on its first guerrilla foray on 13 February 1943. The Chindits

Brigadier Orde Wingate (standing, centre), the eccentric commander of the Chindits who later died in a plane crash, stands beside a large map during a briefing for his officers.

crossed the Chindwin River near the town of Imphal with the mission of destroying bridges and cutting the rail system which conveyed supplies to Japanese troops on the front line.

The Chindits spent more than two months fighting both the Japanese and the terrible hardships of the Burmese jungle climate. The Japanese were initially surprised by the presence of British guerrillas more than 200km (125 miles) from their own territory. However, they counter-attacked ferociously, and Wingate's men, who were sick – many suffering from malaria – and fatigued after weeks fighting, were forced to retire. Divided into five separate columns originally, the Chindits had found the plain beyond the Irrawaddy River wholly unsuitable for continued operations. Wingate ordered them to break up into small units and make their way back to India.

On 29 April, Wingate, leading a column of 34 survivors, reached safety. The expedition had cost the 3000-man Chindit force more than 800 casualties outright, while only about 600 were able to take up arms again. Although many British officers and observers considered the Chindit foray an abject military failure, others cast the operation in a decidedly different light. Chief among these was Prime Minister Winston Churchill, who briefly considered elevating Wingate to command the entire British military effort in Burma.

WINGATE'S WIN

In the wake of shattering Japanese victories in the China-Burma-India theatre in the early months of the war, Wingate had achieved something of military significance. The Chindits had proven that losses could be inflicted on the Japanese, and they had taken on the seemingly invincible foe in his own backyard. The Allied cause was in need of heroes, and Wingate fitted the bill. As a result of his

Left: Their faces etched with the trauma of weeks of combat in an unforgiving climate, a group of Chindits emerges from the Burmese jungle in 1944.

The insignia of the 3rd Indian Division, otherwise known as the Chindits, was a golden Burmese dragon (a Chinthern Pagoda Guardian) on a blue background.

first Chindit expedition, the jungle fighter won promotion to major general, and his command was greatly expanded, even to include his own air support of American transports, bombers, fighters, observation planes and gliders under Colonel Phil Cochran.

Now in command of six brigades – more than 20,000 fighting men – Wingate planned an ambitious operation for February 1944, in concert with the American guerrilla force of Merrill's Marauders and units of the Chinese Army commanded by General Joseph W. Stilwell. The plan involved another foray deep behind Japanese lines. This time a series of fixed bases were to be established and resupplied by air, while armed units struck at Japanese communications and supply routes. The idea was to harass the enemy troops opposing a thrust by Stilwell's Chinese to push the Japanese out of northern Burma, to capture the vital airstrip at Myitkyina and open an Allied land supply route to China.

Glider-borne Chindits landed and established bases with names such as Broadway, Aberdeen, White City and Piccadilly. But the landings were not without incident: a number of Dakota transports and gliders crashed after the Dakota pilots were ordered to tow two of the gliders, which taxed their engines to the point of overheating as they climbed above high mountain peaks. Further compounding the initial insertion intended for Piccadilly was the fact that the area was unfit for glider landings due to numerous felled trees. Diverted to Broadway, only 35 of 61 gliders managed to land safely. Marching overland, the Chindit 16 Brigade, commanded by Brigadier Bernard Ferguson, did not reach its halfway point, the banks of the Chindwin River, for 23 days, hacking its way through the thick Burmese jungle.

The Japanese moved decisively to eliminate these

thorns in their side, as Lieutenant General Masakuzu Kawabe ordered more than 10 battalions of troops against the British. Two brigades hit Broadway, and hand-to-hand fighting raged at White City between the Chindit 77 Brigade, commanded by Brigadier Mike Calvert, and a huge Japanese force of 6600 men.

In his book *The Road Past Mandalay*, Chindit officer John Masters wrote of the carnage: '… Blasted trees, feet and twisted hands sticking up out of the earth, bloody shirts, ammunition clips, holes half full of water … and over all the heavy, sweet stench of death, from our own bodies and entrails lying unknown in the shattered ground, from Japanese corpses on the wire, or fastened, dead and rotting, in the trees …'

With his force reduced to less than 2000 men, Calvert and 77 Brigade succeeded in capturing the town of Mogaung, but at a cost of more than half of its already reduced number. By this time Broadway and White City had been abandoned, and the Japanese pressed 111 Brigade at its hastily erected strong point called Blackpool. Ultimately the Chindits were spent as a fighting force, and were ordered to withdraw via air and land at the end of August, having suffered 5000 casualties during their second operation.

At the end of the campaign the remnants of the Chindit force were under new leadership. Brigadier Joe Lentaigne, previously at the helm of 111 Brigade, had assumed overall command at the end of March. Wingate had flown to Aberdeen on 24 March to survey the situation, and on his return flight the B-25 bomber which was carrying him crashed into the side of a mountain southwest of Imphal. One of the most brilliant yet controversial commanders in the British Army was dead.

CHINDIT LEGACY

The legacy of the Chindits is one of endurance and ferocity in combat. During the second campaign, the average weight loss per man was 19kg (42lb). Malaria and dysentery were rife among the ranks. Routinely, the Chindits marched many kilometres in a single day through some of the world's thickest jungle, carrying 27kg (60lb) packs and doing battle with mosquitoes, leeches, flies, ticks, snakes and

huge spiders. For the Chindit, simply enduring was a victory.

The Chindits paid a heavy price, particularly when employed as assault troops or in the defence of fixed fortifications, operations for which they were not originally intended. However, they succeeded in boosting Allied morale; tying down significant Japanese troops which otherwise might have been deployed against the Chinese troops in the Assam Valley; and in just about every case of direct combat, inflicting serious casualties on the enemy.

FOURTEENTH ARMY

- **FOUNDED: 1943**
- **STRENGTH: 120,000**
- **THEATRES: INDIA, BURMA**

The operational life of the British Fourteenth Army may have been relatively short during World War II; however, its significance in hastening the defeat of Imperial Japan cannot be underestimated. It was this army of British, Indian and East African troops which defeated the Japanese at the epic battles of Imphal and Kohima on the India-Burma frontier in the spring of 1944, and subsequently advanced to liberate the great cities of Rangoon and Mandalay.

Formed in mid-1943, the Fourteenth Army was placed under the command of the brilliant General William Slim, who would go on to attain the rank of field marshal, be knighted by King George VI in December 1944, command all Allied land forces in Southeast Asia, and serve as Governor General of Australia after the war. One of the most capable field commanders of World War II, Slim, a lieutenant general at the time of his appointment to command the Fourteenth Army, had already successfully led Commonwealth troops in Africa and the Middle East and been wounded in action.

Although the situation in the China-Burma-India theatre appeared bleak, Slim had managed to extricate much of the 1st Burma Corps and retreat more than 1500km (900 miles) to relative safety in India as the steadily advancing Japanese took

Indian soldiers of the Fourteenth Army prepare to meet the Japanese in Burma in 1944. Indian troops comprised a large percentage of Allied ground forces in the China-Burma-India Theatre.

control of Burma in its entirety during 1942. Following the early disaster in Burma, the British reorganized their Army in the theatre in the hope of retaking the offensive at an opportune time. Slim took command of the Fourteenth Army in October 1943, and undertook a short-lived offensive along the Arakan coast of Burma in December.

JAPANESE ATTACK INDIA

When the British were halted rather quickly, the Japanese seized the initiative and launched Operation U-Go, which, if successful, would threaten all of India, the jewel in the crown of the British Empire. The importance of the town of Imphal and the outpost at Kohima lay in their positions along the single road which ran 210km (130 miles) northward from Imphal to the vital railway transportation hub at Dinapur. The Japanese Fifteenth Army, under General Renya

Mutaguchi, launched its attempt to seize the two communications centres on 4 February 1944.

Soon the garrisons at Imphal and Kohima were imperilled. On 29 March the Japanese succeeded in cutting the road north of Imphal, and for all practical purposes the two positions were besieged. Although the British defenders at Imphal numbered 155,000 at the height of their strength, the only troops available initially at Kohima to stem the tide of the attacking Japanese 31st Division, which totalled 12,000 men, were a relatively small number of soldiers from the 161st Indian Brigade, the Assam Regiment, and the 4th Battalion of the Royal West Kent Regiment. These hard-pressed troops held out for a miraculous two weeks before being relieved by the 33rd Corps.

At Imphal fighting raged for nearly 90 days, much of it taking place between small pockets of opposing infantrymen firing at each other through dense jungle and on steep hillsides. Five British soldiers were awarded the Victoria Cross for heroism at Imphal. Among these were Lieutenant Abdul Hafiz of the Jat Regiment, who fired his Bren gun into the face of an advancing Japanese company

31

General Sir William Slim led the British and Commonwealth troops of the Fourteenth Army against a determined Japanese foe, won the battles of Imphal and Kohima, and liberated Burma.

and was mortally wounded, and Sergeant Hanson Victor Turner, a member of the 1st West Yorkshire Regiment, who, before he died in action, repelled five separate enemy attacks on his position, primarily by throwing hand grenades.

One of the most savage close-quarter gun battles of the war took place at Kohima on the grounds of the district deputy commissioner's bungalow. The centre of the fighting was the narrow expanse of the adjacent tennis court. In early April the Japanese had captured the bungalow and the surrounding area and established a series of strong points along the terraced hillside. The British counter-attacked, and in the following month recaptured all of the overrun territory with the exception of the fortified bungalow and no-man's land of the tennis court.

BATTLE OF THE TENNIS COURT

In an engagement which has gone down in history as the Battle of the Tennis Court, the opposing soldiers often fought literally within feet of one another as hand grenades hissed and skidded along the playing surface. British soldiers who exposed themselves too readily were easy marks for the Japanese riflemen and machine gunners firing through slits in the wall of their bunker which commanded all approaches.

The soldiers of the Dorsetshire Regiment's 2nd Battalion were frustrated as their fire had little apparent effect on the defenders. Finally, Royal Engineers managed to clear a path for a Grant tank, with a 37mm (1.46in) turret-mounted gun and a 75mm (2.95in) cannon in the hull, to be winched and manhandled up the steep hillside. When the tank reached the tennis court on the morning of 13 May its guns blasted the Japanese bunker from point-blank range and finally ended the stalemate.

Along with the courage of the Fourteenth Army, the difference between victory and defeat at Imphal and Kohima was the ability to resupply troops. The Japanese were unable to provide their soldiers with much more than what each man could carry on his back. Conversely, Lord Louis Mountbatten, overall Allied commander in Southeast Asia, marshalled his resources and commenced a combined British-American resupply effort by air. During the three-month ordeal, nearly 19,300 tonnes of supplies and 13,000 reinforcements were delivered by Allied pilots, and more than 40,000 refugees and 13,000 battle casualties were evacuated.

With the onset of the monsoon season, the Japanese were compelled to acknowledge their worst defeat on land in the entire war. They had lost more than 13,000 killed and 47,000 wounded, sickened or taken prisoner. A total of 17,600 Commonwealth troops lost their lives. At Kohima, a simple monument bears mute testimony to the heroism displayed by soldiers of the Fourteenth Army. It reads, 'When you go home, tell them of us, and say: For your tomorrow, we gave our today.'

SLIM VICTORY

Slim had not only secured India from invasion, he had also permanently wrested the initiative from the Japanese. In December 1944 the Fourteenth Army launched Operation Capital. Crossing the

Irrawaddy River in January 1945, the British spearhead liberated Mandalay in March and Rangoon, the Burmese capital, in May. Japanese casualties soared to 350,000 during their retreat. Recognizing the tenacity of his foe, Slim later wrote, 'The strength of the Japanese army lay in the spirit of the individual Japanese soldier. He fought and marched till he died. If 500 Japanese were ordered to hold a position, we had to kill 495 before it was ours – and then the last five killed themselves.'

Undoubtedly, the Japanese held their adversaries of the Fourteenth Army – renamed Malaya Command on 1 November 1945 – in high regard as well.

Upon their return from a raid, rugged SAS men pose in their heavily armed Jeeps. SAS missions often lasted for days, the raiders being sustained by the provisions their vehicles could carry.

LONG RANGE DESERT GROUP

- •FOUNDED: 1940
- •STRENGTH: 112
- •THEATRES: NORTH AFRICA

Almost from the beginning of World War II, Major Ralph A. Bagnold, a New Zealander, had advocated the formation of an elite group of soldiers who could gather intelligence and provide reconnaissance deep behind enemy lines in the desert of North Africa. It was necessary that these soldiers be resourceful and capable of survival in one of the world's harshest climates.

Bagnold was well aware of the type of men required to do the job. For years he had travelled in the region, guiding expeditions across the expanse of

Pausing for a moment, a member of the Long Range Desert Group grabs a quick bite to eat. Exposure during daylight hours risked detection by prowling German aircraft.

the Libyan desert. In the summer of 1940 Bagnold met with General Archibald Wavell, Britain's Commander-in-Chief, Middle East, in the Egyptian port city of Alexandria, and explained his concept. Wavell was also familiar with the desert, having entered Jerusalem decades earlier during World War I in the company of T.E. Lawrence, the fabled Lawrence of Arabia.

Wavell quickly gained confidence in Bagnold and understood fully what a well-trained unit such as the one the Kiwi officer envisaged could accomplish. He not only endorsed Bagnold's idea but enthusiastically assisted in the appropriation of the necessary equipment. Bagnold was also allowed to hand-pick his men, and a number of the original members of what became known as the Long Range

Desert Group (LRDG) were transfers from the 2nd New Zealand Infantry Division.

Much of the rigorous early training, which included survival techniques, radio and communications, demolitions and desert driving, was conducted at Abbassia Barracks near the Egyptian capital of Cairo. The equipment had to be specialized, including high-performance trucks which were capable of taking abuse for weeks at a time in the harsh, unforgiving desert. These American-made Chevrolet vehicles were outfitted with overflow radiator tanks, machine guns and plenty of storage space for ammunition and provisions.

It was not uncommon for LRDG patrols to spend three weeks at a time in the desert and to cover as much as 3200km (2000 miles) while observing German troop movements, harassing columns, destroying enemy supply dumps, raiding bases and gathering intelligence. At times a patrol might spend days in isolation without any enemy contact. Experts in navigation on the vast sea of sand, the LRDG men regularly provided transportation for the elite raiders of the Special Air Service (SAS). A number of joint operations between the groups resulted in spectacular successes.

Often, the LRDG pre-positioned caches of supplies behind German lines to sustain operations; however, it was necessary for each patrol to include several trucks which hauled only provisions. Even then, the standard daily water ration was a meagre 2.8 litres. Supply difficulties sometimes cut that amount to less than half a litre, well under subsistence level.

DAREDEVILS AND ECCENTRICS

For nearly three years of the war in the desert at least one LRDG patrol was deployed constantly. As

initial successes were documented, the force grew to include men from numerous other parts of the far-flung British Commonwealth. Rarely were the rank and file of the Allied armed forces aware that the LRDG was operating, but these intrepid men wore their Arab head dresses, sheepskins and sandals with honour. Military formality was always secondary to esprit de corps, and the LRDG attracted its share of daredevils, eccentrics and academics.

One memorable encounter with the Afrika Korps occurred in 1941, when Captain A.M. Hay led LRDG Patrol G1 in action east of the Libyan city of Benghazi. After emerging unscathed from a pair of bombing and strafing attacks by Italian and German aircraft, Hay chose to spend the night in the relative safety of an ancient wadi before setting off the next morning on foot in search of potential targets. The best of these proved to be a rest area for drivers bringing supplies to the front near the fortified German positions at Beda Fomm.

After stalking enemy traffic on the road to Benghazi for several hours, Hay brought his patrol into position opposite the rest area and proceeded

The LRDG relied heavily on Chevrolet trucks to get them to their targets quickly and with the necessary firepower to carry out the operation.

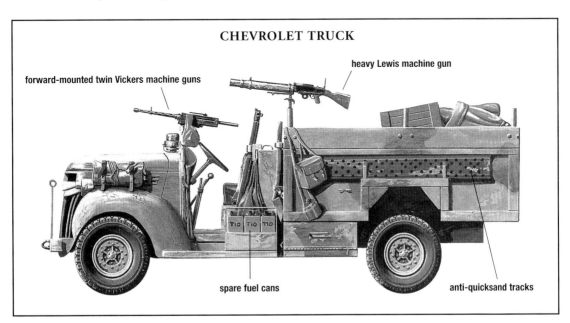

CHEVROLET TRUCK

heavy Lewis machine gun

forward-mounted twin Vickers machine guns

spare fuel cans

anti-quicksand tracks

to wreak havoc with steady machine gun and anti-tank cannon fire, hand grenades and the staccato of the Tommy gun. The Germans were in such disarray that they failed to pinpoint the location of the LRDG team until the raiders had made good their escape. Following the attack, Hay and company dodged enemy patrols and aircraft which had been dispatched to find them and returned to their base at Siwa Oasis unscathed.

The Allied victory in North Africa in the spring of 1943 did not end the useful life of the Long Range Desert Group. Operating on islands in the Mediterranean in Italy, and in the Balkans, the LRDG took its toll in real enemy casualties while also causing the Germans to divert forces from main areas of combat to defend against damaging raids.

One raid in Albania cost the enemy 80 killed in action, and in the autumn of 1944 two LRDG teams parachuted into northern Greece with orders to spread chaos and confusion among the German occupation forces. Preparing an ambush for any unwary enemy traffic which might venture past, the raiders mined a winding road and waited. When a German convoy appeared, the lead truck detonated a mine and the rout was on. When the LRDG men had ceased firing, 50 Germans lay dead.

Although they inflicted many casualties on the enemy and destroyed vital stores of supplies, the LRDG did suffer major losses during the war. One mission ended in disaster with more than 40 men killed, while Colonel Jake Easonsmith, the unit's commanding officer at the time, died in combat on the island of Leros in November 1943, and dozens of his men were taken prisoner.

At the end of World War II, the British War Office declined a request from the leaders of the

LRDG that the unit remain intact for service in Southeast Asia. The successful but relatively brief history of the Long Range Desert Group ended when the unit was disbanded in August 1945.

POPSKI'S PRIVATE ARMY

- •FOUNDED: 1942
- •STRENGTH: 120
- •THEATRES: NORTH AFRICA, ITALY

As desert warriors go, Lieutenant Colonel Vladimir Peniakoff may have been the most unlikely of heroes. Born in Belgium to parents of Russian heritage, Peniakoff had worked in Egypt as an engineer before the war and become enamoured with the life of a desert wanderer. His eccentricities led to early disappointments, particularly his desire to be a member of the elite Long Range Desert Group (LRDG) of the British Army. At the outbreak of war, however, the British military did recognize the value of individuals who were experienced in desert survival and familiar with the North African area. So Peniakoff was commissioned a lieutenant in 1941 and operated initially with an obscure raiding unit known as the Libyan Arab Force.

By 1942, Peniakoff's reputation for daring had been noted, and he had participated in numerous raids in the company of the LRDG. British radio operators had trouble pronouncing his surname, however, so LRDG Intelligence Officer Bill Kennedy Shaw began referring

This lance-corporal typifies Popski's unit in the field. He wears a civilian sweater and a Royal Armoured Corps beret, indicating the mixed military origins of many of Popski's men.

to him as 'Popski'. The name stuck, and in the autumn of that year when Colonel John Hackett offered Popski the opportunity to form a small, independent unit to conduct raids behind Axis lines, he leaped at the chance. The new unit was officially designated No. 1 Demolition Squadron, PPA. Thus, Popski's Private Army was born. Although Popski's Private Army never numbered more than 120 men, which constituted the smallest unit of the British Army under independent command during World War II, its leader made certain that a distinctive insignia and high level of *esprit de corps* contributed to its repute during service in North Africa and Italy. The original complement of soldiers in the unit included five officers and 18 enlisted men.

The initial foray for Popski's Private Army nearly ended in disaster in December 1942, as the unit departed from Cairo and moved into southern Tunisia. German aircraft destroyed all but two of Popski's Jeeps along with all supplies except those the men carried on their backs. Finally making contact with other British Army units in February

Men of PPA in North Africa enjoy a break. In the front, sitting, is Corporal 'Jock' Cameron, who fought as Popski's gunner for much of the war.

1943, Popski's men had covered more than 6400km (4000 miles) and even impersonated a German patrol in order to survive.

DESERT, MOUNTAIN AND SEA

Less than a month later the refitted command crossed mountains on a trail thought only fit for mules, and conducted several successful raids against German fuel dumps and installations. On 19 March 1943, at Sened, three of Popski's enlisted men accepted the surrender of 600 Italian soldiers trapped in a wadi from which there was no escape. During its desert sojourn, Popski's Private Army was credited with destroying 34 Axis planes, six armoured vehicles, 112 trucks and 450,000 gallons of fuel. In contrast, only two of the raiders were wounded and a single soldier captured. Miraculously, none were killed.

In the final phase of the war in North Africa, the ranks of Popski's Private Army steadily grew, and the

Lieutenant Colonel David Stirling founded the Special Air Service and proved to be an outstanding leader of the elite force. His successor in command was the legendary Blair 'Paddy' Mayne.

unit took part in the Anzio campaign supporting the Allied Fifth Army in Italy in the winter of 1944. The following summer, elements of the force made an arduous crossing of the Sibellini Mountains and captured the town of Camerino prior to halting before the formidable German defences at the Gothic Line.

Using stealth and deception as well as the concentrated firepower of 12.5mm (.50 cal) machine guns and other small arms, Popski led several amphibious operations along the coast of the Adriatic Sea. During an amazing display of almost reckless audacity, 45 of Popski's men surprised the German garrison at the medieval fortress of Caserma dei Fiumi Uniti. As the raiders observed the enemy soldiers' routine, they captured the position without firing a shot. A German patrol which arrived a few hours later was also captured intact. A third group of heavily armed German soldiers was then confronted

and forced to surrender. For the loss of three killed and five wounded, Popski's Private Army had killed 40 Germans and captured 152.

In the spring of 1945 the German forces defending the coastal town of Chioggia surrendered nearly 700 men and a complement of heavy artillery to what they thought was a large contingent of Allied troops. The Germans were shocked to learn that they had capitulated to 12 of Popski's men who had reached the town in five Jeeps.

Popski's unorthodox methods of operation may have been risky, but more often than not they produced memorable successes. On 14 September 1945 the unit was officially disbanded. Popski died in 1952 at the age of 55.

SPECIAL AIR SERVICE

- •FOUNDED 1941
- •STRENGTH 2000
- •THEATRES: NORTH AFRICA, MEDITERRANEAN, WESTERN EUROPE

While recovering from a serious spinal injury he had suffered during an unauthorized parachute training exercise, Lieutenant Colonel David Stirling formulated the idea of an elite unit of the British Army which was destined to become the stuff of legend.

Stirling's concept was that of a highly trained and motivated force which could operate in small groups far behind enemy lines, inflicting casualties, destroying equipment and supply depots, and generally creating chaos and confusion. Before the Special Air Service (SAS) was officially activated on 1 July 1941, the innovative Stirling discovered that he had nearly as great a battle at hand with the British bureaucracy as he was hoping to take on with the Germans.

A former member of No. 8 Commando, which was a part of Layforce in the early days of the war, Stirling scribbled his SAS proposal on a scrap of paper and stole his way into the building which housed the offices of General Sir Claude Auchinleck, Commander-in-Chief of British Forces in the Middle East. Ducking guards who had tried to halt his unauthorized entry, the visionary officer accidentally found himself before Lieutenant General Sir Neil Ritchie, Deputy Chief of Staff for Auchinleck. The meeting was fortuitous, as Ritchie chose to endorse the proposal and presented it to the commander-in-chief, who approved.

Although war materiel was in short supply everywhere, the initial 66 recruits to the newly formed unit managed to scrounge and 'borrow' the necessary items to facilitate their organization and training. Officially designated L Detachment, Special Air Service Brigade, the SAS adopted the motto 'Who Dares Wins'.

1 SAS REGIMENT

The unit's official title was meant to confuse the Germans more than to describe its actual method of deployment. As the enemy became more familiar with the irregular force causing so much trouble in rear areas, they might begin to wonder about other units, designated Detachments A to K, descending from above in large numbers. Although the men of the SAS did engage in airborne training, they were capable of insertion by land and sea as well. Most of their raids were actually initiated overland, with the raiders covering the final distance on foot. By September 1942 the unit was renamed as the British Army's 1 SAS Regiment.

The first SAS mission, a November 1941 parachute drop in support of the Army's ground offensive in North Africa, encountered high winds,

Outfitted against the wind and dust of the desert, an SAS patrol scout a section of road. The SAS often operated miles behind enemy lines.

sandstorms and significant enemy resistance. The disastrous debut cost the SAS one-third of the strength employed, 22 men killed or captured. Undaunted, Stirling managed to coordinate a second raid, this time against three airfields at Sirte, El Agheila, and Aqedabia. With transportation provided by the Long Range Desert Group (LRDG), the SAS attackers destroyed more than 60 enemy aircraft on the ground without the loss of a single man. This was the beginning of a productive association between the SAS and the LRDG, which often utilized its specially equipped Chevrolet trucks to insert SAS fighters behind enemy lines.

Stirling was more than a planner and desk soldier, often leading his men from the front and exposing himself to enemy fire. One memorable expedition which he led has become known as 'the Jeep Raid'. In July 1942 he decided to set in motion a new plan for attacking enemy airfields. The recently acquired Jeeps were heavily armed with twin Vickers machine guns, and the drivers would approach the target, take up a V formation for the attack, and move in quickly with guns blazing.

On 26 July a complement of 18 Jeeps, mounting more than 60 machine guns, pulled away from the desert base at Bir Chalder and headed toward the German airfield at Sidi Haneish 64km (40 miles) northwest. Suddenly, out of the trackless desert the airfield loomed ahead, flooded with light. It seemed that the Germans might have been alerted to the coming attack, but then a bomber appeared out of the darkness, slowing for a landing approach. As the bomber touched down, Stirling touched off the raid with a signal flare.

The raiders charged ahead, shooting up row after row of Junkers Ju-87 dive bombers, Heinkel He-111 bombers and valuable Junkers Ju-52 transport aircraft. The startled Germans replied with mortar, cannon and small arms fire. Stirling's Jeep was disabled and three others were put out of action. During the frenetic battle three other vehicles were damaged, one of which was to give out later on, but the SAS men, splitting back into smaller groups,

SAS men pose with locals in Italy during operations in 1943. Canadian Captain MacDonald (standing) was commander of 2 SAS in the area.

made good their escape while the Germans searched fruitlessly for them.

Stirling's group found a depression and covered its Jeeps with camouflage netting and scrub brush. Travelling by daylight was dangerous as *Luftwaffe* planes would surely be on the prowl. Under cover of darkness the party reached its rendezvous point and headed for home. The tally had been impressive with at least 25 German aircraft destroyed. An LRDG team had successfully completed a diversionary raid, destroying another 15 enemy planes. Only one SAS man had been lost in the operation, killed by a fragment from an exploding

Ammunition bandoleers strung across their chests, a trio of SAS men walks along a dirt road at Cassino, Italy. The soldier in the centre is shouldering a Vickers machine gun barrel.

mortar shell. In truth, more was accomplished than the destruction of 40 German aircraft. The frayed nerves which the raid left behind and the need for security in rear areas obliged the Germans to divert forces from the front to guard vital installations.

In January 1943 Stirling's luck ran out. He was captured in Tunisia by the Italians and spent the rest of the war as a prisoner. Although he escaped five times he was recaptured during each effort and eventually endured his final months in captivity in the high security Colditz Castle.

The capture of Stirling was a blow to the SAS, but into his considerable shoes stepped one of the outstanding combat soldiers of World War II, Lieutenant Colonel Robert Blair 'Paddy' Mayne. An original member of the SAS, Mayne was a rough-and-tumble character who spent a fair amount of time in trouble with the military authorities. At

1.93m (6ft 4in) tall he was an imposing figure from Northern Ireland who had played rugby and been a champion boxer before the war. Mayne and David Stirling's brother, Bill, led the SAS during fighting in several European countries in 1944 and 1945, including the Netherlands, Belgium, France, Norway and Germany. By the end of the war Mayne was said to have personally destroyed as many as 130 aircraft. He received the Distinguished Service Order with three bars, and today a review is being conducted to right a potential wrong and award Mayne the Victoria Cross for an action near Oldenburg, Germany, on 9 April 1945.

BEHIND GERMAN LINES

As the reputation of the SAS grew, so did its ranks, and by 1944 the force had grown to five regiments, two British, two French and one Belgian. Harassing the enemy at every turn, up to four SAS teams were at work behind German lines at any given time during the Italian campaign. In one raid a team attacked the headquarters of the German Fifth Army Corps, killing numerous officers and burning the buildings to the ground.

Prior to D-Day and in the weeks that followed, SAS teams were able to move freely in daylight because of Allied mastery of the air. Working in cooperation with resistance groups the SAS spread chaos and confusion among the Germans with highly mobile firepower and nocturnal ambushes. During Operation Dunhill in August 1944, the SAS deployed 59 men in five teams to support Operation Cobra, the US Third Army's breakout from the hedgerow country of Normandy. One team liberated 200 captured Allied airmen before linking up with the Americans after three weeks in the field.

In September 1944, during the ill-fated Operation Market-Garden in the Netherlands, the SAS scouted drop zones and harried the enemy. On 25 March 1945 the SAS supported the crossing of the Rhine River at Wesel on the German frontier with reconnaissance efforts by 450 soldiers.

ENEMY ATROCITIES

On at least two occasions during the war in Europe SAS troops were the victims of German atrocities.

OPERATION LOYTON

The disaster of Operation Loyton occurred when Lieutenant Colonel Brian Franks led 91 men of 2 SAS and Phantom, a radio transmission group, on a parachute insertion in the Vosges Mountains of France on 12 August 12 1944. Their intelligence gathering mission lasted until 9 October, but the men were harassed constantly by two German divisions, which had been dispatched to defend the nearby Belton Gap. Occasionally, the raiders were assisted by members of the French Resistance. Regrettably, 31 members of the SAS team were taken prisoner and later put to death. Numerous family members of the Resistance were also executed.

From August to October 1944 SAS troopers conducted Operation Loyton, in which 91 men performed reconnaissance and hit-and-run raids. From the outset the mission was plagued by bad weather and supply difficulties, while compounding the problem was a build-up of German forces in the Vosges Mountains. By the end of the harrowing experience, 31 SAS men had been captured and summarily executed. On another occasion, 24 SAS soldiers and a captured American airman were massacred. As the war neared its end, the SAS participated in the rounding up and apprehending of Nazi officials and senior officers.

Given the risky nature of its operations, SAS units compiled an outstanding combat record during World War II. Through 18 months of war in the desert the SAS destroyed at least 350 German aircraft along with countless stores of supplies, and inflicted casualties on the enemy well in excess of those expected from the relatively low combat strength of the SAS units deployed. At its peak during the war in Europe, the SAS brigade totalled about 2000 men, while 330 soldiers were killed in action. The tally of enemy losses in 1944 and 1945 reads impressively: 7733 killed, 4784 taken prisoner, 89 wagons, 29 locomotives and seven trains destroyed, 740 vehicles destroyed or captured, 33 derailments, and approximately 400 targets identified for attacks by Allied air forces.

The modern SAS traces its lineage back to its

World War II ancestor, and the armed forces of numerous nations have based fighting units on this elite force, whose insignia of the winged dagger is instantly recognizable among military units around the world. Since World War II the SAS has operated in numerous locales. Among them are Malaya, Korea, Oman, Indonesia, the Falklands, Iraq and Afghanistan.

79TH ARMOURED DIVISION
- •FOUNDED: 1942
- •STRENGTH: 10,000
- •THEATRE: WESTERN EUROPE

When Allied soldiers waded ashore on the beaches of Normandy on 6 June 1944 they were accompanied by a number of very specialized armoured vehicles. Critical to the success of

Operation Overlord, these specialized Sherman tanks, called DD for duplex drive, had been modified with canvas skirts which could be raised on a metal framework, allowing the tank to float. When a pair of propellers was engaged the Shermans were able to move forward and waddle onto the beach under their own power, delivering much-needed fire support to the landing infantry.

The DD Sherman was only one of several armoured vehicle modifications which were conceived, developed and tested by the tankers of the 79th Armoured Division. These 'Funnies' supported the Allied advance across Western Europe and proved highly successful.

Shortly after D-Day, General Dwight D. Eisenhower, the Supreme Allied Commander, acknowledged the contribution these specialized

The Churchill AVRE was equipped with 290mm (11.5in) spigot mortar that could throw an 18kg (40lb) high-explosive shell at heavy fortifications.

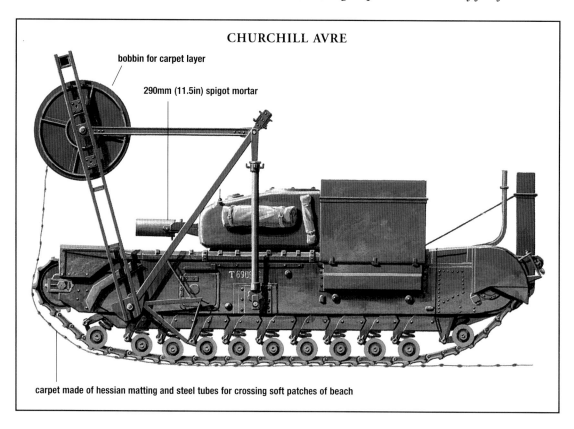

CHURCHILL AVRE

bobbin for carpet layer

290mm (11.5in) spigot mortar

T 6909

carpet made of hessian matting and steel tubes for crossing soft patches of beach

vehicles had made in Normandy. 'The comparatively light casualties which we sustained on all the beaches except Omaha were in large measure due to the success of the novel mechanical contrivances which were employed. It is doubtful if the assault forces could have firmly established themselves without these weapons,' he wrote.

The 79th Armoured Division had been formed along standard lines on 14 August 1942, during the same month that the ill-fated Operation Jubilee, a raid composed mainly of Canadian commando units against the French coastal city of Dieppe, took place. One of the significant lessons learned from the disaster at Dieppe was that armoured support would be a critical element in the success of future amphibious operations.

The problem was that most of the engineers who were to clear paths through beach obstacles and minefields so that tanks could advance had been killed in the opening moments of the Dieppe landing. Standard tanks foundered at the water's edge, bogged down in loose sand and gravel, and became easy marks for well positioned German anti-

An AVRE Churchill tank, with its menacing 290mm (11.5in) spigot mortar, clanks down a dirt road past the demolished houses of a French village shortly after the D-Day landings.

tank gunners. In the hours after the raid, the blackened hulks of numerous British armoured vehicles smouldered among the bodies of dead and wounded soldiers.

SPECIALIZED TANKS

In April 1943, to address the issue of armoured support in preparation for D-Day and beyond, Prime Minister Winston Churchill and General Sir Alan Brooke, Chief of the Imperial General Staff, refocused the 79th Armoured Division and its commander, Major-General Percy C.S. Hobart, on the design and development of specialized tanks and the training of the crews which would man them upon allocation to units throughout the Allied armies in Europe.

Originally a member of the Royal Engineers, Hobart was a veteran of World War I, having

Squatting along a beach in France, a Churchill tank has been equipped with a bullshorn mine clearing device.

participated in campaigns on the Western Front and in the Middle East. He had joined the fledgling Royal Tank Corps in 1923, rising to command a brigade and eventually the nucleus of the 7th Armoured Division. He had officially retired in 1939, and according to some that retirement had been forced upon the 54-year-old officer due to his pronounced eccentricities. In the opening months of the war, Hobart was serving as a colonel in the Home Guard. The army's need for every experienced officer to return to active duty breathed new life into Hobart's career. Following a brief stint as commander of the 11th Armoured Division he was transferred to the 79th. The division's new role suited its commander perfectly.

Hobart's gift for innovation was readily apparent in the breadth of tank designs translated from mere ideas to military vehicles which served a variety of purposes and undoubtedly saved thousands of Allied lives. Among those which saw action in addition to the DD Sherman were a modified Churchill tank

called the Bobbin, which carried a 100m (110-yard) coil of coir, a material made from coconut hulls, which could be unrolled over loose ground to enable following vehicles to gain traction. The Crab was a Sherman fitted with a spinning metal drum, 3m (10ft) wide, to which were attached a number of chain flails. When the tank crawled forward at just over 1.5km (1 mile) per hour, the spinning flails would detonate any land mines in the vehicle's path.

CROCODILE AND THE CHURCHILL

Two fearsome combat tanks were the Crocodile and the Churchill AVRE. Instead of a main cannon the Crocodile was fitted with a flamethrower capable of spewing a stream of napalm a distance of 110m (120 yards). The jellied gasoline was stored in a

400-gallon trailer which was towed on heavy rubber tyres directly behind the Crocodile. This flamethrower version of the Churchill was particularly effective against fortified enemy positions, although the napalm-filled trailer also offered a highly flammable target. The Churchill AVRE (Armoured Vehicle Royal Engineers) mounted a squat 290mm (11.5in) mortar, which hurled an 18kg (40lb) shell against hard targets such as bunkers or pillboxes.

Other 79th Armoured innovations included the ARV (Armoured Recovery Vehicle), equipped with a heavy winch to extricate vehicles damaged in combat or mired in mud or sand. Often, the ARV cleared roadways and enabled advancing columns to maintain their timetables and avoid prolonged exposure to enemy air attack or artillery fire. The ARK (Armoured Ramp Carrier) was a turret-less Churchill with a pair of ramps at either end. These could be raised or lowered in order to allow vehicles to cross ditches or small streams or to traverse a sea wall several feet high. A larger version of the ARK was developed from a Churchill AVRE, which could deploy a 9.1m (30ft) bridge capable of supporting a weight of 40 tonnes.

Hobart commanded the 79th Armoured Division throughout the campaign in Western Europe as part of the 21st Army Group under Field Marshal Bernard Law Montgomery. For eight years after the war he served as lieutenant governor of the Royal Hospital. He died in 1957. Many of the concepts originally developed by Hobart and the 79th Armoured Division survive to this day in modern armies.

ROYAL MARINE COMMANDOS

- •FOUNDED: 1900
- •STRENGTH: 2000
- •THEATRES: WESTERN EUROPE

Perhaps no other descriptive word for a soldier in World War II conjures up such images of courage and daring against long odds as that of 'Commando'. In the spring of 1940, Great Britain

Royal Navy Commandos were attached to the Royal Marines and responsible for beach head and naval gunfire support.

stood alone as Nazi Germany, seemingly everywhere triumphant, gripped Western Europe from the Arctic Circle to the Mediterranean.

In the days after the evacuation of the British Expeditionary Force at Dunkirk it became apparent to Prime Minister Winston Churchill that a force must be assembled and equipped for the purpose not only of inflicting casualties on the Germans but also of bolstering British morale for the long fight which lay ahead.

'I look to the Joint Chiefs of Staff to propose measures for a ceaseless offensive against the whole German-occupied coastline, leaving a trail of German corpses behind,' he asserted. 'Enterprises must be prepared with specially trained troops of the hunter class who can develop a reign of terror down the enemy coast.'

One British staff officer had already considered what should be done to revive the flagging offensive spirit of the British Army. Lieutenant Colonel Dudley Clarke had put pen to paper and submitted a proposal to Sir John Dill, Chief of the Imperial General Staff. Spurred on by his own conviction and Churchill's directive, Dill approved Clarke's proposal and added tersely, '… I want you to get it going at once.'

Just three weeks later the first Commando raid of the war took place as 115 volunteers, their faces blackened, were bounced across the English Channel near Boulogne. This initial foray accomplished little, with one party milling about in darkness before heading back to its boat. Commandos killed two hapless German sentries but failed to gather any intelligence or damage any enemy installations.

The second Commando raid, carried out on 14 July 1940 against Germans on Guernsey, one of the occupied Channel Islands, fared little better as new

electric wiring made compasses gyrate wildly and one unit found itself on the wrong island. Another offloaded from its launch in water nearly over the Commandos' heads. Where they expected to find a barracks full of German troops they encountered only an empty building. Swelling seas had forced their launch away from the beach and the tired soldiers were forced to swim to their transportation home.

SPECIAL SERVICE BRIGADE

As inauspicious as the initial Commando raids were, they did signal the start of something very big. Organization and training were obvious keys to future success, and hard lessons in what not to do would prove to be of value in the coming months. By the autumn of 1940 more than 2000 Army personnel had volunteered for Commando training,

Knife clenched in his teeth, a Commando gazes toward his objective during training. The British Army disbanded its Commando units after the war, but Commandos serve in the Royal Marines today.

and what was known as the Special Service Brigade was organized into 12 units called Commandos. As the ranks swelled, Commando units would number around 450 men and be commanded by a lieutenant colonel. In turn, these were divided into troops of 75 men and then sections of 15 soldiers each.

Early Commando units were all from the British Army but they required cooperation with other services, and Admiral Sir Roger Keyes, Chief of Combined Operations, was originally in charge of Commando organization and operations. In October 1941 Keyes resigned and was replaced by Lord Louis Mountbatten. By February 1942 the

Royal Marines had issued a call to organize Commando units of their own, and 6000 men responded. Through to the end of the war an inter-service rivalry between Army and Royal Marine Commandos simmered.

Following months of training and on-again, off-again rumours of impending action, the Commandos were put to the test in the Lofoten Islands off the coast of Norway, where processing plants took fish oil and produced glycerine for use in the manufacture of German munitions. On 1 March 1941, No. 3 and No. 4 Commando loaded 500 men aboard two steamers and headed for the Lofotens. Two days later they reached their target. In the pre-dawn hours of 4 March they landed virtually unopposed and set about taking 216 prisoners and destroying 18 factories and 800,000 gallons of fuel oil. The Commandos sustained only one casualty due to a self-inflicted gunshot wound.

Commandos of the Royal Marine Boom Patrol Detachment train in a small boat. Known as the Cockleshell Heroes, a small group of these men raided the harbour at Bordeaux.

In December 1941, another raid against German economic interests in Scandinavia was executed on the island of Vaagso. No. 3 Commando, supported by Royal Air Force bombers dropping smoke bombs and fire from the light cruiser *HMS Kenya* and four destroyers, quickly took control of Maalo Island, while on nearby Vaagso a spirited fight went on for several hours while fish oil factories were blown up. By mid-afternoon the Commandos were on their way back to England with more than 100 prisoners, having lost 20 dead and 57 wounded.

On 27 February 1942 the 2nd Parachute Battalion assaulted a German radar station on the Normandy coast at Bruneval, taking photos of the top secret Wurzburg radar apparatus, removing parts as they could for transport back to England, and taking prisoners. The raiders lost only one killed, five wounded and seven missing.

COCKLESHELL HEROES

However, not every raid was successful. On 7 December 1942 a group of 10 Royal Marine Commandos, officially known as the Royal Marine Boom Patrol Detachment, set out in five two-man

folding boats, called Cockles. The men became known as the Cockleshell Heroes. Their target was German merchant shipping in the harbour of Bordeaux. Over four arduous days the Commandos paddled under cover of darkness and hid during daylight hours after launching from a British submarine. Two men drowned when they were unable to right their capsized boat, and another four were captured and shot after their boats capsized as well. Of the four Commandos who reached Bordeaux, two were captured and executed while two managed to escape to neutral Spain. Five ships were damaged by the mines that were planted.

The men of No. 4 Commando accounted for the greatest single success of a dark, desperate day during the 19 August 1942 raid on the French coastal city of Dieppe. Under the command of Lieutenant Colonel Lord Lovat, the 250 Commandos silenced a German artillery battery at Varengeville but lost 45 men in the process. At Berneval, only a small fraction of No. 3 Commando was able to assault a second battery. Unable to take the well defended position, the Commandos harassed the gunners with sniper fire so efficiently that the crews were prevented from servicing the guns. Most of No. 3 Commando failed to reach the battery. Only six of its 23 landing craft actually made the narrow beach. Pinned down for a time, about 120 men of No. 3

This illustration shows a sergeant from No. 1 Commando prior to the raid at St Nazaire. As part of a demolition team, he is armed with plentiful hand grenades and a Browning automatic pistol.

Right: Distinguishable by their Bergen rucksacks, Commandos under Lord Lovat go ashore at Sword Beach, D-Day, 6 June 1944.

Commando were captured. On 13 November 1942, Lieutenant Colonel Geoffrey Keyes, the youngest officer of such rank in the British Army at age 24, led an ill-fated raid against the headquarters of Field Marshal Erwin Rommel, the Desert Fox and commander of the vaunted Afrika Korps, at Beda Littoria, 18km (11 miles) inland from the Mediterranean coast of Libya. Faulty intelligence had led the British to believe that Rommel would be at Beda Littoria, and the opportunity to capture or kill him was quite appealing. Keyes was mortally wounded and received a posthumous Victoria Cross, but the raid was a shambles. Only two Commandos returned to British lines after surviving in the desert wilderness for 36 days.

FLOATING BOMB

Perhaps the most celebrated Commando raid of the war in Europe was against the mammoth dry dock at the French port city of St Nazaire. The dry dock had been built before the war in order to service the luxury liner *Normandie*, and it was the only one on the Atlantic coast which could accommodate the massive, 43,700-tonne German battleship *Tirpitz*. If the dry dock could be destroyed *Tirpitz* might be compelled to remain in the relative safety of Norwegian waters and constitute less of a threat to Allied convoys.

On 27 May 1942 Royal Navy Captain Robert 'Red' Ryder and Lieutenant Colonel Charles Newman of No. 2 Commando led the assault toward its target aboard Motor Gunboat (MGB) 314. The only hope to inflict appreciable damage on the dry dock lay with an antiquated destroyer, HMS *Campbeltown*, originally of the United States Navy. The old destroyer had been modified to resemble a German destroyer, and her hull had been packed with thousands of kilograms of explosives.

If all went according to plan the *Campbeltown* would ram the steel gates of the dry dock, lodging inside. Her delayed action bombs would explode hours later and destroy it. Aboard the floating bomb were 75 Commandos, who would leap to shore and blow up port installations. The entire Commando-Royal Navy flotilla included the old destroyer, MGB-314, two escort destroyers and 16 motor launches carrying a total of 611 Commandos.

With the *Campbeltown* in the mouth of the Loire River and less than 1.5km (1 mile) from the dry dock, the Germans suddenly sprang to life and began firing at the attackers. At a speed of 20 knots the old destroyer rammed the gate and Commandos clambered down her sides. One intrepid group of five Commandos reached the pump house at the dock, raced down 12m (40ft) of stairs, set demolition charges to explode in 90 seconds, and darted back out in 60.

Accurate fire from the Germans ashore wrecked several of the motor launches, and casualties began to mount among the Commandos. Eventually, 397 of them were killed or captured. As for the dry dock, more than 12 hours after the raid on St Nazaire began the *Campbeltown* exploded violently, killing 380 Germans and destroying it completely. Five Victoria Crosses were awarded for heroism during the raid.

Commando operations supported Allied offensive efforts in Sicily, Italy, Normandy, and against the Japanese on the Asian continent. The British Army disbanded its Commando units in 1946 but the tradition lives on today in the modern Royal Marines. The successes of the British Commandos inspired the formation of similar elite forces around the world, including the US Army Rangers.

SPECIAL BOAT SERVICE

- •FOUNDED: 1940
- •STRENGTH: 100 (ESTIMATED)
- •THEATRES: NORTH AFRICA, MEDITERANNEAN, INDIAN–BURMA

Formed in July 1940 by Captain Roger J.A. Courtney upon the authorization of Admiral Sir Roger Keyes, Chief of Combined Operations, the Special Boat Service was originally known by the nondescript moniker of the Folboat Troop, after the folding canoes which carried its raiders on covert missions throughout the war.

It was Courtney's premise that small groups of highly trained men could slip undetected into enemy harbours and destroy or damage shipping by attaching limpet mines or other explosives to hulls. In its early period the name of the Special Boat Service (SBS) and its functionality continued to evolve. From the Folboat Troop the unit became the Special Boat Section, then Z SBS, and later the Special Boat Section, before it ultimately came to be known as the Special Boat Service. By the time Courtney had left the Mediterranean Theatre the unit had

An SBS man, armed with an M1 carbine and other equipment, beams after returning from a raid. Operating in small groups, these seaborne Commandos gained notable successes.

grown appreciably, and approximately 18 months after its formation the SBS was absorbed by the Special Air Service (SAS).

Another unit, which operated as the Special Boat Section of the Combined Operations Special Service Brigade, should not be confused with the Special Boat Service. The primary function of the Special Boat Section became coastal reconnaissance in advance of amphibious landings on hostile shores, such as Operation Torch, the Allied landings in North Africa in November 1942. The Special Boat Service often attacked targets on land along the

Major Anders Lassen, known to the Germans as the 'Terrible Viking', was the most famous of the SBS men. He received the Victoria Cross and other awards for bravery.

coast of North Africa, Italy and the Greek Isles, but the unit was not limited to the European Theatre of Operations, conducting dozens of raids against the Japanese in the China-Burma-India theatre. During one raid against a moored target in the French harbour of Boulogne, two SBS men were delivered to a point offshore by a motor torpedo boat (MTB).

From there they paddled their folboat into the harbour and attached limpet mines to the hull of a German freighter carrying 5000 tonnes of copper ore. The mines exploded with a roar, and the ship settled to the bottom of the harbour as the raiders watched from the safety of the MTB, having eluded all efforts to locate them.

SBS raiders hit an Axis airfield on the Greek island of Rhodes in September 1942, blowing up three Italian Savoia-Marchetti bombers, a fuel dump and numerous buildings. The attackers then hid out for more than four days under the noses of the enemy. Although one party was captured, the other, nearing the end of its endurance, managed to reach the coastline and signal a waiting submarine offshore. Their small watercraft had been discovered by an Italian patrol, and the SBS men had no choice but to swim to the rendezvous point, nearly 5km (3 miles) from the beach.

Once aboard the submarine the raiders were still not safe. A prowling Italian destroyer depth charged the vessel before it made good its escape. One of the SBS men, Captain David 'Dinky' Sutherland, was seriously ill and hospitalized after the raid. He recovered and rose to command all SBS unit operations in Italy, Greece and the Aegean Sea later in the war.

THE TERRIBLE VIKING

By far the most celebrated SBS raider was Major Anders Lassen, an expatriate Dane who became one of the most highly decorated soldiers in World War II. Lassen was awarded the Victoria Cross and three Military Crosses for valour in action and was reputed to have killed more Germans than any other British soldier during the war.

Lassen became known to the Axis enemy in the Mediterranean as the 'Terrible Viking'. One raid graphically illustrates his boldness and no-quarter attitude. On the island of Santorini in the Aegean Sea he chose the small Santorini town as the focus of his party's attention while other groups were active elsewhere. In company with 11 SBS men, Lassen found the local bank building, which 68 Germans and Italians had decided to use as a barracks. Moving from room to room, the SBS team killed all but 10 of the enemy soldiers, some

of whom leaped from upper story windows to get away.

Lassen lost his life during a mission in Italy on 9 April 1945. After silencing a number of German bunkers near the village of Comacchio in support of a large commando raid, he noticed a white flag hanging from a strong point still occupied by the Germans. As he approached to accept their surrender he was gunned down.

The Special Boat Service survives today as an independent unit of the Royal Marines. The SBS is currently based with 1 Assault Group Royal Marines and 148 Commando Forward Observation Battery of the British Army located at Poole, Dorset.

X-CLASS SUBMARINES

- **FOUNDED: 1942**
- **STRENGTH: 100 (ESTIMATED)**
- **THEATRES: WESTERN EUROPE, FAR EAST**

While the defeat of Nazi Germany on land was an essential component of victory in World War II, an equally important fight for survival was waged on the high seas. The Battle of the Atlantic preserved the lifeline of supply to both the island nation of Great Britain and the beleaguered Soviet Union, but the cost was high as Germany's marauding U-boat wolf-packs of Admiral Karl Doenitz very nearly succeeded in their mission to thoroughly disrupt Allied supply and troop movements.

Improvements in technology, growing numbers of convoy escort vessels and escalating U-boat losses eventually tipped the balance of power in the Atlantic in favour of the Allies; however, equally unsettling to Allied leaders was the threat of German warships which might intercept Allied shipping and decimate vital convoys. In mid-1942 one German battleship loomed as a greater threat

Right: The crew of a British X-Class submarine conducts training prior to Operation Source, which was conceived to attack the German battleship **Tirpitz** *in a Norwegian Fjord.*

An X-Class submarine underway, with a crewman standing on its hull, practices manoeuvres in preparation for one of several clandestine operations conducted during the war by these small submersibles.

than any other – the mighty 43,000-tonne *Tirpitz*. The elimination of this potentially devastating enemy warship had become a priority for the Allies, particularly British Prime Minister Winston Churchill.

Ensconced safely in the shelter of Kaafjord on the coast of Norway, *Tirpitz* was a frustrating target. The sheer cliffs of the fjord and formidable anti-aircraft defences made successful air attack virtually impossible, and submarines could not safely operate in such narrow confines, particularly when their target was undoubtedly protected by heavy harbour patrols and ringed with anti-torpedo netting.

TIRPITZ TEST

Churchill deemed the very existence of *Tirpitz*, which obliged the Admiralty to maintain a deterrent force of capital ships at the Royal Navy's Scapa Flow anchorage in the Orkney Islands of

Scotland, as intolerable. A single option, fraught with risk, appeared to be the only card left for the British to play.

Well aware of the potential of the midget submarine to effectively pull off an attack on the *Tirpitz*, the Royal Navy had begun design work on such a craft in late 1941. The result was the X-Craft, a submersible 16m (51ft) in length, weighing about 30 tonnes, and with room for a crew of four in quite cramped quarters. Two prototypes, X-3 and X-4, were constructed, and the first X-Craft was launched in March 1942. Five more midget submarines, X-5 to X-10, were built and the force was designated the 12th Submarine Flotilla.

X-Craft crewmen were selected during rigorous training, and a number of volunteers were unable to cope with the claustrophobic conditions and extremely hazardous nature of the duty. Specific training for the attempt to sink the *Tirpitz* began in the spring of 1943 at a top secret base referred to as Port HHZ in Loch Cairnbawn on the coast of northern Scotland.

On the night of 11 September 1943 the five X-Craft departed from the Scottish shore under tow by conventional Royal Navy submarines. Dubbed

Operation Source, the mission began with an arduous trek of more than 1700km (1100 miles). The X-Craft were to be manned by transit crews which would then be replaced by the combat crews once the rendezvous point at Soroy Sound, 160km (100 miles) from Kaafjord, had been reached. The voyage was hazardous to say the least, particularly when the weather turned nasty on 15 September. Three towlines snapped in the heaving seas; X-8 foundered and was scuttled, while the waterlogged

The cramped interior of an X-Class submarine reveals the close quarters shared by the midget submarine's crew of four. The small craft could not remain submerged for extended periods of time.

towline of X-9 dragged the submersible and its transit crew to the bottom of the sea.

Initially, the six X-Craft were to attack *Tirpitz* and her consorts, the battle-cruiser *Scharnhorst* and the pocket battleship *Lutzow*, which were thought also to be at Kaafjord. However, down to only four midget submarines the Admiralty decided that all of them would attack the *Tirpitz*. As it turned out, *Scharnhorst* and *Lutzow* were not anchored in Kaafjord at the time of the attack anyway. Each of the X-Craft was armed with a pair of 2-tonne explosive charges affixed externally to its hull. Once inside Kaafjord the plan was to manoeuvre under the battleship and release the explosives, timed to detonate one hour later on the seabed.

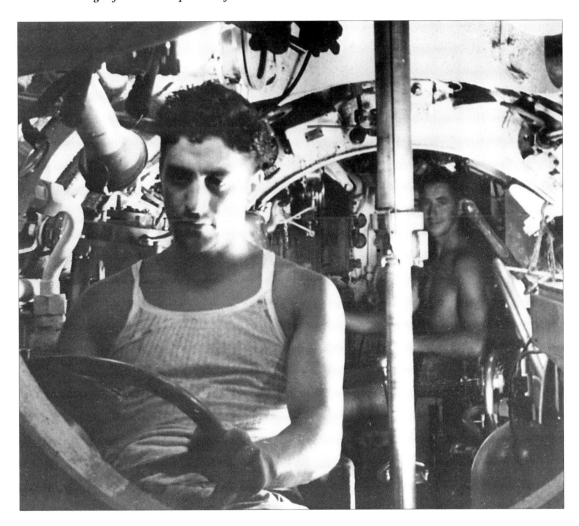

By the time the X-Craft attack commenced on 21 September only three of the midget submarines remained in service. X-10 had experienced an electrical failure which forced the craft to withdraw from the fjord. The three, X-5 commanded by Lieutenant Henty Henty-Creer, X-6 commanded by Lieutenant Duncan Cameron, and X-7 commanded by Lieutenant Godfrey Place, managed to penetrate the defences and reach the *Tirpitz* anchorage.

Cameron followed a German patrol craft through an opening in the anti-torpedo netting and then attempted to orient X-6 for the final run below the battleship. When he surveyed the scene through the periscope of X-6 he spotted the *Tirpitz* 180m (200 yards) away. Diving again, X-6 crashed into a submerged rock formation and bounced to the surface only 68m (75 yards) from the giant warship. This time the tiny submarine was spotted and came under fire from the *Tirpitz*. Cameron quickly ordered the charges jettisoned under the ship's forward 380mm (15in) gun turrets and surrendered to a launch which had been put in the water by the Germans.

Aboard X-7, Place struggled with entanglements in the anti-torpedo netting and popped to the surface a scant 22m (25 yards) from the target. The X-Craft actually scraped the battleship's hull as Place released one charge forward and his second amidships but again became entangled in the netting. At 8.12 a.m. a huge explosion rocked the *Tirpitz*, as all of the placed charges were apparently detonated by the shock of the first to go off. X-7

MIDGET SUBS IN SINGAPORE

In August 1945 the midget submarines XE-1 and XE-3, an improved version of the X-Craft, attacked Japanese warships in Singapore harbour. XE-3 attached limpet mines to the hull of the cruiser Takao and dropped two external explosive charges nearby. The XE-1 was unable to locate its target, the cruiser *Myoko*, and attacked the Takao as well, and the target was sunk. XE-4 and XE-5 participated in operations Sabre and Foil, which succeeded in cutting Japanese communications cables between Singapore, Saigon, Hong Kong and Tokyo.

was blown free from its entanglement but severely damaged. Under heavy fire from *Tirpitz* Place and another crewman survived and were captured, while two others perished, trapped inside the small vessel.

The fate of X-5 remains something of a mystery as the midget submarine was taken under fire and depth charged by at least one German destroyer and several smaller patrol craft, and there were no survivors. It is unknown whether Henty-Creer actually was able to plant his charges beneath the battleship's hull. However, in 2003 Norwegian marine archaeologists and divers discovered the hull of a midget submarine thought to be X-5 – without its charges. They may actually have been successfully placed.

Regardless, the *Tirpitz* suffered significant damage, a gaping hole blown in her hull, steering gear wrecked, and turrets displaced from their mountings. The ship would never become fully operational again, although it would require a raid by Royal Air Force heavy bombers dropping 6000kg (13,000lb) tallboy bombs to finally sink the behemoth in Tromso Fjord on 12 November 1944.

Cameron, Place and the surviving British crewmen remained prisoners of the Germans until the end of the war. Both commanders received the Victoria Cross for their daring, and a movement is under way to petition for the award of a third to Henty-Creer.

The raid on the *Tirpitz* was not the only employment of X-Craft midget submarines during World War II. In the spring of 1944, X-24 attacked the Laksevag floating dry dock at Bergen, mistakenly laying its charges underneath the 7650-tonne merchant ship *Barenfels*, which was sunk while the dry dock sustained little damage. On 11 September 1944 the X-24 made a second attempt and successfully sank the dry dock. Prior to the D-Day invasion X-Craft performed reconnaissance of the Normandy beaches by periscope and ferried divers close to shore to collect specimens of sand and assess the disposition of landing obstacles.

The X-Craft submariner of World War II was a rare breed, accepting the great risk involved in such operations yet willing to venture into enemy territory aboard a vessel which could utilize only stealth in its own defence.

6TH AIRBORNE DIVISION

- •FOUNDED: 1943
- •STRENGTH: 8000
- •THEATRES: WESTERN EUROPE

The weather was far from ideal, but the word had been passed and the mighty Allied invasion force poised to begin the liberation of Western Europe from Nazi domination had been unleashed in the pre-dawn hours of 6 June 1944. The first Allied troops to set foot in occupied France were to be the paratroops and glider-borne soldiers of three airborne divisions, the American 101st and 82nd, and the British 6th.

These elite soldiers were tasked with securing the western and eastern flanks, respectively, of the Normandy invasion beaches, silencing enemy gun emplacements, and seizing key bridges and road intersections in German-held territory. The 6th

On 6 June 1944, elements of the 6th Airborne Division captured the bridge over the Caen Canal. Three paras take a much needed break after being relieved.

Airborne, officially formed in England on 3 May 1943, had trained intensely for months to achieve its D-Day objectives – the capture of the bridges over the Caen Canal and Orne River, the destruction of a battery of heavy guns at Merville, which could devastate the landings on Sword beach if left intact, and the destruction of five key bridges across the Dives River on the extreme left flank in order to delay the German counter-attack which would surely come.

Lieutenant General Richard N. Gale, the 6th Airborne Division's commander, may rightly be called the father of the British Army's airborne forces. A veteran of World War I, he had served in France nearly three decades earlier. Between the world wars he posted to India where he spent 15 years without advancement above the rank of lieutenant. By 1940 he was in command of a battalion, and the following year he was ordered to organize the army's first parachute brigade. Elevated to the position of Director of Airborne Forces with the War Office for a time, he was eventually granted field command of the 6th Airborne, and landed with glider troops in Normandy.

D-DAY GLIDERS

The first British forces in action on D-Day were to land via glider at 12.15 a.m., while pathfinders jumped to illuminate landing zones for the waves of paratroopers which would be descending in the coming hours. In six Airspeed Horsa gliders towed behind Douglas C-47 Dakota transports, five platoons of the 2nd Battalion, Oxfordshire and Buckinghamshire Light Infantry, along with a company of Royal Engineers, were to capture the bridges across the Caen Canal and the Orne River near Bénouville.

Right on schedule the Dakotas released their tow lines and the gliders whisked free. At the Caen Canal bridge Private Helmut Romer walked sentry duty. Suddenly, he saw the looming form of a large aircraft heading into a field a scant 20m (22 yards) from the far end of the bridge. In rapid succession

Officers from the 22nd Independent Parachute Company stand waiting in front of a C-47 transort plane on 5 June 1944, prior to the D-Day air drop.

two more careened in, landing within 22m (25 yards) of the first. The Germans were taken completely by surprise, and Romer was one of several who quickly fled the scene.

Led by Major John Howard, the glider troops captured the Caen Canal bridge within 10 minutes. Resistance had been light but a burst of machine-gun fire had killed Lieutenant Den Brotheridge, who was perhaps the first of many Allied soldiers to die in action during the effort to liberate Western Europe. Air Chief Marshal Sir Trafford Leigh-Mallory called the accurate glider landing the most outstanding example of airmanship in the entire war. Since 6 June 1944 the Caen Canal bridge has been called Pegasus Bridge, a reference to the 6th Airborne insignia featuring the mythical winged horse and in honour of the nearly flawless operation.

Two of Howard's three remaining gliders were more dispersed on landing, while the third failed to reach the landing area altogether. Nevertheless, these glider troops were equally successful in capturing the Orne River bridge, and the code words 'ham and jam' were broadcast to signal the capture of two objectives. At about 12.50 a.m. 6th Airborne reinforcements

A British glider pilot clutches his red beret. British pilots were fully-trained soldiers who were expected to fight on the ground.

parachuted near Ranville, reinforced Howard's men at the bridges, and cleared landing zones for the arrival by glider of the headquarters group along with Jeeps and heavier weapons such as anti-tank guns scheduled for 3.20 a.m. The soldiers at the bridges held their positions against counter-attacks and were relieved by commandos under Lord Lovat around 1.30 p.m.

For everything that had gone well for Howard, something else went very wrong for 29-year-old Lieutenant Colonel Terence Otway and the 650-man 9th Parachute Battalion charged with reducing the Merville Battery. A pre-jump aerial bombardment by Royal Air Force Avro Lancaster bombers had missed the mark, succeeding only in killing a few cows and levelling a small village. Gliders carrying the unit's anti-tank weapons and Jeep transportation broke their towlines and took their precious cargoes to the bottom of the English Channel. Heavy anti-aircraft fire caused the transport pilots to begin manoeuvring violently, throwing the paratroops around inside the planes.

Once they hit the silk the paratroops were badly scattered. Otway landed on top of a German command post and had to scurry to safety as scores of enemy soldiers poured out the front door. Weighed down with heavy gear, some unfortunate paratroops landed in the marshes near the Dives River and drowned. With only one machine gun and 155 men, Otway started toward the Merville Battery just before 3 a.m. Shortly after they reached their objective, Otway and his company watched as two gliders filled with reinforcements, which should have landed on top of the battery, overshot the area and landed too distant to help with the difficult task ahead.

HAND-TO-HAND COMBAT

With no other course of action available the young officer ordered an attack. Gaps were blown in the barbed wire and hand-to-hand fighting ensued in the trenches surrounding the blockhouse whose concrete walls were 1.86m (6ft) thick. While one group of paratroops took on the German machine-gunners, a second raced for the battery's steel doors, two of which were open. Forcing their way inside, they killed the German artillerymen and destroyed

On the day after their glider landing in Normandy, paras of the 6th Airborne Division dig a defensive trench around their landing zone. A damaged glider is visible at right.

the guns with explosives. The Merville Battery was no longer a threat. Otway had lost 65 men killed or wounded, while German casualties totalled more than 100. A recognition flare went up, notifying an observation plane that the battery had been silenced just 15 minutes prior to the commencement of a naval bombardment, which would have been unleashed on the assumption that the airborne operation had failed.

Near Troarn, two brigades of the 3rd Parachute Battalion ran into high winds, mis-marked drop zones and anti-aircraft fire, which scattered the paratroops over a wide area. Still, four of the five bridges were blown up in short order. The fifth proved more difficult, but an enterprising group of nine soldiers found a Jeep equipped with a trailer which had been dropped for medical corps use. The soldiers sped away toward Troarn, extricated themselves from a barbed wire entanglement and

drove down the town's main street with guns blazing. Moments after reaching the bridge, demolition charges sent the span crashing into the river below.

The exploits of the 6th Airborne Division on D-Day secured the left flank of the Normandy beachhead and delayed a counter-attack by the veteran German 21st Panzer Division for several hours. Over the following two months the 6th Airborne was engaged east of the Orne. Finally returning to England in September, the division had sustained 4000 casualties.

Later in the war, under the command of Major-General Eric Bols, the 6th Airborne Division fought in Belgium during the Battle of the Bulge from December 1944 to January 1945, and participated in the airborne crossing of the Rhine River, Operation Varsity, in March 1945. In late April, elements of the 6th Airborne linked up with units of the Soviet Red Army at the Baltic seaport of Wismar, Germany. Gale's illustrious military career continued after the war, as he was appointed NATO Deputy Supreme Commander in Europe and Commander-in-Chief of the British Army of the Rhine. He died in 1982 at the age of 86.

COMMONWEALTH & EXPATRIATE ROYAL AIR FORCE PILOTS

- **Founded: 1940**
- **Strength: 244**
- **Theatres: Western Europe**

Great Britain's Royal Air Force (RAF) may be distinguished as having written one of the most heroic chapters of World War II, and indeed in all the history of armed conflict. When the Battle of Britain was over, Prime Minister Winston Churchill summed up the sublime sacrifice and triumph saying: 'Never in the field of human conflict has so much been owed by so many to so few.' The Royal Air Force withstood the full fury of the mighty German Luftwaffe during the summer and autumn of 1940 and until Hitler was obliged to cancel Operation Sealion, his planned invasion of the island nation. The RAF was also visible and active in the campaigns to defeat the Nazis from the Arctic to the deserts of North Africa, as well as the Japanese from the subtropics of the South Pacific to the jungles of Burma.

Among the pilots who flew their Supermarine Spitfire and Hawker Hurricane fighters and their Handley-Page Halifax and Avro Lancaster bombers into legend were a number of outstanding young men from the nations of the British

Standing in front of a Hawker Hurricane fighter, Belgian pilots serving in the RAF watch as one of their number comes in to land.

Hawker Hurricanes of a Canadian fighter squadron fly in formation toward the English Channel to intercept a German air raid. A large contingent of Canadian pilots flew in the RAF.

Commonwealth and from countries which had been occupied by the Nazis during their lightning conquest of Europe, both East and West. Some of these pilots flew in squadrons which were solely made up of their own countrymen, while others were engaged in standard Royal Air Force squadrons throughout the war. For example, the Royal Canadian Air Force (RCAF) contributed 48 squadrons to the war effort, but only about 40 per cent of the personnel committed served in Canadian squadrons. Roughly 60 percent served in the RAF.

Following the swift conquest of most of Europe by the German *Wehrmacht*, pilots from countries such as France, Poland, Belgium, Czechoslovakia, Norway, the Netherlands, Yugoslavia and Greece managed to reach the relative safety of Great Britain

and volunteered their services. Some of these, particularly the Poles and the French, were experienced combat pilots, having fought the Germans earlier. Canada, Australia, South Africa, New Zealand and Ireland committed fliers to the war effort as well.

TOP 10 ACES

Among the highest scoring British and Commonwealth aces during the war, the top 10 included two South Africans, an Irishman, a Canadian and an Australian. Squadron Leader M.T. St. J. Pattle, known as 'Pat' to his comrades, is reputed to be the top scoring ace of Great Britain and the Commonwealth during the war. Pattle is credited with shooting down approximately 51 Axis fighter planes in North Africa and Greece. His first two victories came while flying with No. 80 Squadron on 4 August 1940, but the feat nearly cost him his own life as he was shot down in turn.

In the autumn of 1940 the squadron was transferred to Greece to assist the Greek Army in its

FRENCH FIGHTER ACE

The leading French ace flying with the RAF was Wing Commander Jean Demozay, who had shot down 21 German aircraft by the end of 1942, while using the nom de guerre of Moses Morlaix. Demozay escaped to England after serving as an interpreter for RAF No. 1 Squadron, which had been based on the continent. Flying Hurricanes, he gained five victories by the spring of 1941, then switched to Spitfires with No. 91 Squadron. He was killed in an air accident shortly after the war.

fight with the invading Italians. Soon, Pattle's score increased with 10 more individual kills and partial credit for two more. In late February and early March 1941 his tally continued to rise with multiple kills on at least two days. With his score at 24 he was promoted to command No. 33 Squadron. Due to the destruction of Allied records in the retreat following German intervention in Greece, it is difficult to confirm Pattle's number of victories during the spring of 1941. However, conservative estimates place his score at a minimum of 40 by this time. During a five-day period from 15-19 April he was reported to have shot down 14 enemy planes. However, during his third sortie of the final day he spotted a fellow pilot under attack above Eleusis Bay near Athens. Pattle dived to the rescue but was shot down and killed.

Wing Commander Brendan 'Paddy' Finucane, an Irishman, was third on the RAF ace list with 32 victories, a total matched by Group Captain A.G. Malan from South Africa. Finucane was killed in action in 1942, while Malan's career as a fighter pilot, much of which was spent with No. 74 Squadron, concluded at the end of 1941, when he was transferred from active flying.

'SCREWBALL' BEURLING

Although his own country's air force, the RCAF, had rejected him due to his lack of education, Flight Lieutenant George 'Screwball' Beurling was welcomed into the RAF and proved to be a formidable fighter pilot with a total of 31 victories by the end of the war. For all his flying skill,

Beurling displayed a penchant for getting into trouble, and eventually he was exiled from No. 41 Squadron in England to the island of Malta in the Mediterranean.

History remembers the Canadian as the greatest Allied ace during the long, difficult defence of the fortress island. Flying with No. 249 Squadron, he shot down three enemy aircraft on at least two occasions and flamed four in one day on 27 July 1941. Twenty-six of Beurling's victories were scored in the skies above Malta. At the end of 1943 he returned to England and finally joined the RCAF, downing three German fighters as a member of No. 412 Squadron. Other high scoring Canadian aces included Flight Lieutenant V.C. Woodward with 22 and Squadron Leader H.W. McLeod with 21.

Wing Commander Clive Caldwell became the top Australian ace of World War II with twenty-eight-and-a-half aerial victories. As a member of No. 250 Squadron, he claimed 18 kills in North Africa between June and December 1941, flying the Curtiss P-40 Tomahawk fighter. During a single air battle on 5 December he downed five Junkers Ju-87 Stuka dive bombers. Later, he led No. 112 Squadron.

ACE ON BOTH SIDES

Lieutenant Pierre LeGloan shot down 20 aircraft before dying in a fiery crash on 11 September 1943, caused by an overheated engine. Although he was never a member of the RAF his story is interesting. While a member of the French Air Force LeGloan shot down several Italian aircraft, five in one day. Ironically, his squadron was transferred to Syria. Flying for the Vichy government he shot down seven RAF fighters. When his squadron was transferred to Algeria in 1942 LeGloan would undoubtedly have opposed Operation Torch, the Allied landings in North Africa; however, bad weather kept his plane grounded. Eventually, his squadron received American planes, and LeGloan shot down six German aircraft.

Although a number of skilled Polish pilots reached Great Britain early in the war, it was not until the British Government and the Polish Government in exile concluded an agreement on 11 June 1940 that all-Polish squadrons were formed in the RAF. The Polish pilots were required to wear British uniforms, but on 5 August these airmen were recognized as part of the Polish Army and allowed to wear Polish rank insignia. The first Polish units were bomber squadrons No. 300 and No. 301 and fighter squadrons No. 302 and No. 303. By the end of the war, 14 Polish air squadrons had been formed, Polish pilots had flown more than 73,000 fighter sorties and claimed more than 1200 enemy aircraft destroyed or damaged, and Polish bomber crews had flown more than 11,700 missions.

The pilots of No. 303 Squadron were the first to enter combat, and quickly established themselves as one of the best performing squadrons in the Battle of Britain. Wing Commander Witold Urbanowicz scored 17 victories in Europe with No. 303 Squadron and went on to fly with US forces in China, where he downed three Japanese planes. Six more pilots of No. 303 Squadron became aces during 1940.

The highest scoring Polish ace of World War II, edging Urbanowicz by only a fraction with just under 21 kills, was Wing Commander Stanislav Skalski. The only confirmed Polish ace during the fighting in the skies above his native country in 1939, Skalski then flew with No. 306 Squadron and led No. 316. He volunteered to transfer to the desert and fly Spitfires in 1943, earning at least seven more victories. Following a brief respite, he returned to action over France as commander of 133 Polish Wing, flying American P-51 Mustang fighters and claiming his final two victories above the Normandy invasion beaches.

A ground crewman for a Polish fighter squadron has written a message of defiance to the Nazis on the fuselage of a Hawker Hurricane. The artist has also supplied a caricature of Hitler.

CZECH POINTS

Sergeant Joseph Frantisek, flying with the air forces of Poland, France and Great Britain, was the leading Czech ace of World War II with 28 victories. The only Czech pilot flying Hurricanes with the famous No. 303 Squadron,

Frantisek racked up an impressive 17 victories in September 1940 alone, at the height of the Battle of Britain. Frantisek's score would undoubtedly have been substantially higher had he not been killed during a landing accident on 8 October.

The highest scoring Czech in the service of the RAF was Flight Lieutenant Karel Kuttelwascher, who reached England in 1941 after brief service with the French Air Force and the Foreign

Four Czechoslovakian pilots from a Hurricane fighter squadron watch some of their colleagues in flight, 4 January 1940.

Legion. During one sortie Kuttelwascher miraculously shot down three German bombers in four minutes. He also successfully engaged in night fighter operations.

Two Free Norwegian fighter squadrons, No. 331 and No. 332, were organized in Britain, and Captain Sven Heglund emerged as his country's top ace of the war with fourteen-and-a-half aerial victories. Heglund flew with No. 331 Squadron from the spring of 1942 until the autumn of 1943, and shot down 11 German planes. His final three victories were with RAF No. 85 Squadron, flying De Havilland Mosquito night fighters.

Fighter pilots of the Commonwealth nations and those who flew while in exile from their native lands contributed greatly to the establishment of Allied air supremacy in the skies over Europe and the ultimate defeat of the German Luftwaffe.

Not only did they augment the rolls of the Royal Air Force; in many cases they led by heroic example.

RAF EAGLE SQUADRON

- •FOUNDED: 1940
- •STRENGTH: 244
- •THEATRES: WESTERN EUROPE

Alerted to an impending German air raid, pilots of an RAF Eagle Squadron scramble for their Hurricane fighters. In the background, ground crewman assist one pilot into his cockpit.

With the outbreak of war in Europe, a number of American pilots made their way to Great Britain, many of them through Canada, and volunteered for service in the Royal Air Force. Although they were violating their country's Neutrality Acts, their presence was welcomed and the pilots were placed in various RAF squadrons.

These pilots joined other Americans who had ventured to Europe to fly for Finland against the Soviet Union during the Winter War but had seen no action before that conflict ended. Numerous American fliers also served in the Royal Canadian Air Force (RCAF). During the Battle of Britain at least eight Americans flew missions against the Germans, several as members of No. 609 Squadron, RAF.

The concept of the Eagle Squadron, an all-American fighter unit, was originally proposed by Charles Sweeney, a wealthy American businessman living in London. In the opening days of the war Sweeney had been actively recruiting Americans to fly with the French Air Force in a squadron reminiscent of the famous Lafayette Escadrille of World War I. He also cooperated with Canadian World War I ace Billy Bishop to recruit American pilots into the RCAF. After the fall of France, 12 of Sweeney's recruits reportedly joined the RAF. Sweeney also paid the cost of transportation and training, about $100,000, for each American pilot who came to England.

The first Eagle Squadron, No. 71, was formed in September 1940, and based initially at Church Fenton, approximately 320km (200 miles) north of

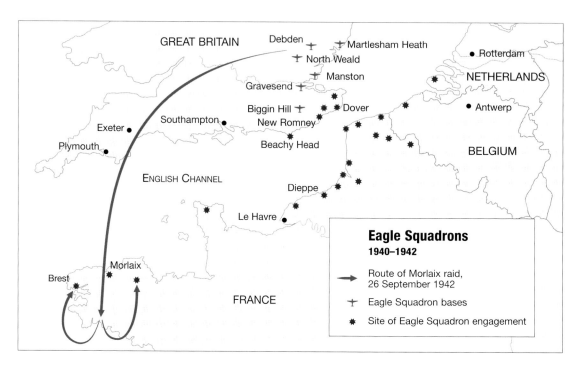

No. 133 Squadron escorted some B-17s on a bombing raid on 26 September 1942. High winds and poor navigation meant the fighters did not have enough fuel to get back to England, and 10 of the Eagle Squadron's new Spitfire Mk IXs were lost.

London. The first three American fliers on the roster were Eugene 'Red' Tobin, Andrew Mamedoff and Vernon 'Shorty' Keough, each of whom had flown previously with No. 609 Squadron. In November, No. 71 Squadron received nine Hawker Hurricane fighters, and on 5 February 1941 the unit was declared operational. It was then based at Martlesham Heath, 105km (65 miles) northeast of London.

Formed in the spring of 1941, the second Eagle Squadron, No. 121, was based at Kirton-on-Lindsey, and the third, No. 133, came into being in August of that year, based at Duxford. Each of these was originally to fly Hurricanes, but within days of their formation these two units were given Spitfires, as was No. 71. Altogether, 244 American pilots would ultimately fly as members of Eagle Squadrons, and 16 British officers acted as commanders of squadrons or flights at various times. Eighty-two

of these pilots, 77 of them American, were killed in action.

On 2 July 1941, pilots of No. 71 Squadron shot down three German Messerschmitt Me-109 fighters in the unit's first aerial contact with the enemy. Gregory A. 'Gus' Daymond shot down seven German planes, received the Distinguished Flying Cross, and rose to command No. 71 Squadron in 1942. William R. Dunn became the first Eagle Squadron pilot to shoot down an enemy aircraft and the first Eagle Squadron ace with five victories before being wounded on 27 August. On that day, Dunn shot down two Me-109s and was attacking a third when no less than four German fighters pounced on him. Seriously wounded, he managed to maintain consciousness and land his badly shot-up Spitfire at Hawkinge, Kent, barely inland from the English Channel. After he had sufficiently recovered, Dunn was transferred to Canada to train new pilots.

'RED' McCOLPIN'S TALLY

The top scoring Eagle Squadron pilot was Carroll W. 'Red' McColpin, who tallied eight victories, six with No. 71 Squadron and two more as commander of No. 133. On two occasions he claimed a pair of Me-109s. McColpin ended his career flying with the US Ninth Air Force, after raising his victory total to 12. He also accomplished one of the more notable feats of the air war, forcing three Messerschmitts to crash into the ground without ever opening fire on them.

In the wake of the Japanese attack on Pearl Harbor, representatives of the Eagle Squadrons demonstrated a desire to join their country's war effort in the Pacific. However, for the time being, the Americans would stay with the RAF due to

logistic challenges and the fact that negotiations would be necessary to compensate the British for their relinquishing three fully trained and equipped fighter squadrons to the United States Army Air Forces (USAAF).

The three Eagle Squadrons flew together only once, during the large scale raid on the French port

Flying their Supermarine Spitfire fighters in formation, a group of Eagle Squadron pilots roar above their airfield as others watch from the ground near the posting of a US flag.

city of Dieppe in August 1942. The following month, the Eagle Squadrons and their beloved Spitfires were formally incorporated into the USAAF as the 334th, 335th and 336th Fighter Squadrons of the 4th Fighter Group of the US Eighth Air Force. Most of the pilots received a USAAF rank equivalent to the one they had held with the RAF. During less than two years of active service the Eagle Squadrons claimed seventy-three-and-a-half German planes shot down, 41 of these by No. 71 Squadron, 18 by No. 121, and fourteen-and-a-half by No. 133.

After a slow start, the 4th Fighter Group eventually accounted for more German aircraft destroyed on the ground and in the air than any other unit of comparable size in the Eighth Air Force. In March 1943 the group was re-equipped with Republic P-47 Thunderbolt fighters, and in April 1944 these were traded in for the superb North American P-51 Mustang fighter.

A pair of former Eagle Squadron pilots went on to achieve great success with the 4th Fighter Group. Captain Don Gentile was the group's highest scorer of the war with 22 victories, two of which were claimed as a member of No. 133 Squadron. Colonel Don Blakeslee commanded the 4th Fighter Group from January to October 1944, and ended his career with 15 and-a-half victories. Three of these were scored during 120 sorties with No. 121 and No. 133 Squadrons.

RAF LYSANDER PILOTS

- FOUNDED: 1939
- STRENGTH: 1000 (ESTIMATED)
- THEATRES: WESTERN EUROPE

One of the most unlikely successes as a modern combat aircraft of World War II was the Westland Lysander, an ungainly looking single-engine aircraft which was conceived as an artillery spotting and reconnaissance plane and as a link between Royal Air Force (RAF) ground attack squadrons and troops of the British Army. Characterized by oversized fixed landing gear and

wings of fabric and wood, the Lysander appeared to be something of a flying anachronism.

In the early days of the war, the RAF threw aircraft of every kind against the German Luftwaffe, and although it was a reliable performer in its intended role, the Lysander was slow and lightly armed and proved to be an easy mark for enemy fighters. Interestingly, prior to the evacuation of the British Expeditionary Force at Dunkirk, a Lysander shot down the first German bomber, a Heinkel He-111, to come down behind British lines. The Lysander also flew ground attack missions early in the war and airlifted supplies to the defenders of the French port city of Calais.

A modified version of the Lysander, equipped with a 682-litre long-range fuel tank and a ladder which allowed quick access into its rear seating area, earned the aircraft a lasting place in history. The most significant attribute of the aircraft was its ability to take off and land in places where other aircraft simply could not operate. Needing only a small area of pasture, field or even a forest clearing, the plane was perfect for inserting and recovering covert agents in German-occupied areas.

MYSTERY FLIGHTS

Flying from bases in Newmarket and later Tempsford, these modified Lysanders, called 'Black Lysanders', completed more than 400 missions with Squadron Nos. 138, 148 and 161 in Europe and No. 357 in the Pacific. In the months prior to D-Day, Lysanders flew more than 60 missions into enemy controlled territory, losing two planes while inserting 101 agents and recovering 128. Even today, more than 60 years after the end of the war, many of the activities in which Lysander pilots were engaged remains shrouded in secrecy.

Under the direction of the British Government's Special Operations Executive, pilot Lewis Hodges flew Lysanders, Handley Page Halifax bombers and Lockheed Hudson bombers on clandestine missions in Europe before transferring to the Far East to lead No. 357 Squadron. At the height of a long career in the RAF, Hodges rose to the rank of air chief marshal. After flying Supermarine Spitfire and North American P-51 Mustang fighters, Flight Lieutenant Peter Arkell joined No. 161 Squadron in 1944. During one mission, which involved another Lysander, he watched the loss of the second plane, resulting in the death of that pilot and two agents aboard. Flying with No. 357 Squadron in Burma, he was seriously injured in an attempt to land during a monsoon. He was eventually rescued, along with his injured passenger, by another Lysander.

Flying with three different photographic reconnaissance units, Flight Lieutenant Murray Anderson photographed the German heavy cruiser *Prinz Eugen* in the harbour at Kiel. In 1943 he transferred to No. 161 Squadron and was once again flying the Lysander, the aircraft in which he had

originally trained in 1940. Six times he piloted a plane during risky missions involving two Lysanders. Anderson is also remembered for his remarkable navigational abilities, helping one lost pilot in his flight of three aircraft to regain his bearings based solely on a description of the terrain below.

Between stints as a fight pilot, Flight Lieutenant

Standing before Squadron Leader Hugh Verity's Lysander, with its distinctive 'Jiminy Cricket' insignia, are (from left to right): Flight Lieutenant J. McCairns, Verity himself, Group Captain P.C. Pickard, and Flight Lieutenants P. Vaughan-Fowler and F. Rymills.

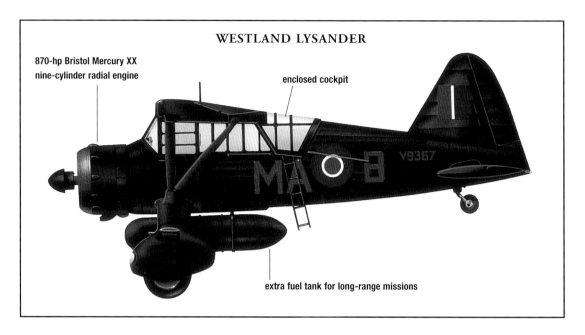

WESTLAND LYSANDER

870-hp Bristol Mercury XX nine-cylinder radial engine

enclosed cockpit

extra fuel tank for long-range missions

R.G. Large flew solo, double and triple Lysander missions with No. 161 Squadron. He later became one of the first British pilots to fly the country's new jet fighter, the Gloster Meteor.

The Lysander was a remarkable aircraft because of its Short Take-Off and Landing (STOL) capabilities, which allowed it to land on small airstrips with the minimum of fuss, making it ideal for clandestine operations behind enemy lines.

RAF PATHFINDER SQUADRONS

- •FOUNDED: 1942
- •STRENGTH: 8000 (ESTIMATED)
- •THEATRES: WESTERN EUROPE

The Allied bomber offensive in the skies over Nazi Germany and occupied Europe was a costly affair; however, it was a critical component of the ultimate victory in World War II. While there was much debate as to the relative merits of daylight precision bombing versus night time area bombing, it was eventually decided that the US Eighth Air Force would bomb by day and the squadrons of Royal Air Force (RAF) Bomber Command by night.

Chief among the reasons for the RAF tactical decision was the lack of long-range fighter escort early in the war and the sizable losses incurred in

previous daylight efforts. Still, the debate was vigorous. Once the course had been charted it became apparent that some method of assisting bomber pilots in identifying targets and delivering their explosive payloads at night had to be devised.

The answer, according to Group Captain Sidney Bufton, was to cull the finest bomber crews in the RAF and employ them in advance of large formations to drop target indicators as aiming points for the waves of aircraft to follow. These so-called 'Pathfinders' were themselves the subject of heated debate even before their first mission was flown. Air Chief Marshal Sir Arthur 'Bomber' Harris, head of RAF Bomber Command, opposed the formation of the Pathfinder Force (PFF), fearing that an elite among the ranks of the RAF might result in a negative effect on morale.

Harris also harboured a particularly healthy dislike for Bufton. Despite his vocal opposition, however, Harris was forced to accede to the necessity of creating the Pathfinders. He then asserted that each Bomber Group should have its own Pathfinder unit but was again compelled to relent, and a separate PFF was officially formed on 15 August 1942.

In the early days the PFF flew the same aircraft as other RAF bomber formations, including the Avro Lancaster and Handley Page Halifax bombers. When the De Havilland Mosquito, a sleek, twin-engine light bomber constructed largely of wood and canvas, was introduced in quantity, equipping the PFF with these became a priority. As the PFF grew, volunteers were accepted from standard bomber squadrons, while some air crews showing

particular talent might be transferred for a two-week course in target-marking methods prior to joining a PFF unit.

THE SILVER BADGE
PFF airmen wore a distinctive silver badge on their uniforms, received an advance of one rank, and were paid more than other RAF personnel.

On 12 August 1944 Nos 235 and 248 squadrons of the Portreath Strike Wing attacked enemy minesweepers in the Gironde estuary, France, in their Mosquito FB.Mk VIs.

However, the hazardous nature of their duty was acknowledged by all, and rather than a standard rotation of 30 missions, PFF crews were required to complete 45.

A premiere unit of the PFF was 8 Group, commanded by Donald C.T. Bennett, an Australian who became the youngest officer in the RAF to achieve the rank of air vice marshal, which took place in 1943. An experienced pilot before the war, Bennett had flown seaplanes with Imperial Airways, the predecessor of BOAC. He was shot down during a bombing raid on the giant German battleship *Tirpitz*, evaded capture and eventually managed to return to England through Sweden along with his co-pilot.

Bennett is also given credit for a major contribution to the development of the Pathfinder concept. Interestingly, Bennett's willingness to speak his mind and his somewhat confrontational personality earned him the animosity of numerous RAF colleagues. He was the only RAF group commander who did not receive a knighthood after serving a complete term as air officer commanding in World War II.

Bennett's main rival in the PFF was Sir Ralph Cochrane, commander of 5 Group, who challenged convention and boldly stated that his command could execute precision, low-level missions and mark targets which other units could not. Cochrane was allowed to demonstrate his pilots' abilities during Operation Chastise, an attack against the dams in the Ruhr, the industrial heart of Germany. Planes of No. 617 Squadron flew in at an altitude of a mere 19m (60ft).

Later, they utilized the stabilized automatic bomb sight from extremely high altitude on 16 December 1943, to drop bombs within 84m (94 yards) of a German V-1 buzz bomb launch site near Abbeville, France. Cochrane was an innovator as well, as the pilots of 5 Group invented a 'quick' landing system and the '5 Group Corkscrew', a technique for eluding German fighter planes.

Swift, agile De Havilland Mosquitoes of No. 139 Squadron fly above Nazi-occupied Europe, their hazardous mission to illuminate targets in advance of raids by heavy bombers of the RAF.

CHESHIRE'S 100 MISSIONS

Group Captain Leonard Cheshire, the commander of No. 617 Squadron, deserves special mention for formulating much of 5 Group's specialized tactics and improving the results of night bombing raids. Cheshire flew an incredible 100 missions with Bomber Command, received the Victoria Cross and three awards of the Distinguished Service Order, and was the RAF observer aboard the aircraft responsible for photographing the mission to drop the atomic bomb on the Japanese city of Nagasaki.

Pathfinder tactics steadily evolved and usually included aircraft called 'Finders' whose job was to drop flares along the bombing routes, keeping the formations together and on course to, and then over, the target. Illuminators flew directly ahead of the main bomber formations and dropped target indicators (TI) on the bombers' aiming point, which should already have been visible from flares dropped by the Finders. Planes serving as Markers then dropped incendiary bombs above the TIs to keep routes and targets

This wing commander from No. 617 Squadron wears the standard blue-grey battledress of RAF personnel of the period, with a life jacket, leather flying helmet and fleece-lined flying boots.

illuminated. Other PFF aircraft, designated Supporters and Backers-Up, were present to drop more TIs on an as-needed basis.

The TIs were usually distributed in various colours to prevent Germans on the ground from lighting decoy flares which might lure the bombers away from their intended target and into a concentration of anti-aircraft fire or night fighters. Some of these TIs were called red spots, pink pansies and smoke puffs. During missions which encountered cloud cover or bad weather, markers could be dropped with the aid of Oboe, H2S, Gee, or other navigational radar.

While a number of the PFF illumination efforts were amazingly accurate, one regrettable event occurred on 16 April 1943 during a raid on Pilsen, Czechoslovakia. The target was misidentified, and the RAF bombs fell on an insane asylum.

In World War II, Pathfinder squadrons flew more than 50,000 missions, illuminating nearly 3500 targets. More than 3700 PFF airmen lost their lives in combat.

RAF NO. 617 SQUADRON 'DAMBUSTERS'

- •FOUNDED: 1943
- •STRENGTH: 78
- •THEATRES: WESTERN EUROPE

Their motto 'Après Moi, Le Deluge', or 'After Me, The Flood' was certainly appropriate for the pilots of Royal Air Force No. 617 Squadron. The squadron was officially formed at RAF Scampton on 15 March 1943 for the purpose of carrying out Operation Chastise, a bombing raid against the vital dams on the Mohne, Eder and Sorpe rivers in the Ruhr Valley, the industrial heart of Germany. The dams supplied hydroelectric power and water to the factories which produced much of the material used by the Nazi war machine.

Heavily defended, these dams stood approximately 46m (150ft) high, were constructed of concrete, earth and masonry work, and were up to an astounding 35m (112ft) thick at the base.

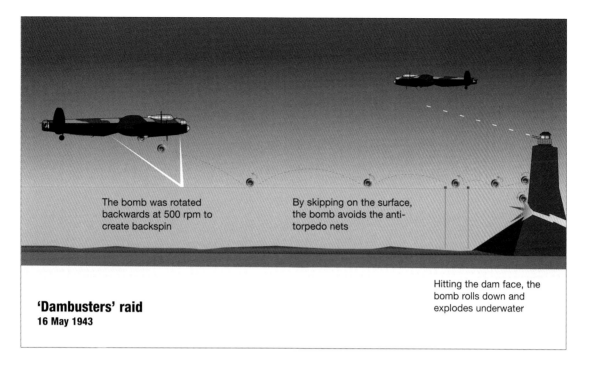

The bomb was rotated backwards at 500 rpm to create backspin

By skipping on the surface, the bomb avoids the anti-torpedo nets

Hitting the dam face, the bomb rolls down and explodes underwater

'Dambusters' raid
16 May 1943

One of them was 775m (2500ft) long with a 7.75m (25ft) wide roadway running across its top. Virtually impossible to attack effectively by conventional means, two of the dams were ringed with anti-aircraft guns, and anti-torpedo netting was strung underwater across their expanses. In response to the difficulty posed by this situation, British design genius Barnes Neville Wallis devised a large, specialized bomb codenamed 'Upkeep'.

The idea had come to Barnes while he was playing with his daughter's marbles, watching them bounce from one surface into another. Weighing more than 4000kg (9000lb), with an identical height and width of 1.4m (4ft 8in), a single Upkeep bomb carried 2900kg (6600lb) of explosives. Simply dropping these behemoths, however, would not do. The barrel-like weapons would be released from just above the surface of the water at a certain angle and rotation, then skip into the face of the target dam before exploding. Such a specialized bomb would naturally require a specialized aircraft for its delivery. Avro Lancaster heavy bombers were modified with a release mechanism and bomb bay structure which could accommodate Upkeep, and it was determined that in order for the entire scheme to work the

For the 'Dambuster' raid to be successful, the 'bouncing bomb' had to be released at a height of 18.3m (60ft) above the water at a speed of precisely 354km/h (220mph).

aircraft would skim the deck at only 18.6m, releasing its payload a mere 360-390m (400-425 yards) from the target while flying at a speed of 354km (220 miles) per hour.

The obvious choice, thought many, to command No. 617 Squadron was an officer who was already something of a legend in the RAF. Wing Commander Guy Penrose Gibson was only 24 years old. Already, he had flown 173 combat missions in bombers and fighters. Once rejected by the air service because his legs were too short, Gibson earned the Distinguished Flying Cross during his first bombing mission in July 1940. As a fighter pilot he shot down four German planes and received a second Distinguished Flying Cross.

'SQUADRON X'
Because of his experience, Gibson was allowed to select his own group of fliers, eventually settling on 147 intrepid men to constitute what was first

mysteriously known as 'Squadron X'. In a remarkably short period of two months, crews were trained and aircraft and bombs were readied. The mission against the Ruhr dams was scheduled for 16 May 1943.

With a full moon providing excellent visibility, Gibson led 19 Lancasters in three groups from their base at Scampton. One plane experienced engine trouble and the crew was forced to move to an alternate aircraft, resulting in its departure half an hour behind the other bombers. Some of the planes encountered stiff winds and veered off course for a while, then were bathed in the beams of German searchlights and roughed up by flak.

One Lancaster suddenly plunged into the ground and exploded. Eyewitness accounts of the incident are contradictory, some saying that the plane was shot down by anti-aircraft fire, others observing it flying so low that it struck power lines. Altogether, five bombers either crashed or were forced to turn back prior to reaching the targets.

As he started his run toward the Mohne dam, Gibson commented nonchalantly: 'Well boys, I suppose we'd better start the ball rolling.' The release went flawlessly, and the first Upkeep exploded with a roar and a geyser of water. The second Lancaster released its bomb too late, and the projectile crashed into a power plant beyond the wall of the dam.

Seconds later, the plane ignited in a brilliant flash. Two crewmen managed to parachute safely but were captured. It was the third Lancaster whose bomb actually opened a breach in the Mohne with a direct hit. At first it was thought

'ENEMY COAST AHEAD'

In his autobiography, *Enemy Coast Ahead*, Gibson remembered: 'The whole valley was beginning to fill with fog from the steam of the gushing water, and down in the foggy valley we saw cars speeding along the roads in front of this great wave of water, which was chasing them and going faster than they could ever hope to go … The floods raced on, carrying everything with them as they went – viaducts, railways, bridges and everything that stood in their path.'

to have caused no damage. However, water suddenly began to pour through a 90m (100-yard) gash in the wall.

LANCASTERS SCORE AND MISS

The Eder dam was situated between cliffs which reached as high as 310m, and the Germans had not deemed it necessary to place anti-aircraft guns in the vicinity. Still, this was a formidable target. Several runs were aborted with the planes still carrying their bombs. Finally, the Lancasters scored back-to-back hits and breached the Eder dam. The first of these actually damaged the bomber as well, which crashed killing everyone aboard.

One Lancaster of the second wave was shot down by flak, and another crashed in northern Germany. Its bomb was recovered intact and later studied by German scientists. A third Lancaster was heavily damaged by anti-aircraft fire and forced to return to Scampton. Still another was flying so low that it hit the water, which ripped the Upkeep from its bomb bay and tore the plane's tail wheel off. This one, too, had to turn back.

The only plane of the second wave to attack the Sorpe dam was piloted by American Flight Lieutenant Joseph McCarthy, who hailed from Brooklyn, New York, and had remained with Bomber Command even after the United States entered the war. McCarthy released his bomb, which struck home but failed to breach the structure.

FINAL ATTACK

The final attack against the Sorpe was carried out by the single plane of the third wave to reach its destination. This Lancaster attempted eight runs at the target, releasing its Upkeep in an apparent direct hit. However, when the smoke and mist cleared the dam remained intact. A pair of Lancasters, separated from their flights, attacked secondary targets and were unsuccessful in their attempts to breach the Lister and Ennepe dams.

The damage to the two dams which were breached was repaired in about three months, although flooding was widespread for about 80km (50 miles) around the structures and their reservoirs had been drained. About 1300 people were killed by the rushing water, some of whom were Soviet

Conducting a briefing, Wing Commander Guy Gibson, who received the Victoria Cross for leading the Dambuster Raid, references a photo of one of the breaches created during the attack.

prisoners of war whose camp was in the flood plain. Of the 19 Lancasters which had undertaken Operation Chastise, 11 returned to base. Casualties were high, as No. 617 Squadron lost 56 men, three of whom were prisoners of war. Gibson was awarded the Victoria Cross for his leadership, while several other airmen received the Distinguished Flying Cross or Distinguished Service Order. A total of 33 men were decorated.

Later in 1943, Group Captain Leonard Cheshire took command of No. 617 Squadron, and subsequently Wing Commander J.B. 'Willie' Tait took over, leading three raids against the German battleship *Tirpitz* with gigantic Tallboy bombs, weighing 5400kg (12,000lb) each.

Gibson flew only two missions after Operation Chastise. He was killed when his De Havilland Mosquito bomber was hit by anti-aircraft fire over Rheydt, Holland, in September 1944.

The spirit of No. 617 Squadron remains alive today, as the modern unit flies the Panavia Tornado bomber from its base at RAF Lossiemouth, Scotland.

GERMANY

The armed forces of Nazi Germany proved to be some of the most tenacious and resourceful in the world during periods of both conquest and prolonged defence. Throughout World War II, elite units of the German armed forces acquitted themselves bravely. Often led by highly motivated and experienced officers, these formations were well trained and outfitted with the finest weapons and equipment available.

2ND SS PANZER DIVISION DAS REICH

- •FOUNDED: 1939
- •STRENGTH: 18,000
- •THEATRES: WESTERN EUROPE, BALKANS, EASTERN FRONT

Weeks after their successful D-Day landings on the coast of Normandy, Allied forces had successfully executed a breakout of the French hedgerow country and threatened to encircle the German Fifth Panzer and Seventh armies in a ring of steel around the French town of Falaise. Fighting from the outside to keep the only route of escape

*Left: Elite German **Fallschirmjäger**, or paratroopers, pore over a map as they prepare for an operation early in the war. The **Luftwaffe** insignia is prominent on one soldier's smock.*

open, the battle-hardened soldiers of the 2nd SS Panzer Division *Das Reich* managed to hold out long enough to allow thousands of German troops to evacuate.

Nevertheless, at Falaise an estimated 50,000 German troops were captured and 10,000 killed. More than 9000 armoured vehicles, tanks and trucks were also captured. It was a blow from which the German armed forces in the West would never recover, and it would undoubtedly have been worse had *Das Reich* and other units not fought desperately.

The defensive action at Falaise was a far cry from the early days of the war, when soldiers of *Das Reich* were victorious in the 1940 conquest of the Low Countries and France, their 1941 campaigns in the Balkans, and the early successes of Operation Barbarossa, the German invasion of the Soviet Union. Formed in 1939, *Das Reich* was the second of the Waffen (armed) SS divisions created as elite fighting forces independent of the traditional German Army.

The very existence of the Waffen SS caused discord among the leadership of the German war effort. The SS units were, for the most part, fanatically loyal to Nazi doctrine and to Adolf Hitler. They were also the best equipped, best trained and most highly motivated of German ground forces. There was no debate as to their prowess in combat. In the case of *Das Reich*, the division's formation took place six years after the 1st SS Division *Leibstandarte* Adolf Hitler, which in its early days served as the Fuhrer's personal bodyguard, was constituted.

The symbol of the 2nd SS Division was the Wolfsangel rune and the ancient sign became all too familiar across Europe as *Das Reich* fought both East and West. Following its initial successes the division provided seasoned cadre and troops for the formation of the 5th SS Panzer Division *Wiking*.

CAPTURE OF BELGRADE

In the spring of 1941 *Das Reich* took part in the invasions of Yugoslavia and Greece. One of *Das Reich*'s most spectacular successes occurred in April with the capture of the Yugoslav capital of Belgrade.

As SS *Hauptsturmführer* (Captain) Fritz Klingenberg approached Belgrade along the banks of the Danube River accompanied by a small motorcycle detachment, he decided to cross the river with a group of only eight men. Once he was on the south bank Klingenberg sent two soldiers back to the other side to summon reinforcements. He then proceeded into the city's centre, forced the surrender of a band of 20 Yugoslav soldiers without firing a shot, occupied the Yugoslav War Ministry building briefly, and then reached the

This corporal from the **Das Reich** *Division is dressed in the standard field-grey service uniform issued on the Eastern Front in 1943. On his cap is the divisional Death's Head badge.*

Right: **Reichsführer** *SS Heinrich Himmler greets soldiers of the 2nd SS Division* **Das Reich** *in the shadows of their tanks. The 2nd SS Division fought the Allies both East and West.*

German embassy. Klingenberg unfurled a large swastika emblazoned flag and declared to the astonished mayor, who appeared a couple of hours later, that the city had been captured by German forces. The following day a large German force arrived to consolidate the occupation. Klingenberg had pulled off one of the great ruses of the war and received the Knight's Cross for his audacious leadership.

KREMLIN IN ITS SIGHTS

When Germany invaded the Soviet Union on 22 June 1941 *Das Reich* attacked with other units of Army Group Centre from occupied Poland and participated in the battle for Smolensk. In the vanguard of the German advance toward Moscow the division came within 16km (10 miles) of the city. The spires of the Kremlin and the city's large church buildings could be seen through the officers' binoculars. The advance, however, could go no further as mounting losses and a fierce Red Army winter offensive halted progress.

Briefly refitting in France, the division returned to the Eastern Front in 1943, assisted in recapturing the city of Kharkov from the Soviets, and was heavily engaged in Operation Citadel, the effort to reduce a massive Red Army salient which extended deep into German lines. The climax of Citadel was the largest armoured battle in history, which was fought in the vicinity of the town of Kursk in July. Penetrating the Soviet salient more than 48km (30 miles) in some sectors, the division was eventually returned to France for another refit after Citadel ended in failure.

Indicative of the intense fighting on the Eastern Front was the fact that the exhausted SS troops turned back 14 separate Soviet attacks in a single day. By the end of July the division's effective strength had been reduced to a mere 20 assault guns and less than 30 tanks.

In the wake of D-Day, *Das Reich* was ordered from positions near Toulouse in southern France to

Normandy. Impeded along the way by the effective operations of the French Resistance, the division required nearly three weeks to complete a trek which should have been accomplished in three days or less. The Resistance and the French towns along the way, however, suffered bitter reprisals.

TERRIBLE REVENGE

The powerful *Das Reich* comprised more than 15,000 soldiers, 200 tanks and 1400 vehicles at its peak strength in the West. When the town of Tulle had been seized by the Resistance and nearly 150 German soldiers killed, *Das Reich*

A Panzerkampfwagen III tank of **Das Reich***, its protecting infantry riding along, rolls through the outskirts of Kharkov during the battle for the city during March 1943.*

employed overwhelming force to recapture it. Ninety-nine of the townspeople were summarily hanged from lampposts.

Near the village of Oradour-sur-Glane, SS Major Helmut Kampfe, commander of one of *Das Reich*'s battalions, was captured and killed by the Resistance. When SS Major Otto Dickmann and more than 100 panzergrenadiers arrived, they exacted terrible revenge. The town was burned, and 642 people, a number of them women and children, were indiscriminately killed. Many of the civilians perished after being herded at gunpoint into a church, which was subsequently set ablaze. Oradour-sur-Glane was never rebuilt, and its ruins continue to serve as mute testimony to SS brutality. After the war, numerous participants in the atrocity were tried for war crimes.

While fighting to keep the Falaise escape route

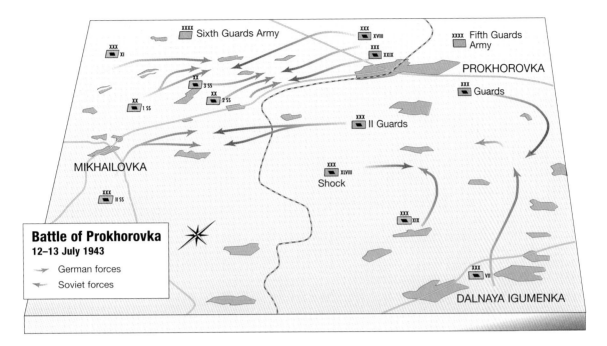

Battle of Prokhorovka
12–13 July 1943

→ German forces
← Soviet forces

The II SS Panzer Corps, which included the **Das Reich** *and* **Totenkopf** *divisions, was engaged in what was reputed to be the largest tank battle of the war at Prokhorovka, during the Kursk offensive in July 1943. After 36 hours of heavy fighting, the SS were fought to standstill by Soviet forces, effectively ending German chances of success at Kursk.*

open, *Das Reich* soldiers also assaulted the high ground around the city of Mortain, which had been occupied by elements of the 30th Infantry Division. The reinforced Americans held out but suffered heavy casualties before the SS tanks and panzergrenadiers were withdrawn to assist in the continuing effort at Falaise.

From December 1944 to January 1945 *Das Reich* took part in the Battle of the Bulge, its spearheads very nearly reaching their objective of the Meuse River before strong Allied counter-attacks drove them back to their original positions. Near the end of the war, the division was once again sent to the Eastern Front to participate in the final German offensive against the Red Army, an attempt to relieve the siege of the Hungarian capital of Budapest. By the time Germany surrendered, much of the 2nd SS Division *Das Reich* had made its way westward and

capitulated to American forces.

One of the most effective divisions of the German armed forces, *Das Reich* was a formidable foe on two major fronts. However, its combat record and its honour are very much stained by the atrocities some of its soldiers committed.

3RD SS PANZER DIVISION *TOTENKOPF*

- •FOUNDED: 1939
- •STRENGTH: 15,500
- •THEATRES: WESTERN EUROPE, EASTERN FRONT

As inspector of Nazi Germany's concentration camp system, SS Obergruppenfuhrer (lieutenant general) Theodor Eicke had instilled a ruthlessness seldom seen among civilized people in the soldiers who guarded these centres of death and misery. When he raised the 3rd SS Panzer Division *Totenkopf* (Death's Head) from among these troops in the autumn of 1939, the unit was destined to fight fanatically and perpetrate a succession of serious war crimes.

SS Lieutenant General Theodor Eicke (second from left), the ruthless commander of the 3rd SS Panzer Division Totenkopf, *chats with Field Marshal Keitel (second from right) during a conference at Rastenburg, Hitler's headquarters in East Prussia.*

One of 38 combat divisions of the Waffen (armed) SS, *Totenkopf* spent the vast majority of its fighting tenure on the Eastern Front. However, it was initially employed in the campaign against France and the Low Countries in the spring of 1940. During operations in the West, *Totenkopf* captured more than 15,000 French prisoners northeast of Cambrai, but very nearly met disaster.

On 21 May, near the French village of Arras, two British tank battalions, a pair of battalions of the Durham Light Infantry, and the French 3rd Light Mechanized Division stopped *Totenkopf* and the 7th Panzer Division cold with a ferocious counter-attack. When 75 Allied tanks – many of them the tough,

heavy Matildas – hit the Germans, some SS troops broke and ran. General (later field marshal) Erwin Rommel, commander of 7th Panzer, rushed to the scene and directed that 88mm (3.46in) anti-aircraft guns be used in an anti-tank role. This action, combined with repeated attacks by German dive bombers, finally stopped the Allied thrust. *Totenkopf* had suffered many of the 700 casualties inflicted on the Germans. Twenty tanks were also lost.

In April 1941 *Totenkopf* was transferred to the East in preparation for Operation Barbarossa, the invasion of the Soviet Union, which was scheduled for June. Advancing through Lithuania and Latvia as part of Army Group North, the division drove toward Leningrad and became embroiled in a bitter month-long fight on the city's outskirts.

'THE CAULDRON'

Late in 1941, the Soviet Red Army began a series of counter-attacks, one of which trapped more than

100,000 German soldiers of six divisions, including *Totenkopf*, in the area around the city of Demyansk. The fighting there was so intense that it became known as *Der Kessel* (The Cauldron), and *Totenkopf* took heavy casualties during months of protracted combat. The division had invaded Russia 17,000 strong the previous summer, and by the time it successfully broke out of the Demyansk encirclement more than 9000 casualties had been sustained. In October the division was moved to France to replenish its men and machines.

Seven months later, *Totenkopf* was again on the Eastern Front. This time the division participated in the fighting around Kharkov, which successfully halted a Red Army offensive. Eicke was killed on 26 February 1943 when his Fieseler Storch observation plane was shot down by Soviet infantry.

The tanks and infantry of the Death's Head Division advance through seemingly endless fields of waist-high brush toward the front during the epic tank battle of Kursk, July 1943.

During Operation Citadel the abortive offensive to reduce the Red Army salient in the German lines around the town of Kursk, *Totenkopf* sustained casualties which were almost as heavy as those at Demyansk. After a week's fighting in July 1943 the division's tank strength had been reduced from 117 to less than 60. By the autumn of 1943 the division had lost more than 14,000 men.

As 1944 began, German armed forces on the Eastern Front were clearly on the defensive. *Totenkopf* fought tenaciously at Krivoi-Rog and linked up with 56,000 German troops who had been encircled at Cherkassy. Falling back across the Bug River and into Poland, the division arrived in the Warsaw area in July. Delaying actions briefly stabilized the Eastern Front along the Vistula River late in the year.

BUDAPEST ENCIRCLEMENT

In January 1945 *Totenkopf* and other units nearly succeeded in reaching more than 40,000 German soldiers who had been encircled in the Hungarian

Soldiers of the 3rd SS Panzer Division gather for an assault on a Soviet strongpoint during the invasion of the Soviet Union, July 1941. Their commander peers around a corner, while two men handle a light machine gun.

capital of Budapest. Repeated attacks succeeded in reaching the city's perimeter but could go no further. In March, a Red Army counter-attack nearly succeeded in trapping both *Totenkopf* and the 5th SS Panzer Division *Wiking*. The 9th SS Panzer Division *Hohenstaufen* was able to maintain a narrow avenue of escape, however, and *Totenkopf* fought its way westward into Czechoslovakia.

When the remnants of the 3rd SS Panzer Division *Totenkopf* surrendered to American forces on 9 May 1945, the prisoners were abruptly turned over to the Soviets. Their reputation for ruthlessness on both the Eastern and Western fronts contributed to the demise of many former *Totenkopf* soldiers, who were marched off to prison camps in the Soviet Union and never seen again.

During World War II in the East, *Totenkopf* personnel were responsible for numerous war crimes, sometimes accompanying the Einsatzgruppen death squads behind German lines and actually participating in the slaughter of Jews and Red Army prisoners.

WITHOUT MERCY

Totenkopf's criminal record, which later resulted in a number of war crimes trials, began only days after the division was originally deployed. On 26 May 1940, at the French town of La Paradis, the

Totenkopf 2nd Infantry Regiment, commanded by *Obersturmführer* (1st lieutenant) Fritz Knöchlein, captured 99 soldiers of the British Royal Norfolk Regiment. The prisoners were taken to an open field near a farmhouse and outbuildings and mowed down by machine gun fire. Only two of the British soldiers escaped with their lives. After the war Knöchlein was hunted down, tried and convicted of war crimes. He was hanged on 28 January 1949.

While it is reasonable to assert that the 3rd SS Panzer Division *Totenkopf* was one of the most heavily engaged and tenacious fighting units of the German forces in World War II, its lasting legacy is one of pitiless brutality.

5TH SS PANZER DIVISION WIKING

- •FOUNDED: 1940
- •STRENGTH 14,500
- •THEATRES: EASTERN FRONT

One week after Adolf Hitler launched Operation Barbarossa, the 22 January 1941 invasion of the Soviet Union, the first of a new breed of Waffen (armed) SS divisions made its combat debut on the Eastern Front. The Waffen SS, considered to be the elite military arm of the fanatically loyal Schutzstaffel, had originally been composed only of Germans. However, as Germany appeared everywhere victorious, foreign volunteers came forward in increasing numbers.

In late 1940 the nucleus of the 5th SS Panzer Division *Wiking* was formed from existing motorized German units and volunteers from the Netherlands and Scandinavian countries of Denmark, Norway, Sweden and Finland. Its training complete in the spring of 1941, *Wiking* was placed initially under the command of SS *Brigadeführer* (brigadier

Holding an automatic weapon, a panzergrenadier of the 5th SS Panzer Division **Wiking** *scans the horizon through binoculars. Soldiers who hailed from Scandinavian countries formed the nucleus of the* **Wiking** *Division.*

general) Felix Steiner, who had already proven himself a cool and capable leader of troops under fire. *Wiking* deployed with Army Group South and supported the *Wehrmacht* summer offensive in the Ukraine, capturing Rostov and advancing into the Caucasus.

TOUGHEST ON EASTERN FRONT

Although many top German field commanders were initially sceptical of the fighting ability of a division comprising so many foreign volunteers, *Wiking* proved early in its combat career to be one of the toughest and most resilient formations of the German armed forces. Like other Waffen SS divisions, *Wiking* began as an infantry division before being expanded to a panzergrenadier division and finally to a full panzer division. Typically, the elite Waffen SS forces also received the best equipment. Fighting entirely on the Eastern Front, *Wiking* personnel were awarded more than 50 Knight's Crosses for bravery in action.

As the autumn of 1942 approached in the Caucasus, *Wiking* was ordered to take a

commanding hill in the vicinity of the city of Grozny and then move on to capture the city itself. During two days of savage fighting on September 25-26, one regiment lost 50 per cent of its troops within half an hour, and the division suffered 1500 casualties. The hill was taken but the Germans could advance no further. When the Soviets surrounded the German Sixth Army at Stalingrad and efforts to relieve the besieged troops failed, *Wiking* was transferred northward in support of the Fourth Panzer Army, which was falling back through Rostov.

By early 1943 *Wiking* was back in the Ukraine, fighting near the industrial centre of Kharkov until the city was recaptured. Following the epic tank battle at Kursk, in which *Wiking* defended positions around Kharkov against Soviet attacks, the division

was moved southward to the vicinity of the Mius River. In company with the 2nd SS Panzer Division *Das Reich* and the 3rd SS Panzer Division *Totenkopf*, the troops of *Wiking* engaged two Soviet tank armies and destroyed more than 800 of an estimated 1000 tanks sent against them.

At Cherkassy in the winter of 1943-44 *Wiking* narrowly escaped complete destruction. Acting as the rearguard for German units slipping through a narrow corridor to safety, the division was forced to abandon much of its equipment while taking heavy losses. With virtually no time to rest, *Wiking* was

Outfitted with camouflage covers, soldiers of the 5th SS Panzer Division **Wiking** *trudge through knee-deep snow on the Eastern Front during the fighting retreat before the Soviet Red Army.*

again thrown into a desperate battle. This time elements of the division fought their way through a Red Army cordon, linking up with encircled German forces at Korsun and compelling the Soviets to give ground.

From August until the end of 1944 *Wiking* occupied more or less stationary positions around Warsaw. Although the division was not engaged in the defeat of the Warsaw Uprising it was prominent in holding the line against a Red Army offensive. By January 1945, increasing Soviet pressure all along the Eastern Front produced numerous critical situations. Fighting alongside *Totenkopf*, the division came within a few kilometres of rescuing thousands of German troops trapped in the Hungarian capital of Budapest. The two SS Panzer divisions suffered more than 8000 casualties, and the relief attempt was ultimately unsuccessful.

RETREAT AND SURRENDER

In the final weeks of the war, *Wiking* fought a series of delaying actions and retreated into Austria and Czechoslovakia. On 9 May 1945 the remnants of the division surrendered to advancing US forces at Furstenfeld, Austria.

In contrast to other Waffen SS divisions, the record of the 5th SS Panzer Division *Wiking* does not include convictions for any war crimes. However, the SS itself had been declared a criminal organization during the Nuremberg Trials, and some witnesses reported *Wiking* troops had taken part in hundreds of murders. Some of these were alleged to have been perpetrated while working behind the lines with the dreaded *Einsatzgruppen*, or death squads.

The 5th SS Panzer Division *Wiking* earned grudging respect during some of the most difficult fighting of World War II. The division compiled an excellent combat record and penetrated deeper into the Caucasus during the summer offensive of 1942 than any other unit of the German armed forces.

12TH SS PANZER DIVISION HITLER JUGEND
- **FOUNDED:** 1943
- **STRENGTH** 19,500
- **THEATRES:** WESTERN EUROPE

The youthful notion of invincibility and Nazi idealism combined to produce one of the most fanatical fighting units of World War II in the 12th SS Panzer Division *Hitler Jugend*. When the division was authorized by Hitler on 10 February 1943, its teenage rank and file could hardly remember any other Germany than the nation ruled by Nazi doctrine. The original members were all born in 1926, and at 17 years of age their world view had been shaped by compulsory participation in the *Hitlerjugend* (Hitler Youth).

The formation of the division also bolstered the manpower shortage which had been suffered by veteran units of the Waffen (armed) SS, the military wing of the fiercely loyal *Schutzstaffel* headed by *Reichsführer* Heinrich Himmler. After less than a year of training, much of which took place in occupied Belgium, the 12th SS Panzer Division was placed in combat ready status. To compensate for the fact that time was limited and much of the standard training programme would be eliminated or abbreviated out of necessity, officers and non-commissioned officers of the battle-hardened 1st SS

INFAMOUS VETERAN

The most infamous veteran of *Wiking* was undoubtedly Dr Josef Mengele, who was reported to have served as a combat medic during some of the division's early campaigns. Mengele received the Iron Cross for rescuing two wounded men under fire and was, in turn, wounded himself. The severity of his injuries prevented him from returning to the Eastern Front, and he was assigned to work at the Auschwitz-Birkenau concentration camp in Poland.

At Auschwitz, Mengele conducted a number of heinous experiments on the camp's prisoners. Particularly grotesque were his experiments on children, including many sets of twins. After the war, Mengele escaped prosecution for war crimes. He lived in obscurity for decades in South America and drowned in Brazil in 1979.

Panzer Division *Leibstandarte* Adolf Hitler were interspersed with the young soldiers.

The *Leibstandarte* was the original Waffen SS formation, which had been created in 1933 as Hitler's personal bodyguard. The leadership of the original commander of the 12th SS, *Oberführer* Fritz Witt and the veteran cadre subjected the troops to lengthy periods of live fire and situational training.

OPERATION OVERLORD

The 21st Panzer Division and the 12th SS Panzer were situated in the vicinity of the city of Caen in Normandy on 6 June 1944, when the Allies launched Operation Overlord and assaulted Hitler's Fortress Europe. Hitler retained personal control over the vast majority of the German armoured forces in France, and although 21st Panzer went into action somewhat earlier in the day, the 12th SS was not ordered forward until approximately 3 p.m. Movement was hampered by general confusion caused by the French Resistance and Allied airborne operations which disrupted communications near the invasion beaches. Allied air supremacy was nearly total, and any appreciable movement by armoured columns also attracted the attention of enemy fighter bombers.

When elements of the 12th SS Panzer Division went into action the following day they faced Canadian troops who had come ashore at Juno Beach. With orders to halt the Canadian advance, move on to the coast and drive a wedge between two of the Allied beaches, the *Hitler Jugend* SS

Left: The youthfulness of the fanatical members of the 12th SS Panzer Division **Hitlerjugend** *is apparent on the face of this heavily armed soldier, leaning on his machine gun during a rest.*

Heavily armed and wearing the standard camouflage of the SS, this soldier of the **Hitler Jugend** *Division is typical of those who fought the Western Allies in France in 1944.*

troops displayed a ferocity which shocked the Canadians. Casualties were heavy on both sides, but the Canadians managed to hold.

Although the 25th and 26th regiments of the 12th, commanded by *Standartenführer* (colonel) Kurt 'Panzer' Meyer and *Obersturmbannführer* (lieutenant colonel) Max Wunsche respectively, had initially made gains, the attack bogged down as the Canadians established strong defensive positions. One regiment, the Sherbrooke Fusiliers, sacrificed itself in allowing other Canadian units to consolidate, losing nearly 30 tanks in the process.

When a regiment of the North Nova Scotia Highlanders was overrun and dozens of prisoners taken, a number of them were shot by men of the 12th SS. After the two sides had fought to a bloody stalemate on 7 June, Meyer and his staff reportedly interrogated a group of prisoners who were then summarily executed.

Estimates of the total number of Canadian prisoners murdered on 7 June top 100. This was only the first of numerous criminal acts attributed to the troops of the division.

FANATICAL COURAGE

One week later, a barrage of heavy gunfire from British naval vessels scored a direct hit on the division's command post, killing Witt. Meyer promptly became the youngest division commander in the German armed forces at the age of 33 and was promoted to the rank of *Gruppenführer* (major gene al). The fanatical courage of the *Hitler Jugend* soldiers cost them dearly. During a month of nearly

continuous fighting, the division lost approximately 4000 dead and 8000 wounded.

Caen had been designated a primary objective of the British on D-Day; however, the city was vital to the Germans in maintaining lines of communication. Bitter fighting raged for control of Caen, and the 12th SS Panzer Division was instrumental in delaying its capture. On 26 June the division became heavily engaged with troops of the British VIII Corps southwest of the city near the town of Cheux. Along with the 21st Panzer and Panzer Lehr divisions, the *Hitler Jugend* managed to halt Operation Epsom. Caen fell on 9 July during Operation Charnwood, after German armoured forces had been pulled back to high ground at Bourquébus Ridge. In mid-July, Operation Goodwood consolidated the Allied hold on Caen, but at a fearful cost as the British lost nearly 200 tanks and more than 5000 casualties in two days.

By August the Allies were threatening to encircle the entire German Seventh Army in the Falaise Pocket during Operation Totalize. The 12th SS Panzer Division, its armour outnumbered nearly ten to one, fought to keep the escape route open for an extended period before withdrawing across the natural barrier of the Seine River. While fighting along the frontier between France and Belgium the division was reduced to an effective strength of less than 3000 men. Meyer was captured and eventually replaced in November by *Brigadeführer* (brigadier general) Hugo Kraas, who led the division until the end of the war.

BATTLE OF THE BULGE

During the Battle of the Bulge in December 1944 and January 1945 the *Hitler Jugend* troops were primarily engaged in the attempt to capture the vital Belgian crossroads town of Bastogne. The under-strength unit was a division in name only as its number of tanks had been reduced from 100 to about 25, while its panzergrenadier battalions numbered less than 150 men. Eventually, the US

US military police keep a watchful eye on two **Hitler Jugend** *soldiers captured during the failed German winter offensive of 1944–45, which became known as the Battle of the Bulge.*

Third Army reached the trapped 101st Airborne Division, and the siege was lifted. Within three weeks most German units were pushed back to the positions they had occupied when the offensive began.

Transferred to the Eastern Front in January 1945, the 12th SS Division participated in an abortive attempt to relieve a garrison of 45,000 German mountain troops who were surrounded in the Hungarian capital of Budapest. The following month, an offensive called Operation Spring Awakening, which was intended to retake the Hungarian oil fields, ended in failure. Continuing attacks by the Soviet Red Army pushed German forces steadily westward, and in May 1945 the remnants of the 12th SS Panzer Division *Hitler Jugend* were close enough to Allied lines to surrender to American forces.

After the war, the entire SS was condemned by the Allies as a criminal organization. The documented litany of atrocities committed by the zealots of the 12th SS Panzer Division resulted in the prosecution of a number of individuals. Meyer was convicted by a Canadian tribunal for the slaying of 40 Canadian prisoners of war at the Chateau Andrieu in June 1944. In January 1946 his sentence was commuted to life in prison when most of the evidence against him was deemed circumstantial. In September 1954 he was released from prison due to failing health. He died later that year at the age of 43.

THE BRANDENBURGER REGIMENT

- •FOUNDED: 1939
- •STRENGTH: 3200
- •THEATRES: WESTERN EUROPE, EASTERN FRONT

They appeared to be a nondescript group of Polish coal miners, common in the area and working for a living. They attracted no special attention. On 1 September 1939, however, these seemingly innocent men sprang into action. Specially trained to seize communications and industrial centres ahead of advancing German units which would roll across the Polish frontier on the first day of World War II in Europe, these were agents of the Abwehr, Germany's intelligence service.

Known as Kampf-Truppen, these intrepid special forces personnel seized objectives such as the power station at Chorzow in Upper Silesia and held them until units of the *Wehrmacht* arrived. The valuable service of the Kampf-Truppen paved the way for the rapid success of the German invasion of Poland. With the electrical facility at Chorzow in their hands, for example, the Germans cut power over a wide area and threw the Polish armed forces into confusion.

Ironically, after their spectacular successes in Poland, the Kampf-Truppen were to be disbanded. One adventurous Abwehr officer, however, had other ideas. Captain Theodor von Hippel petitioned Admiral Wilhelm Canaris, the chief of the Abwehr, to form a permanent special forces unit which would conduct covert operations in enemy-held territory and facilitate the advance of German troops wherever possible. Canaris reluctantly agreed to the experiment, and on 25 October 1939 the clandestine unit officially known as the 800th Special Duties Construction Company came into being. Almost from the beginning the formation was known as the Brandenburgers.

DECEPTION AND DISGUISE

The Brandenburgers often relied on stealth and deception to carry out their missions. Although they were required to complete a rigorous course of several weeks' training, it was of paramount importance that they were at least bilingual, preferably speaking the languages of one or more neighbouring countries. Many of the men had lived in other countries and were familiar with their customs and mannerisms. The Brandenburgers also learned the importance of disguise. During future offensive operations both East and West, the Brandenburgers would precede standard German Army formations.

When Hitler unleashed his *Blitzkrieg* against Denmark in April 1940 the Brandenburgers donned Danish Army uniforms and captured every objective they were assigned. Weeks later, during the invasion of France and the Low Countries, what appeared to

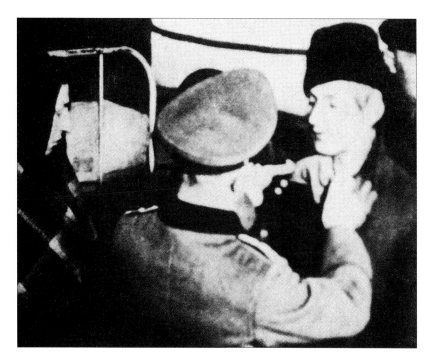

A Brandenburger is fitted for an upcoming operation in Poland. The Brandenburger infiltrators seized communications and industrial centres on 1 September 1939, the first day of World War II.

be a group of Dutch policemen escorting prisoners near the town of Gennep reached a bridge over the Maas River. Suddenly, both prisoners and police produced weapons and took the bridge. Attempts by other units to seize bridges in the area were unsuccessful, and the Brandenburgers' capture of the Gennep span proved to be a significant contribution in maintaining the timetable for the invasion.

In Belgium the Brandenburgers captured locks to prevent flooding in the path of the oncoming army. More than 100 agents, dressed in civilian clothes and some of them pushing baby carriages, seized key bridges over the Dender and Meuse rivers and a tunnel near the Scheldt Estuary. The men of No. 3 Brandenburg Company, commanded by Captain Hans-Jochen Rudloff, were awarded more than 90 Iron Crosses for their efforts in Belgium. In mid-May the battalion size Brandenburger unit was raised to regimental strength.

Although they were frustrated by the cancellation of Operation Sealion, the invasion of Great Britain, and Operation Felix, conceived to take control of the British bastion at Gibraltar, the Brandenburgers infiltrated the Balkans and prepared the way for offensive operations there in the spring of 1941.

Posing as crewmen for river craft along the Danube, they captured a number of vessels before they could be sunk by the Yugoslavs to block the waterway.

One formation of ethnic Ukrainians served with distinction among the Brandenburgers. Known as the Nightingale Group, they crossed the border into their homeland on the first day of Operation Barbarossa, the invasion of the Soviet Union. Even though they were dressed in German uniforms, the Nightingales convinced a Red Army patrol that they were Soviet soldiers returning from a secret mission. Escorted safely into the town of Przemysl, the Nightingales waited patiently until the approaching *Wehrmacht* caused the Russians to pull out of the city. They rounded up stragglers and maintained control of Przemysl until relieved.

FOOLING THE RED ARMY

Perhaps the most spectacular success of the Brandenburgers was a mission carried out by approximately 60 agents under the leadership of Adrian von Folkersam, whose grandfather had served Russia as an admiral in the Czarist navy. In August 1942 Folkersam and company dressed in the uniforms of the NKVD, the Soviet secret police, and joined a retreating column of Red Army troops.

For days the Brandenburgers maintained their ruse as members of the NKVD, and Folkersam reported to the Soviet general commanding the garrison of the town of Maikop. That evening he was invited to the general's quarters for drinks, and the following day he was given a tour of the town's defences. At Folkersam's suggestion the general weakened a concentration of artillery which had been positioned to fire in the precise direction from which German forces would approach.

When it became apparent that the *Wehrmacht* was near, the Brandenburgers, still in NKVD uniforms, destroyed a communications centre and spread confusion in the rear of the Red Army. They went about ordering Soviet units to retreat or countermanding instructions in the name of the general they had met a few days earlier. With their communications network a shambles, the recipients of these orders had no way to confirm them and were left with little alternative but to comply. Throngs of confused Red Army troops, some advancing and some falling back, clogged the roads

and made a coordinated defence virtually impossible. Elsewhere, a number of nearby oil fields which had been slated for demolition were captured intact due to fictitious orders.

In the autumn of 1942 the Brandenburger Regiment grew to division status. However, the German Army was no longer conducting the type of offensive operations which were so well complemented by these special forces. Many of the soldiers were assigned to duty as panzergrenadiers.

A major factor in the Brandenburgers' undoing was Adolf Hitler's disdain for Admiral Canaris, whose Abwehr had diminished greatly in stature due to a number of apparent intelligence failures. By 1943 *Reichsführer* SS Heinrich Himmler, a rival of Canaris, had seized the opportunity to create an elite special forces unit of his own, which was headed by Major Otto Skorzeny. Disillusioned by recent events, many of the Brandenburgers joined Skorzeny's ranks.

While Canaris was being investigated for conspiring against the Nazi regime, the Brandenburgers faded into relative obscurity. In the autumn of 1944 the unit was dissolved.

SKORZENY'S SS COMMANDOS

- •FOUNDED: 1943
- •STRENGTH: 1200
- •THEATRES: ITALY, WESTERN EUROPE

The small Fieseler Storch observation plane was built to carry the pilot and one passenger safely. On the afternoon of 12 September 1943, however, the light aircraft was dangerously overloaded. Aboard were the nervous pilot, SS Captain Otto Skorzeny, and Benito Mussolini, the deposed dictator of fascist Italy. Although the Storch was well known for its ability to take off and land in a

Otto Skorzeny, known as the most dangerous man in Europe, masterminded German commando raids such as the rescue of Mussolini and Operation Greif during the Battle of the Bulge.

relatively confined space, this departure from the Gran Sasso in the Abruzzi Mountains of northern Italy would be a stern test.

A short slope ended abruptly on the mountainside, and a sheer 2015m cliff left virtually no margin for error. The little plane bounded the short distance to the edge and dropped from view. Seconds later, the pilot fighting to maintain control, it began to rise. German paratroopers and commandos gave a lusty cheer. Their mission had been accomplished in only 12 minutes, and without firing a shot.

The reputation of Skorzeny as a daring, high stakes special forces leader was already growing before his 90-man force stunned the world and plucked Mussolini, who had been removed from power by King Victor Emmanuel when a new government headed by Marshal Pietro Badoglio was formed days earlier, from his mountaintop prison. Anti-fascist troops loyal to the king were holding Mussolini at the Campo Imperiale Hotel, and Hitler charged Skorzeny with bringing his Axis partner to safety.

Benito Mussolini, the former Italian dictator, prepares to board a Storch aircraft at Gran Sasso in Italy's Abruzzi Mountains, while his German rescuers look on.

A force of 12 gliders had originally been intended for the operation, and Mussolini was to have been taken to the valley floor aboard a cable car. Only eight of the gliders reached the Gran Sasso on that September day and skidded to a stop, but the force of German rescuers executed its mission flawlessly. Communications problems forced a change in the evacuation plan, and it was decided to fly the former dictator directly from the top of the mountain. Shortly afterwards, Mussolini and Skorzeny boarded a Heinkel He-111 bomber and flew on to Berlin where a grateful Hitler awarded the commando leader the Iron Cross.

Skorzeny's elite commando unit had been formed as a company in mid-1943 and quickly grown to battalion size. *Reichsführer* SS Heinrich Himmler authorized the new formation as a successor to the Brandenburger Regiment. The Brandenburgers had been controlled by German Intelligence, the Abwehr, and rendered outstanding service before being relegated to lesser roles as Abwehr chief Admiral Wilhelm Canaris fell from favour with Hitler.

Austrian by birth, Skorzeny had joined that nation's Nazi party in 1931. He was turned away when he tried to join the *Luftwaffe* early in the war, but found his opportunity as a member of the Waffen (armed) SS. As a junior officer with the 1st SS *Leibstandarte* Adolf Hitler, the original Waffen SS division formed as Hitler's personal bodyguard, Skorzeny saw combat in France and the Low Countries and was seriously wounded on the Eastern Front in December 1942. The following April he was placed in command of two battalions which subsequently trained in special operations for only about four months before executing the Mussolini rescue operation.

'MOST DANGEROUS MAN IN EUROPE'

Skorzeny's reputation continued to grow in the spring of 1944 when his command took part in Operation Rosselsprung, fighting communist partisans in Yugoslavia and very nearly capturing their leader, Yosip Broz, popularly known as Tito. On 20 July 1944 Skorzeny took prompt action in Berlin and contributed to restoring order after an unsuccessful attempt to assassinate Hitler at his Wolf's Lair headquarters at Rastenburg, East Prussia.

By the autumn of 1944, the Allies knew Skorzeny as 'the most dangerous man in Europe'. When Hitler became convinced that Hungarian regent Miklos Horthy's commitment to the Axis was wavering, the Fuhrer ordered Skorzeny to action on 15 October. Peace negotiations Horthy was conducting with the Soviet Union ended abruptly when Skorzeny and his commandos kidnapped the regent's son, Milos Horthy, who had been acting as chief negotiator, and spirited him off to Berlin. The following day, Miklos Horthy was taken into custody and a pro-German regime was installed, ensuring that Hungary would remain in the war on the side of the Axis.

A week later, Skorzeny was promoted to the rank of SS *Obersturmbannführer* (lieutenant colonel) and given command of the 150th Panzer Brigade with the additional task of organizing groups of English-speaking German soldiers who were to dress in American uniforms and infiltrate behind enemy lines, some using captured vehicles. These Germans were to be fluent in English, even to the extent that they were familiar with American slang.

ARDENNES OFFENSIVE

When the German winter offensive in the Ardennes, which came to be known as the Battle of the Bulge, commenced on 16 December 1944, Skorzeny also implemented Operation Greif, sending his infiltrators behind Allied lines to raise havoc and seize key bridges across the Meuse River. A few of these specially trained troops actually did manage to create confusion, but most of them were killed or captured and subsequently executed as spies. The greatest damage inflicted upon the Allies by these covert operatives was the spreading of wild rumours that a major German raid was under way behind the lines and even that Skorzeny was personally on the move toward Paris to kidnap General Dwight D. Eisenhower.

On 21 December Skorzeny led elements of his brigade in an abortive attack near the Belgian town of Malmédy. After the failure of the Ardennes offensive, Skorzeny's brigade was dissolved and its survivors allocated to other combat units.

For the remainder of the war Skorzeny fought to defend Prussia and Pomerania against the advancing Soviet Red Army. He commanded a stubborn defence of a vital bridge across the Oder River and authorized a failed attempt by frogmen to destroy the Ludendorff Bridge across the Rhine River at Remagen after its capture by American troops. Skorzeny received the oak leaves to the Knight's Cross near the end of the war and was preparing defences in Bavaria prior to surrendering at Salzburg on 19 May 1945.

After the war Skorzeny was tried for war crimes by a military tribunal at Dachau. He was acquitted but not released from prison, finally escaping to

Right: American military police tie one of SS Major Otto Skorzeny's Operation Greif *infiltrators to a post in preparation for his execution by firing squad during the Battle of the Bulge.*

Spain in 1948. There he married and resumed his civilian career as an engineer. His business was highly successful, and he worked as a consultant to the Egyptian and Argentine governments. Skorzeny was also reputed to have assisted in the organization of the Odessa escape network for former SS men. He died in Madrid in 1975 at the age of 67.

In light of the accomplishments of his special forces, Skorzeny is considered by many to be the most outstanding commando of World War II.

21ST PANZER DIVISION

- •FOUNDED: 1941
- •STRENGTH: 16,000
- •THEATRES: NORTH AFRICA, WESTERN EUROPE

Early on the morning of 6 June 1944, Lieutenant General Edgar Feuchtinger and the German 21st Panzer Division occupied positions near the Norman village of Caen. Obviously something was up. The sound of gunfire and the smoke of battle were readily apparent. As the intensity of the disturbance grew and reports of British airborne troops and landings on the nearby beaches filtered in, Feuchtinger was certain that his field telephone would ring.

Commanding the only panzer division of the German Army then stationed in Normandy, Feuchtinger expected orders to move against the D-Day invaders. However, the German high command was not convinced that the Allied operation in Normandy was the real invasion. They still expected the main landings to occur to the northeast at the Pas de Calais, where the distance across the English Channel from Great Britain to France was at its narrowest. Besides, foul weather had lulled many of the commanders into a temporary false sense of security. Finally, when he could wait no longer, Feuchtinger struck out on his

General Edgar Feuchtinger led the 21st Panzer Division, the only German armoured unit to counterattack the Allied landings on D-Day. The division reached the sea but was forced to retire.

own initiative and attacked British paratroopers who had landed behind the invasion beaches with orders to seize a key bridge across the Caen Canal near the Orne River along with the town of Ranville and a battery of heavy German guns at Merville. While engaged in this independent action, 21st Panzer finally did receive orders – to attack the British at Sword Beach to the north. So Feuchtinger was obliged to move his armoured forces back through Caen and redeploy, a movement which required several hours to complete.

When 21st Panzer counter-attacked in support of the 716th Infantry Division late in the afternoon of 6 June, one spearhead managed to reach the coastline, driving a wedge between Sword and Juno beaches. However, the concentrated fire of numerous warships offshore had a telling effect. When no reserves appeared to exploit the penetration, the panzers, low on supplies, were forced to retire. Caen itself had been a D-Day objective of the British, and the actions of 21st Panzer were instrumental in preventing the city's

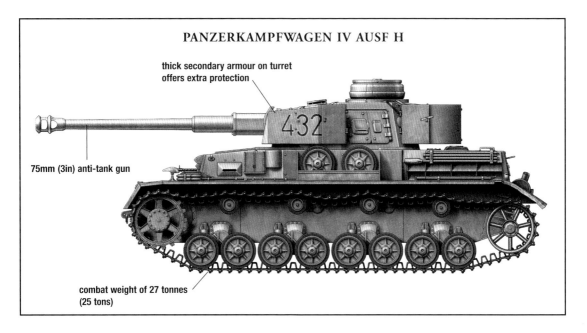

PANZERKAMPFWAGEN IV AUSF H

thick secondary armour on turret
offers extra protection

75mm (3in) anti-tank gun

432

combat weight of 27 tonnes
(25 tons)

When the Allies landed at Normandy on 6 June 1944, the 21st Panzer Division was equipped with the ubiquitous Panzer Mk IV, the mainstay of the Werhmacht for much of World War II.

capture. A month of difficult fighting lay ahead before the *Wehrmacht* was forced out of Caen. By that time the division had lost nearly all of its tanks.

Exhausted from the fighting around Caen, the division was pulled out of the line for rest and refitting. Within weeks, however, the Allies had succeeded in breaking out of the hedgerow country of Normandy and had begun a relentless advance across France.

WHILE HITLER SLEPT

The battle for Normandy had actually been lost on 6 June, when the German high command had refused to commit armoured reserves located near Paris and in the Pas de Calais to counter-attack in a timely manner. Hitler retained personal control over the disposition of all armoured reserves, and none of his subordinates in Berlin believed the situation warranted disturbing his sleep. He woke at noon and finally released the reserve panzer divisions around 4 p.m., much too late to make a difference on D-Day.

When the Normandy campaign commenced, the 21st Panzer Division included a few combat veterans who had survived the retreat and evacuation of German forces from North Africa. Originally called the 5th Light Afrika Division, 21st Panzer had been formed in early 1941 from available forces in North Africa. Its purpose was to prop up the faltering Italian Army, which the British had handled roughly. As part of Field Marshal Erwin Rommel's famous Afrika Korps, the 21st Panzer Division took part in bitter fighting against the British at the Sidi Rezegh, the Gazala Line and Mersa Matruh.

Opposing Field Marshal Bernard Montgomery's offensive at El Alamein on the Egyptian frontier in the autumn of 1942, the 21st Panzer Division was heavily engaged during the fight for a key position called Kidney Ridge. The division made five separate attempts to take the high ground over a two-day period, only to be repulsed by anti-tank and artillery fire four times and by heavy air attacks during the fifth assault. Eventually, all of its tanks were disabled.

Following the American landings on the North African coast during Operation Torch, 21st Panzer was moved to the west and participated in the rout of American units at Sidi Bouzid and Kasserine Pass in February 1943. In the first week of March three panzer divisions, 21st, 15th and 10th, were mauled by anti-tank guns and air strikes at Medenine.

The 21st Panzer Division was subsequently withdrawn to France, offering the only German counter-attack of any consequence on D-Day and resisting the Allied push across France in the regions of Alsace and the Saar. Near the end of the war the division was transferred to the Eastern Front, where it surrendered to the Soviet Red Army in 1945.

PANZER LEHR DIVISION

- **FOUNDED: 1943**
- **STRENGTH: 14,699**
- **THEATRES: WESTERN EUROPE**

At the time of its formation in the winter of 1943-44, the Panzer Lehr Division was the elite armoured division of the German Army. Equipped with the latest in tanks and armoured vehicles, the unit was composed of demonstration (lehr) troops from the army's panzer training schools. The combat history of Panzer Lehr spans the final 12 months of the war in Europe, during which the unit opposed the Allied D-Day landings in Normandy, the fighting around the strategically vital towns of Caen and St. Lo, the Ardennes Offensive, and the Ruhr Pocket.

After a brief deployment to Hungary on the Eastern Front, in which the division was augmented by a regiment of elite Lehr infantry, Panzer Lehr returned to France in the spring of 1944. When the Allies landed in Normandy on 6 June, Panzer Lehr was positioned in the vicinity of Caen. Hitler maintained personal control of virtually all panzer forces in Western Europe, and Panzer Lehr was not released to advance toward the invasion beaches until late in the afternoon of D-Day. Allied air superiority hampered daylight movement, and the division did not fully engage the British and Canadian troops in its front until 9 June.

TIGERS EARN STRIPES

One of the single most spectacular feats of arms during World War II occurred on 13 June at the

Lieutenant Michael Wittman and his 501st Heavy Tank Battalion decimated a British armoured unit at Villers-Bocage in Normandy, destroying 23 vehicles.

hamlet of Villers-Bocage. During an attempt by the British 7th Armoured Division, veterans of the fighting in North Africa, to bypass Caen, a strong column consisting of the 4th County of London Yeomanry and the Rifle Brigade had halted for a rest. Panzer Lehr's 2nd Company, 501st Heavy Tank Battalion, equipped with the formidable 88mm-gunned Tiger tank, was in the vicinity and under the command of Lieutenant Michael Wittman, who was already famous as a tank ace on the Eastern Front with 119 enemy vehicles destroyed in combat.

Wittman left a blocking force of three Tigers and a Mark IV medium tank outside the town and warily moved in. When gunner Bobby Woll spotted four British Cromwell tanks neatly parked on the side of the road, he aimed and fired, sending all four up in flames. When Wittman ordered the rest of the tanks forward they moved methodically from one end of the British column to the other. Twenty-three British vehicles were destroyed, and more than 100 of the accompanying infantry were killed or captured. Wittman was awarded the swords to his Knight's Cross for the accomplishment and was promoted to major, but two months later he was killed in action when a single British Sherman Firefly tank of the 1st Northamptonshire Yeomanry destroyed his Tiger.

After a month of hard fighting, the German hold on Caen was finally broken and Panzer Lehr retired westward to the vicinity of St. Lo, leaving 2500 dead and wounded and more than 100 destroyed tanks at the Caen battleground. Defending in the French hedgerow country, Panzer Lehr held its line at Pont-Herbert for several days but lost a number of tanks to incessant Allied air attacks.

OPERATION COBRA

American forces captured St. Lo in mid-July, and on the 25th, Operation Cobra, the attempt to break out of the hedgerow country commenced with a devastating carpet bombing of German positions. Panzer Lehr, positioned astride the main American line of advance on the St. Lo-Périers Road, was stunned by the savagery of the bombardment. Although some of the ordnance fell on American troops and inflicted a number of casualties unintentionally, Panzer Lehr was virtually

incapacitated. Its commander, Major General Fritz Bayerlein, reported that by noon 70 per cent of his troops were unfit for combat, either 'dead, wounded, crazed, or numbed ...'

By the time Hitler launched his Ardennes offensive on 16 December 1944 Panzer Lehr had been refitted, but it barely resembled the elite unit it had been at its inception. The division was thrown into the drive to capture the vital Belgian crossroads town of Bastogne and the advance toward one of the offensive's major objectives, the Meuse River.

While elements of the division combined with the 26th Volksgrenadier Division and other units to encircle Bastogne, the remainder of Panzer Lehr was heavily engaged at Dinant, Rochefort and Celles. Bad weather lifted, and Allied air power decimated the German armoured columns. Bastogne did not fall, having been relieved by a spearhead of the American Third Army's 4th Armoured Division on 26 December, and the thrust toward the Meuse was abandoned by 1 January 1945.

In March 1945 the 9th Armoured Division of the US First Army captured the Ludendorff railroad bridge over the mighty Rhine River at the town of Remagen. Panzer Lehr was among the German forces sent to wipe out the bridgehead, but the depleted division was unable to do much more than slow Allied progress into the Ruhr, the industrial heart of Germany. As the Third Reich crumbled, Panzer Lehr was reduced to relatively few armoured vehicles. Its surviving combat troops were among the 325,000 German soldiers who surrendered to the American First and Ninth armies after being encircled in the Ruhr pocket in April 1945.

BATTLESHIP *BISMARCK* CREW
- **LAUNCHED:** 1939
- **STRENGTH:** 2200
- **THEATRES:** ATLANTIC

The epic of the chase of the battleship *Bismarck* and its eventual sinking by warships of the British Royal Navy is one of the greatest stories in the history of conflict on the high seas. Perhaps the most famous battleship ever constructed, the short combat career of the *Bismarck* lasted only nine days, from 18-27 May 1941.

The *Bismarck*, pride of the Kriegsmarine, Germany's Navy, had been laid down on 1 July 1936. She was launched on 14 February 1939 and commissioned on 29 August 1940. The massive vessel, nearly 255m (823ft) in length with a beam of 37m (118ft), displaced more than 51,000 tonnes fully loaded. The *Bismarck*'s main armament consisted of four turrets, each mounting a pair of

The massive beam of the battleship **Bismarck** *is visible in this image, as are her forward 15-inch guns. The Royal Navy sank the warship during an epic chase in May 1941.*

380mm (15in) guns which could hurl a shell more than 32km (20 miles). The ship's all-volunteer crew numbered more than 2200 officers and sailors. During its fateful voyage the crew also included a complement of 500 naval cadets, all of them in their teens. In the spring of 1941 Grand Admiral Erich Raeder, commander of the Kriegsmarine, authorized Operation Rhine Exercise. The *Bismarck* was ordered to sortie from the port of Gotenhafen on the coast of the Baltic Sea in occupied Poland and attack convoys of merchant ships supplying the island nation of Great Britain with a lifeline of supplies and war materiel.

When the *Bismarck* weighed anchor on 18 May she was accompanied by the 19,380-tonne heavy cruiser *Prinz Eugen*. The two warships then made for the open sea and eventually the Atlantic

In this image taken from the cruiser **Prinz Eugen,** **Bismarck** *is captured firing a broadside during the encounter with the battlecruiser HMS* **Hood** *and the battleship HMS* **Prince of Wales.**

shipping lanes via the Denmark Strait.

The hope of maintaining secrecy faded when the two German vessels were spotted by a Swedish cruiser in the Skagerrak between Denmark and Norway about 48 hours later. When the British Admiralty received word that the *Bismarck* and *Prinz Eugen* were under way and a reconnaissance aircraft confirmed that the battleship was no longer in port, the race was on. The Admiralty dispatched two battle groups from the Royal Navy anchorage at Scapa Flow in Scotland's Orkney Islands and summoned forces from as far away as Gibraltar to hunt down and sink the *Bismarck*.

UNDOING OF THE HOOD

British cruisers patrolled the potential entry points for the *Bismarck* and *Prinz Eugen* into the Atlantic, and on the evening of 23 May the cruisers HMS *Norfolk* and HMS *Suffolk* spotted the giant battleship in the Denmark Strait and began to shadow her. On the morning of 24 May the brand new battleship *Prince of Wales*, with some workmen still aboard, approached the German ships. Sailing

with the new 35,700-tonne battleship, which mounted 356mm (14in) main armament, was the 42,840-tonne battlecruiser HMS *Hood*, the pride of the Royal Navy. Commissioned in 1920, the *Hood* was known the world over. With 380mm (15in) guns, she matched the *Bismarck* in firepower. Her Achilles heel, however, was a thin layer of protective armament, little more than 76mm (3in) on top of the hull. The *Hood's* designers had sacrificed armament for speed, and this was to prove the undoing of the great ship.

During a battle which lasted less than nine minutes, the *Hood* was hit by gunfire from both German vessels and erupted in a gigantic explosion. She sank in seconds, and only three sailors survived the debacle.

One German sailor described the demise of the *Hood*. 'There was an explosion of quite incredible violence … Through huge holes opened up in the grey hull, enormous flames leaped up from the depths of the ship … and blazed for several seconds through an ashen pall of smoke in two billowing columns … Below them formed something like an incandescent dome.'

The *Prince of Wales* was damaged during the exchange and turned away. *Bismarck*, too, was hit and began to leak a telltale oil slick from a gashed fuel bunker. The death of the *Hood* shocked the

Royal Navy leadership and served to intensify the hunt for the Germans.

Admiral Guenther Luetjens, overall commander of the German task force, and Captain Ernst Lindemann, commander of the *Bismarck*, decided to head for the safety of a French port, either St. Nazaire or Brest, as the great battleship sailed bow-down, having taken on water. The *Prinz Eugen* was detached, and the *Bismarck* made her way alone, straining to reach the cover of *Luftwaffe* aircraft based in France.

THE CRIPPLED GIANT

On the evening of 26 May the British launched a last-ditch effort to slow the *Bismarck* down. Fifteen Fairey Swordfish torpedo planes appeared out of the gloom and pressed home their attacks. Launched near the limit of their range from the pitching deck of the aircraft carrier HMS *Ark Royal*, the Swordfish were flying anachronisms, constructed mainly of wood and canvas. A previous Swordfish raid, launched from the aircraft carrier HMS *Victorious* on 24 May, had resulted in a single torpedo hit which caused inconsequential damage.

This time, however, these slow flying biplanes were equal to the task at hand. One torpedo slammed amidships and did little damage; a second smashed into the battleship aft of the stern 380mm (15in) gun turrets, jamming the ship's twin rudders so that she could turn only in a circle. All hope of reaching safety evaporated when divers, put over the side to assess the damage, reported that it could not be repaired. Admiral Luetjens subsequently sent a message to Berlin: 'We shall fight to the last shell. Long live the Fuhrer, the Chief of the Fleet.'

As British warships closed in on the crippled giant, the *Bismarck*'s fate was sealed. On the morning of 27 May the battleships HMS *King George V*, with main guns of 356mm (14in), and HMS *Rodney*, armed with 406mm (16in) naval cannon, appeared on the horizon along with several accompanying cruisers and destroyers. Admiral Sir John Tovey, commander of the Home Fleet, ordered the British warships to open fire at 8.47 a.m. from a range of more than 19km (12 miles). Although the *Bismarck* fought back, several shells caused telling damage aboard the German ship. One 406mm (16in) shell

from the *Rodney* disabled both forward 380mm (15in) turrets, while a 203mm (8in) shell from the HMS *Norfolk* destroyed a fire control director and another smashed the forecastle.

Closing to less than 3km (2 miles), the equivalent of point-blank range for naval gunfire, the British warships pounded their quarry incessantly. The *Bismarck* was turned into a blazing pyre as the dead and wounded piled up on her decks.

Approximately 300 shells had hit the *Bismarck* during a 40-minute bombardment, but the proud ship refused to sink. For decades, historians have argued over whether torpedoes fired by the cruiser HMS *Dorsetshire* delivered the *coup de grâce* or *Bismarck* crewmen opened the sea cocks to finally scuttle the ship. Regardless, the *Bismarck* had heeled over on its side and slipped beneath the waves in 4650m (15,000ft) of water by 10.45 a.m.

Admiral Luetjens was killed by a British shell, and Captain Lindemann was seen saluting as the battleship went down. Only 110 survivors were rescued by British vessels before a report of a lurking U-boat forced them to retire. 'In the water we were pushed together in a bunch, as we bobbed up and down like corks,' remembered one former crewman. 'We swam away from the sinking ship as hard as we could to escape her suction.'

The *Hood* had been avenged, and the greatest chase in naval history was over. Decades after the battle the wreck of the *Bismarck* was discovered and explored by an oceanographic team lead by Robert Ballard, who had previously discovered the remains of another famous vessel, the passenger liner *Titanic*.

SUBMARINE U-47 CREW

- **FOUNDED: 1938**
- **STRENGTH: 44**
- **THEATRES: NORTH ATLANTIC**

Their average age was 20 and their commander, known affectionately as the 'old man', was a mere 30 years of age. The crewmen of the German submarine *U-47* were, in many ways, typical of the young, highly motivated sailors of the Kriegsmarine, the German Navy, who volunteered for the most hazardous duty in World War II.

A type VII-B submarine, the *U-47* was the most advanced of its kind available to the Kriegsmarine with the outbreak of war. With a displacement of 285 tonnes and a length of 44m (48.12yds), the boat was armed with an 88mm (3.46in) deck gun, a 20mm (1.6in) anti-aircraft cannon and a cargo of 15 deadly torpedoes.

Admiral Karl Doenitz, commander of the U-boat fleet and a veteran of the unrestricted submarine warfare campaign which had nearly brought the British

Gunther Prien (wearing the dark suit of a U-boat captain) poses with the crew of U-47 *after their triumphant return from sinking the battleship* **Royal Oak** *at Scapa Flow.*

to their knees in World War I, recognized less than a month after hostilities had begun on 1 September 1939, that his elite naval force needed to make a bold statement of its worth in the current struggle.

SCAPA FLOW DARE

Did he dare to send a U-boat against the anchorage of the British Royal Navy's Home Fleet? The base at Scapa Flow in the Orkney Islands of Scotland was assumed to be heavily defended, but if a U-boat could successfully penetrate the anchorage and send a shock wave through the British Admiralty, then Doenitz could make a case for the allocation of more resources to build great numbers of U-boats which could then sever the merchant shipping lifeline of supplies to Great Britain. Doenitz ordered a reconnaissance of the Scapa Flow area, and even

though it was obvious that the anchorage was protected by heavy nets, cables and sunken block ships, he determined that the effort was worthwhile.

When Doenitz began looking for a commander and U-boat crew to undertake the perilous mission, he quickly settled on Lieutenant Commander Gunther Prien and his *U-47*. The crew had already proven itself efficient and effective, scoring some of the first successes for the U-boat service in the Atlantic. Prien was an experienced seaman, having sailed with the German merchant fleet as a boy of 16. He was said to have an innate ability to sense both danger and opportunity, and these were invaluable attributes for a U-boat commander.

On 8 October 1939 Prien and his complement of 44 sailors glided out of the harbour at Kiel and slipped into the North Sea, the conning tower of *U-47* emblazoned with the caricature of a snorting bull. Five days later, the submarine had reached the coast of Scotland. Proceeding on the surface, Prien ordered a crash dive to avoid detection by a merchant ship. Scraping across large cables strung between barrier ships, the submarine ran aground temporarily, unable to wedge free by reversing engines and manipulating the rudder. Finally, Prien ordered the release of all air pressure valves and the flooded dive tanks to be blown. Immediately *U-47* shook loose.

When the dangerous passage resumed, the headlights of a taxi silhouetted the boat against the horizon as the northern lights glimmered, but the vehicle continued on its way. Aerial reconnaissance photos taken only a week earlier indicated that the bulk of the Home Fleet was anchored in Scapa Flow. Prien scanned the harbour, searching the inlets and coves for targets, but to no avail. Nearly all the Home Fleet had relocated to Loch Ewe following an effort to corner the German battlecruiser *Gneisenau*.

ROYAL OAK FELLED

Only the World War I-vintage battleship *Royal Oak*, a formidable sight at 31,875 tonnes with a 380mm (14.96in) main armament, and the seaplane tender *Pegasus* were located in Scapa Flow. *Royal Oak* had put in for repairs after a heavy gale had battered the fleet and she had been unable to keep pace with the rest of the warships. When Prien sighted the vessels he mistook the *Pegasus* for the battlecruiser *Repulse* and moved into position for the attack.

The forward torpedo tubes were loaded and flooded. At Prien's command, a spread

Although not the highest scoring U-boat ace of the war, Gunther Prien was by far the most famous because of U-47's *exploits at Scapa Flow.*

GUNTHER PRIEN

Prien was the U-boat ace who became one of the Third Reich's earliest war heroes because his attack on HMS *Royal Oak*. He was awarded the Knight's Cross – the first to any U-boat commander – and each member of his crew received the Iron Cross (Second Class). Born in Thuringia, Prien was a merchant seaman before joining the German Navy in 1934. He transferred to U-boats in 1935, and by the outbreak of war was in command of *U-47*. Described by William L. Shirer as 'clean-cut, cocky, a fanatical Nazi and obviously capable', he was one of the most successful of all U-boat commanders, sinking over 180,000 tonnes (177,158 tons) of British shipping in 18 months. He was awarded Oak Leaves in October 1940. Prien was killed in action on the night of 7/8 March 1941, when *U-47* was thought to have been sunk by the British destroyer HMS *Wolverine*. However, recent research indicates that the destroyer actually attacked *U-A* and that *U-47* was lost to unknown causes.

of four torpedoes was fired, but one of these jammed in its tube. In three-and-a-half minutes a single torpedo covered 3000m (3281yds) and slammed into the bow of the *Royal Oak*. Prien believed he had hit the *Repulse*, and he noticed little apparent damage to either ship. Amazingly, no significant alarm was raised as a result. Fearing that he would be discovered, Prien turned to engage his stern tubes. A single torpedo was loosed but missed wide of its mark. Then three more were launched from the stern, running straight and true. All three found the mark, detonating against the starboard side of the battleship's hull and probably igniting an ammunition magazine.

'Flames shot skyward, blue, yellow, red,' Prien wrote later. 'Like huge birds, black shadows soared through the flames, fell hissing and splashing into the water, huge fragments of the mast and funnels.'

HITLER'S HERO

In 15 minutes, the *Royal Oak* heaved, rolled over and sank in 19m of water, carrying 833 of its 1200-man crew to their deaths. Unmolested, the *U-47*

reached the safety of the open sea. Only a brief attack by British minesweepers which dropped depth charges impeded the U-boat's progress. On 17 October the submarine arrived at Wilhelmshaven to a hero's welcome. Brass bands, adoring civilians and envious Kriegsmarine personnel choked the docks. Prien and his crew were flown to Berlin, where Hitler personally awarded the intrepid officer the Knight's Cross. Each sailor received the Iron Cross 2nd Class for their tremendous feat of arms.

CBS News correspondent William L. Shirer reported from Berlin on the electrifying news that Prien and the crew of *U-47* had pulled off the daring attack inside Scapa Flow. He remembered talking to a friend who had skippered a German submarine in World War I. The former commander told Shirer that two attempts had been made to penetrate the anchorage during the Great War and that both U-boats had been lost.

Shirer described the U-boat captain who arrived one day in Berlin: '… Tripping into our afternoon press conference at the Propaganda Ministry this afternoon, followed by his crew – boys of 18, 19, 20. Prien is 30, clean-cut, cocky, a fanatical Nazi, and obviously capable. Introduced by Hitler's press chief, Dr Dietrich, who kept cursing the English and calling Churchill a liar, Prien told us little of how he did it. He said he had no trouble getting past the boom protecting the bay. I got the impression, though he said nothing to justify it, that he must have followed a British craft, perhaps a minesweeper, into the base. British negligence must have been something terrific.'

The British had, in fact, identified the potential for a breach in the security at Scapa Flow earlier in the summer. Just days after the *U-47*'s victory, an elderly steamer was detailed for sinking at the point where Prien had guided the submarine into the anchorage on 14 October 1939.

Prien continued to command the *U-47*, although U-boat crews frequently changed. It is thought he was killed when the submarine was lost with all hands around 8 March 1941. Prien's final tally was 33 ships grossing more than 200,940 tonnes sunk.

During World War II, a total of 1155 U-boats were commissioned. Of these, 725 were lost. Approximately 35,000 men went to sea in the

POCKET BATTLESHIP
ADMIRAL GRAF SPEE CREW

- •FOUNDED: 1936
- •STRENGTH: 1150
- •THEATRES: ATLANTIC

Captain Hans Langsdorff chats with members of the crew of the pocket battleship **Graf Spee** *after they scuttled the warship at the mouth of the harbour at Montevideo. Langsdorff later committed suicide.*

With its imposing main armament of six 279mm (11in) guns and a maximum speed of twenty-eight-and-a-half knots, the pocket battleship *Admiral Graf Spee* was one of a new breed of warships which became a mainstay of the Kriegsmarine, the German Navy, during the 1930s. Known to the Allies as pocket battleships, *Graf Spee* and her sisters *Deutschland* (later *Lützow*) and *Admiral Scheer* were employed during the war primarily as commerce raiders.

Graf Spee was the third of the pocket battleships. Her keel was laid in 1932. She was launched in 1934 and commissioned two years later. Her crew

numbered 1150 officers and sailors. *Deutschland* (*Lutzow*) and *Admiral Scheer* survived until 1945, but *Graf Spee* was involved in one of the early engagements of the war near the harbour of Montevideo, Uruguay, at the mouth of the River Plate in December 1939.

With the outbreak of war *Graf Spee* was already at sea. Her commander, Captain Hans Langsdorff, undertook a successful four-month campaign against British shipping below the Equator. Beginning on 30 September, the raider sank nine merchantmen in the South Atlantic and Indian oceans without any loss of life on either side. The crews of the British ships were taken aboard the tanker *Altmark* for transport back to Europe. Later, in a stunning raid by the crew of the British destroyer *Cossack* under the command of Captain Philip Vian, more than 300 of these prisoners were rescued from the *Altmark* in Norwegian territorial waters.

ATTACK AT MONTEVIDEO

Meanwhile, in December 1939, Langsdorff proceeded into waters off the coast of South America in search of an expected British convoy. In response to the pocket battleship's success, the British Admiralty dispatched no less than seven naval squadrons to search for the raider. Rather than finding a merchant convoy, the *Graf Spee* was confronted off Montevideo on 13 December by three Royal Navy warships. The heavy cruiser *Exeter* mounted 203mm (8in) main armament, while the light cruiser *Ajax* had 152mm (6in) guns, as did the New Zealand light cruiser *Achilles*.

At first Langsdorff believed the British ships were convoy escorts which might easily be brushed aside. However, he soon found himself engaged from three different points. The *Exeter* was ordered to draw fire from the *Graf Spee* while the smaller cruisers moved as close as possible for a torpedo attack. A running battle developed and all three of the British ships suffered considerable damage. The *Graf Spee* absorbed 17 hits but only the 203mm (8in) shells of the *Exeter* had been capable of penetrating the pocket battleship's armour.

When Langsdorff entered the neutral harbour of Montevideo he was accorded only a matter of hours to bury his dead and make temporary repairs. The *Exeter* had been so grievously wounded that she was ordered out of the battle. With only the damaged *Ajax* and *Achilles* available to confront the *Graf Spee* if hostilities were renewed, the British commander Commodore Henry Harwood summoned another cruiser, the *Cumberland*, to assist as quickly as possible. Though Harwood considered his battered force's chances of thwarting an escape attempt by the German raider to be slim, Langsdorff was under the impression that a much more powerful British battle group was waiting outside Montevideo.

Rather than fight, Langsdorff made the fateful decision to scuttle the *Graf Spee*. On the evening of 17 December the pocket battleship was blown up by three explosive charges placed over the ship's

ammunition magazines. The crew of the *Graf Spee* was transferred to Buenos Aires, Argentina, and interned for the duration of the war. Langsdorff, on the other hand, was despondent over what he considered to be his failure in command.

During the funeral for his sailors killed in the fight with British cruisers the captain had offered the traditional German naval salute rather than the Nazi salute. On 20 December, after seeing to the safety of his crew, he wrote a final letter explaining his actions, wrapped the naval ensign of the old Imperial German Fleet around himself, and committed suicide with a pistol.

Six decades after the demise of *Graf Spee*, salvage operations have recovered artifacts from the ship's wreck, including a 150mm (5.9in)gun mount, which is on display at a museum in Montevideo, and the warship's figurehead, a swastika-emblazoned eagle.

FALLSCHIRMJÄGER
- **FOUNDED:** 1938
- **STRENGTH:** 160,000
- **THEATRES:** WESTERN EUROPE, MEDITERRANEAN

The elite light infantry of the *Luftwaffe*, the *Fallschirmjäger* (parachute/air landing) divisions of the German armed forces were engaged on every front during the war in Europe. The original airborne formation, the 7th Flieger Division, was constituted in October 1938 on orders from *Luftwaffe* Chief Hermann Goering.

Reichsmarshal Goering's choice to command the new airborne forces was General Kurt Student, a former fighter pilot who had been wounded in aerial combat in World War I. Student was convinced that the *Fallschirmjäger* could make a significant contribution to the German war effort, performing vertical envelopment operations and seizing objectives in advance of ground troops.

In the opening campaign of the war two battalions of airborne troops captured airfields in Poland. Seven months later a large-scale operation facilitated the occupation of Denmark and Norway. On 10 May 1940 Hitler unleashed his assault

against France and the Low Countries.
Fallschirmjäger were inserted by parachute and glider
to seize key objectives, including several bridges in
Belgium and the major obstacle of Fort Eben Emael.

EBEN EMAEL SPECTACULAR
The lightning strike against Fort Eben Emael,
situated on a rocky bluff above the Albert Canal
only 24km (15 miles) across the German border in
Belgium, was one of the most spectacular successes
of World War II. Eben Emael appeared impregnable,
with an array of heavy artillery and a sheer 40m
(130ft) precipice below. The fort defended three
bridges, which, if captured intact, would allow
German forces to pass swiftly to the southwest.

In the pre-dawn hours of 10 May the
Fallschirmjäger struck. Nine gliders whistled to
pinpoint landings on the roof of Eben Emael.
Seventy troopers swiftly emerged from the gliders to
confront the nearly 800 Belgian defenders. Within
20 minutes the Germans had overrun 14 of the
fort's gun emplacements, while stunned enemy
soldiers retreated to positions underground. The
Belgians put up stiff resistance at one gun
emplacement near the western end of the fort but
the Germans used a hollow charge and a
flamethrower to capture the position.

*A Junkers Ju-52 transport plane, hit by anti-aircraft
fire, burns furiously as it plummets earthward.
Operation Mercury, the airborne invasion of Crete,
proved to be a costly affair for the Germans.*

By noon the following day the fort was entirely
in German hands, and the Belgians had suffered 25
dead and 59 wounded. Altogether, 424 men in 42
gliders towed by Junkers Ju-52 transport planes had
participated in the attack, capturing the fort and
two of the three bridges across the Albert Canal
intact. The victors of Eben Emael were withdrawn
by truck. Days later, the officers who had led the
assault on the fort were awarded the Knight's Cross
by Hitler. Enlisted troopers were given the Iron
Cross, and every *Fallschirmjäger* who had taken part
in the Eben Emael operation was promoted one
rank. Everything did not go according to plan for
the *Fallschirmjäger*, however. One parachute
operation in Norway ended in complete failure, and
an assault on The Hague, seat of the Dutch
Government, was subdued with more than 1200
Germans taken prisoner. In the summer of 1940
planning was under way for Operation Sealion, the
German invasion of Great Britain. The
Fallschirmjäger were expected to play a major role in
the opening phase of the invasion; however, when

the *Luftwaffe* failed to win control of the air over the English Channel during the Battle of Britain, Operation Sealion was called off.

BATTLE FOR CRETE

When German forces invaded the Balkans and defending Allied units withdrew to the island of Crete, the *Fallschirmjäger* faced their toughest test of the war. In April 1941, Student persuaded Hitler that his elite troops should be used in securing the large island. Operation Mercury involved dropping more than 7000 parachutists and glider-borne troops to capture key airfields and strong points. Reinforcements were to land the following day.

One of Student's officers remembered the general's sentiment about Operation Mercury. 'He had devised it, struggled against heavy opposition for its acceptance and had worked out all the details … He believed in it and lived for it and in it.'

However, intelligence had failed the Germans. Rather than a garrison of only 5000 demoralized soldiers, Crete was defended by more than 40,000 Commonwealth troops and Greek irregulars. When the plan was set in motion on 20 May it appeared to be a disaster in the making. Many of the gliders crashed and broke up, killing their occupants, while others were shredded by intense ground fire. By the end of the day, the *Fallschirmjäger* had sustained 40 per cent casualties.

Through 10 days of fierce fighting the Germans gained the upper hand. Eventually they captured the island and inflicted nearly 14,000 casualties on the Allies. Even so, it had been a pyrrhic victory. Two thousand German *Fallschirmjäger*, the cream of the 7th Flieger Division, were dead. Of nearly 500 Ju-52 transport planes involved, 220 had been shot down or crashed. The future shortage of these workhorse aircraft was a blow from which German forces in the Mediterranean never recovered. Overall German casualties in Crete were nearly 7000.

Furthermore, Hitler was appalled at the losses incurred during Operation Mercury. He forbade future large-scale airborne deployments for the rest of the war. In a well orchestrated propaganda ploy the Iron Cross was awarded to a celebrity *Fallschirmjäger*, former world heavyweight boxing champion Max Schmeling.

By September 1941 the *Fallschirmjäger* formations were being employed as elite infantry on the Eastern Front. Fighting mainly around Leningrad, airborne units were used to plug holes in the German lines, blunting Red Army counter-attacks. *Fallschirmjäger* units were also deployed to North Africa, and later in the war to Sicily, Italy and France. In February 1944, *Fallschirmjäger* tenaciously clung to the Italian town of Monte Cassino, defending the ruins of its ancient Benedictine abbey with remarkable resilience. At Carentan in Normandy they held stubbornly to the communications and crossroads centre in the days following the D-Day landings. The Sixth Regiment opposed the Americans at St. Lo and was destroyed in the Falaise Pocket.

Outfitted with the distinctive **Fallschirmjäger** *helmet and smock, a heavily armed German paratrooper prepares to don his parachute for an airborne operation early in the war.*

At its peak strength, Student's command had numbered more than 160,000. He had led the elite *Fallschirmjäger* through training and into protracted, costly combat. By the end of the war he commanded an entire army group. Later, he was tried and convicted of war crimes but never served any time in prison. He died in West Germany in 1978, aged 88 years.

TANK-BUSTING STUKA SQUADRONS

- **FOUNDED: 1942**
- **STRENGTH: 950**
- **THEATRES: EASTERN FRONT**

The ungainly, vulture-like appearance of the Junkers Ju-87 Stuka belied its efficiency as a tactical dive bomber and terror weapon early in World War II. Serving as flying artillery, the Stukas attacked in concert with armoured and infantry formations to perfect the German *Blitzkrieg*, or lightning war. Sirens screaming, the Stukas also rained destruction on several of the major cities of Europe, including Warsaw and Rotterdam.

The Stuka was found wanting, however, when its slow speed and light armament made the aircraft easy prey for Royal Air Force fighters during the Battle of Britain. So many of the Ju-87s were shot down that the type was withdrawn from active participation in the raids on British airfields and cities. As the war dragged on, the Stuka began to fade into functional obsolescence. Variants of the design, however, continued in production, and nearly 6000 Ju-87s were constructed by 1944. The last of these variants was the Ju-87G, up-gunned with a pair of 37mm (1.48in) flak 18 cannon, one slung under each wing. This tank-busting version of the Stuka was developed in late 1942 and tested at *Luftwaffe* facilities in Tarnewitz and Rechlin.

RUDEL'S DIVE BOMBERS

The main advocate of the Ju-87G was Captain Hans Ulrich Rudel, who had already achieved great success flying the Stuka in its original dive bomber

role. Destined to become the most highly decorated *Luftwaffe* pilot of the war, Rudel had dropped a single 450kg (1000lb) bomb on the Soviet battleship *Marat* in the harbour of Kronstadt near Leningrad, sinking the warship on 23 September 1941. He had flown more than 1000 combat missions and destroyed over 200 Soviet tanks.

Rudel endorsed the Ju-87G, and in the summer of 1943 his *III Gruppe, Stuka Geschwader 2* was equipped with the new aircraft and renamed the *10th Panzerstaffel Stuka Geschwader 2*. Eventually, the plane was supplied in limited numbers and only Rudel's group and four additional squadrons received the Ju-87G.

KURSK

After combat testing the new Stuka in the Crimea, Rudel went into action during the Kursk offensive, attacking a column of 12 Soviet T-34 tanks on 5 July 1943. Aware of the weaknesses of the T-34, he consistently fired his cannon at the rear of the tank, where the armour was thinnest and flammable fuel was housed. Ravaging the column, he left all 12 of the T-34s smoking hulks.

The addition of the cannon reduced the speed of the Ju-87G even further; so while the tank busters concentrated on Soviet armour, fighters and other Stukas, still in the dive bomber configuration, flew top cover against Soviet planes. In the hands of a skilful pilots the Ju-87G was a

Major Hans-Ulrich Rudel's Knight's Cross with Sword and Oak Leaves decoration can be seen on the collar of his grey one-piece flying overall.

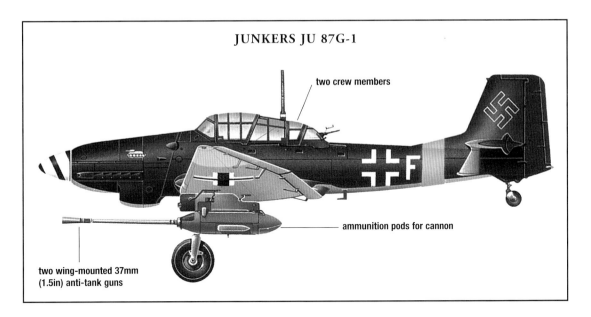

JUNKERS JU 87G-1

two crew members

ammunition pods for cannon

two wing-mounted 37mm
(1.5in) anti-tank guns

weapon to be feared. At Kursk, Rudel and his squadron mates had a field day. 'In the first attack four tanks explode under the hammer blows of my cannons,' Rudel wrote of his attacks on 7 July 1943. 'By evening the total rises to 12. We are all seized with a kind of passion for the chase from the glorious feeling of having saved much German bloodshed. After the first day the fitters have their hands full, for the aircraft have been heavily damaged by flak. The life of such an airplane will always be limited. But the main thing is: the evil spell is broken, and in this aircraft we possess a weapon which can speedily be employed everywhere and is capable of dealing successfully with the formidable numbers of Soviet tanks.'

While the Soviets tried to defend against the marauding Stukas, using smoke bombs to simulate destroyed tanks in the hope of prompting them to hunt elsewhere and bringing more anti-aircraft guns forward, Rudel and his trusty radio operator/gunner, Erwin Hentschel, mounted a phenomenal score of 519 enemy tanks destroyed by the end of the war. At Kursk alone, they reportedly destroyed more than 100.

During six years of combat, Rudel flew 2530 missions and destroyed at least 150 field guns, four armoured trains and 70 landing craft and assault boats. He was shot down several times and was

The Junkers Ju-87 Stuka found renewed usefulness in its tank destroying role on the Eastern Front. The ground attack version of the legendary dive bomber wreaked havoc with Red Army columns.

reported to have had a bounty placed on his head by Soviet Premier Josef Stalin. On 8 February 1945 his Stuka was hit by a 40mm (1.6in) anti-aircraft shell and his leg was shattered below the knee. Just days after his foot was amputated he returned to combat.

Rudel surrendered to American forces in May 1945 and went into self-imposed exile in Argentina three years later. He wrote two books and was an avid skier and mountain climber, who remained a Nazi sympathizer to the end of his life. The only member of the German armed forces to be awarded the Knight's Cross with Golden Oak Leaves, he returned to Germany in 1953, engaged in right-wing political activities and became a successful businessman. He died in 1982 at the age of 66.

The Ju-87G variant of the Stuka exacted a heavy toll on Soviet armour, but too few of the tank busters were produced to change the eventual outcome of the war in the East. Soviet industrial capacity and manpower were immense, and replacements of both tanks and soldiers to operate them were produced more rapidly than even proficient combat pilots could destroy them.

UNITS	SEA
LAND	10th Light Flotilla
Bersaglieri	
Ariete Division	AIR
	Special Air Torpedo Unit

ITALY

Italian involvement in World War II began with Fascist dictator Benito Mussolini and his dream of a reconstituted Roman Empire. However, by the end of the war Italy was a battleground, and its economy was devastated. Mussolini and his mistress, Claretta Petacci, were captured by partisans and executed, their bodies strung up in a Milan square. By then, the government had changed sides, and the military was fighting with the Allies. Although the Italian armed forces were often poorly trained and equipped, the fighting men of the nation's elite combat units displayed extraordinary bravery and accomplished notable feats of arms.

BERSAGLIERI

- •FOUNDED: 1836
- •STRENGTH: 30,000
- •THEATRES: EAST & NORTH AFRICA

Recognized by the distinctive cockerel plumes worn on their helmets, the *Bersaglieri* had been considered the cream of the Italian Army for a century when Fascist dictator Benito Mussolini employed them in his campaign of 1935-36 to conquer Ethiopia, which was followed by the seizure of Albania in 1939, and operations in the Mediterranean theatre during World War II. Generally better armed and equipped than standard

Left: Troops of the elite Italian **Bersaglieri** *pose for the camera during the brutal campaign in Ethiopia in 1936. Mussolini hoped to reestablish the Roman Empire but led his country to ruin.*

units of the Italian Army, the *Bersaglieri* were often attached in regiments to mechanized units and deployed as motorcycle or bicycle troops.

The *Bersaglieri* were founded in 1836 by General Alessandro Lamarmora during the period of the unification of Italy, and at first they functioned as a unit of the Piedmontese Army before becoming part of the Royal Italian Army. Since their inception, the ranks of the *Bersaglieri* have primarily included those of greater than average physical stature and endurance. Twelve of these elite regiments were deployed during World War II, and when the Italian Army organized its armoured divisions in 1939, each was allocated one of these regiments, which had been augmented in strength to three battalions.

After Italy declared war on Great Britain and France, *Bersaglieri* regiments took part in the campaigns in southern France prior to the 1940 invasion of Greece and deployment to North Africa. Eventually, the *Bersaglieri* withdrew to the defence of their homeland. When Mussolini was deposed and a new Italian government installed in mid-1943, *Bersaglieri* soldiers actually fought against German forces which occupied their country.

EARLY DISASTERS
The fighting in North Africa during the first 18 months of World War II proved disastrous for the Italian military. Although the Italians swiftly occupied British Somaliland in August 1940, and launched an offensive against Egypt at the beginning of September, a British counter-offensive initiated from the Sudan in the north and Kenya in the south at the end of the year nearly proved the undoing of Axis intentions in Africa.

On parade in Ethiopia following their victory over the primitive armed forces of the African nation, Italian troops would be roughly handled by the modern British Army in the coming war.

In December 1940 two British divisions faced up to 200,000 Libyan-based Italian troops advancing into Egypt and 300,000 enemy soldiers in East Africa, using Ethiopia as a staging area. Yet the British chased the invaders back into Libya and captured 150,000 prisoners, 40,000 at Sidi Barrani and Nibeiwa, and took 400 tanks and 800 pieces of artillery in the process. In the spring of 1941, all Italian forces in East Africa were forced to capitulate as well. The 10th *Bersaglieri* Regiment was the first unit of its kind to see action in North Africa, roughly handled in a British attack on its transport columns in February 1941. Six of the 12 *Bersaglieri* regiments eventually fought in North Africa and actually gave a good account of themselves.

The Italian Army in North Africa and the Middle East was in great peril when the first German troops and tanks landed at Tripoli to shore up their flagging partners. The vanguard of Panzer Armee Afrika, or the Afrika Korps, had arrived under the command of Field Marshal Erwin Rommel, and the war in the desert would become a protracted affair.

INVASION OF GREECE

Meanwhile, Mussolini had embarked on yet another ill-fated bid for empire. On 28 October 1940 Italian troops invaded Greece from neighbouring Albania. Less than two weeks later, during a three-day battle at Mount Pindus, the Greeks dealt the Italians a major defeat. In mid-November, a Greek offensive drove the Italians all the way back into Albania. Again the Germans intervened, compelling British and Greek forces to withdraw to the island of Crete, which was captured during Operation Mercury in the spring of 1941. Before Nazi Germany invaded Poland on 1 September 1939,

Mussolini had advised Hitler that his armed forces would not be ready for war for another three years. Nevertheless, the Italian dictator signed a treaty with Germany, which he termed the 'Pact of Steel', obliging Italy to go to war in support of the Nazis. In spite of the concerns of a number of his high-ranking commanders, Mussolini was also responsible for ordering an ill-prepared army into action on several occasions. As a result, the armed forces suffered irreplaceable losses, and Fascist Italy remained the junior partner in the Axis alliance until its demise.

The *Bersaglieri* and other units of the Italian Army fought bravely at times; however, these troops were often inadequately organized and poorly led. Modern *Bersaglieri* units have participated in peacekeeping operations in the Balkans and East Africa, as well as in the 'war on terror'.

ARIETE DIVISION

- **FOUNDED: 1939**
- **STRENGTH: 5078**
- **THEATRE: NORTH AFRICA**

In the months leading up to Fascist Italy's entry into World War II, three of its army's armoured brigades were increased in strength to division size, which, at peak strength, consisted of nearly 9000 troops, 200 tanks, 40 armoured cars, 20 self-propelled assault guns, 70 pieces of field artillery and over 1100 other vehicles. The third of these was the *Ariete* Division, formed on 1 February 1939 in Milan.

The *Ariete* Division participated in the North African campaign virtually from start to finish, enduring the hardships of difficult battles against British and Commonwealth troops, the glory of Field Marshal Erwin Rommel's electrifying victories with the German Afrika Korps, and the long withdrawal eastward from defeat at El Alamein and into Tunisia in late 1942 and early 1943.

During the short-lived Italian campaign into France in 1940 the *Ariete* Division was held in reserve, but near the end of January 1941 its troops

and tanks came ashore at the port city of Tripoli on the Libyan coast. For the next two years the division was regularly engaged from one end of the North African desert to the other.

The *Ariete* Division was first involved in combat during Rommel's initial offensive in North Africa, which recaptured the town of El Agheila and laid siege to Tobruk. The success of Operation Crusader, the ensuing British counter-offensive, sapped Rommel's offensive strength and forced him to retire to El Agheila once again. Entrenched at Bir el Gubi, the *Ariete* Division took on the charging Crusader tanks of the British 22nd Armoured Brigade and destroyed 25 of the attackers, forcing the remainder to withdraw.

Always short of supplies and reinforcements, the Axis forces in North Africa rebuilt their strength as British resources were strained by other theatres, particularly in Asia, where the Japanese were advancing through Burma and Malaya.

HEAVY LOSSES

In the spring of 1942 Rommel again went on the offensive and drove the British eastward more than 480km (300 miles) to their strong defensive line at Gazala. The *Ariete* Division, in company with the German 21st Panzer Division, advanced to the southeast and the following week moved north as fighting raged at Bir Hacheim. On 27 May the

This tankman from the **Ariete** *Division is kitted out in leather coat and khaki uniform plus crash helmet with neck protector.*

division advanced in a direct assault on Bir Hacheim. The infantry of the Trieste Division failed to provide anticipated support and the *Ariete* tanks, lightly armed and armoured M-13 types, foundered in minefields and took heavy fire from British anti-tank guns and artillery. The *Ariete* Division fell back, having lost 32 tanks in less than an hour.

On 22 June 1941 Tobruk fell to the *Afrika Korps*, and the British Eighth Army retreated into Egypt. At Mersa Matruh the *Ariete* Division participated in the capture of the town and more than 6000 prisoners. However, at El Alamein, more than 320km (200 miles) inside Egypt, the British and Commonwealth forces were determined to make a stand. Rommel's depleted force had shot its bolt, and the *Afrika Korps* offensive petered out at Alam el Halfa Ridge in September. At first, Rommel believed that his final thrust into Egypt would end with the capture of Cairo. Instead, while his forces grew weaker, the Eighth Army, under the command of Lieutenant General Bernard Montgomery, gained strength almost daily.

An **Ariete** *Division Semovente DA/75/18 armed with a flamethrower engages British forces in North Africa, 1941.*

EL ALAMEIN DEBACLE

On 23 October 1942 the British launched their bid for victory in North Africa at El Alamein. After 11 days of hard fighting the Germans were forced to begin a retreat of nearly 2420km (1500 miles) into Tunisia. El Alamein was one of the turning points of World War II, and the *Ariete* Division was caught up in the Afrika Korps debacle. On the afternoon of 4 November British tanks surrounded the division, which was already at less than 50 per cent of its original strength, and destroyed it.

What was left of the *Ariete* and *Littorio* armoured divisions and the Trieste Infantry Division were combined into the *Ariete* Tactical Group after El Alamein, and continued in the fighting withdrawal along the coast of North Africa, which ended in surrender in Tunisia in May 1943. A second, lesser-known unit, *Ariete* II, was formed in Ferrara,

Italy, on 1 April 1943, and became an Allied formation after the overthrow of Mussolini in July. This division defended Rome against the Germans in September, but was dismantled and its vehicles absorbed by German units following the *Wehrmacht* occupation of the Italian capital.

10TH LIGHT FLOTILLA

- •FOUNDED: 1940
- •STRENGTH: 200 (ESTIMATED)
- •THEATRE: MEDITERRANEAN

The battleships HMS *Valiant* and HMS *Queen Elizabeth* lay berthed in the harbour at Alexandria, Egypt, on the night of 19 December 1941. The great vessels, both more than 30,000 tonnes, were the only British battleships in the Mediterranean at the time, and their presence maintained the balance of naval power in the theatre. Intent on dealing a crippling blow to the Royal Navy, not only in might but also in prestige, six intrepid raiders of the Italian Navy slipped silently into the anchorage.

These were divers of the 10th Light Flotilla, Decima Flottiglia MAS, and they rode innovative two-man human torpedoes, which the men of the 10th had nicknamed *maiali*, or pigs. These contraptions were about 6m in length and carried a detachable warhead weighing 300kg (660lb). The method behind the seeming madness was simple. Two divers, wearing wetsuits and breathing gear, would guide their craft beneath their target and attach the explosive charge, timed to detonate later, to the hull. Then, if all went well, they would make their escape.

The concept of the human torpedo was not new, and the Italian Navy had actually advanced further than any other military organization in the world in their employment. During World War I, an Italian team had sunk an Austrian battleship in the same manner. The 10th Light Flotilla mounted numerous attacks against the British in the Mediterranean in World War II, sinking Allied warships of more than 72,000 tonnes and merchant shipping of nearly 134,000 tonnes. Striking early and often, the Decima MAS attempted its first raid on 21 August 1940, less than two weeks after Italy entered the war on the side of the Axis.

However, the submarine *Iride*, which was transporting four *maiali* to a position to attack Gibraltar, was spotted by British aircraft and sunk en route. A month later, the submarine *Gondar* was spotted and sunk during a run from La Spezia to Alexandria. Its three human torpedoes were also lost. Two more attempts ended in frustrating failures, one mission being scrubbed and the second ending when three *maiali* entered the harbour at Gibraltar but failed to locate a target.

HUMAN TORPEDOES STRIKE

On 10 September the frustration ended when three human torpedoes placed charges which sank the tankers *Fiona Shell* and *Denbydale* and the freighter *Durham* at Gibraltar. All six crewmen survived, swam to the Spanish coast and returned safely to Italy. Three months later, the Decima MAS achieved its most spectacular success of the war.

Detaching from their submarine outside Alexandria harbour on that December night, the six Italian raiders, led by Commander Luigi Durand de la Penne, followed several British destroyers through the defensive boom and netting at the entrance to the anchorage. Two raiders made for the *Queen Elizabeth* and successfully attached their charge,

'HUMAN TORPEDO'

Unlike conventional torpedoes, the 'human' torpedo was designed as means to carry a large explosive device to a defended naval target while avoiding detection. Ridden by frogmen as a human 'chariot', the whole front end was made of an explosive warhead. It was driven by battery-powered electric motor and steered by a control column. The torpedo was also fitted with net cutters and net lifters.
At the target ship it was detached and then held against the target's hull by means of steel cables and magentic clamps. The frogmen were then able to escape riding astride the unburdened tube, but few ever did evade capture.

Italian Motor Torpedo Boats speed through the waters of the Mediterranean Sea. In challenging Britain's Royal Navy for supremacy in the theatre, the Italian Navy employed innovative weapons.

about what had taken place. They were locked up in the *Valiant's* hold just a few metres above the location of the charge they had planted. Accounts vary as to whether they actually disclosed to the British that the explosive was going to detonate, but they did wait for some time. When the explosive went up at 6.20 the following morning, neither raider was injured. The battleship, however, was heavily damaged and settled upright on the floor of the shallow harbour.

Admiral A.B. Cunningham, commander of the Royal Navy in the Mediterranean, was aboard his flagship, the *Queen Elizabeth*, when the vessel was rocked by an explosion which reportedly lifted the admiral 1.5m (5ft) into the air. The *Queen Elizabeth* was seriously damaged, with a huge section of her hull caved in. The flagship also sank into the harbour's mud. Both the *Segona* and the *Jervis* sustained serious damage when the third charge exploded. The four remaining raiders were also taken prisoner.

while a third pair fixed its warhead to the hull of the tanker *Segona*, filled with flammable oil. The destroyer HMS *Jervis* was nearby in position to take on fuel.

Commander de la Penne and his fellow raider, Chief Diver Emilio Bianchi, soon ran into trouble. Bianchi was forced to surface when his breathing apparatus malfunctioned, and the pig's propeller became entangled in cables. Manhandling the little craft, de la Penne managed to set his charge on the bottom of the harbour beneath the hull of the *Valiant*. The raiders swam to a nearby buoy and were picked up by the British.

Tight lipped, the two told their captors nothing

'CONGRATULATIONS ON DESTROYING MY SHIP'

In an ironic twist, de la Penne and Bianchi were repatriated to Italy in 1944, after their country had concluded a treaty with the Allies and changed sides. The raiders were presented the Gold Medal for gallantry. The presenter was none other than the former commander of the *Valiant*, Admiral K.W.

Morgan. The British officer muttered: 'This is ridiculous, but all war is ridiculous. Congratulations on destroying my ship.' The 10th Light Flotilla employed other means of attack as well, including small motor boats called MTMs, which packed a 300kg (660lb) warhead, and frogmen, known as the Gamma Group. The MTM was piloted by a single raider, who ejected after pointing his craft at its target. The frogmen carried explosives weighing up to 4.5kg (10lb) to affix to targets.

On 25 March 1941 a pair of Italian destroyers carried six MTMs to within 16km (10 miles) of Suda Bay on the island of Crete, where the heavy cruiser HMS *York* was anchored. Two MTMs struck the cruiser amidships and she was heavily damaged. The British eventually scuttled the vessel before their forces withdrew from Crete. At least one other MTM struck the Norwegian tanker *Pericles* and damaged her so severely that the ship sank while under tow to Alexandria. Later, an MTM wrecked the destroyer HMS *Eridge* at El Daba, Egypt.

In July 1942 the Gamma frogmen established a base of operations right under the noses of the British at Gibraltar. The hulk of the Italian freighter *Olterra* lay in Algeciras Bay near Gibraltar, and the Italians proceeded to fit the vessel out for operations while the neutral Spanish looked the other way. In just over a year's time the Gamma frogmen damaged or sank 11 ships totalling more than 55,000 tonnes.

Acknowledging the success of the 10th Light Flotilla, the British developed a two-man human torpedo of their own, the Chariot. In January 1945, Italian and British raiders teamed up to sink the unfinished aircraft carrier *Aquila* in Genoa harbour before the Germans could move her to a position to sink her and block the harbour entrance.

Some 10th Flotilla men apparently continued the Fascist fight under the banner of Mussolini's puppet regime in northern Italy. Rather than working in naval operations, they were mainly involved in anti-partisan activities. Numerous reports of their participation in war crimes have surfaced, and some of these were committed while working in cooperation with the SS.

The modern Italian Navy maintains special forces within the umbrella of its Teseo Tesei Underwater and Raiding Grouping Command.

The cigar-shaped SLC-type 'human torpedo' could be taken to a depth of 25 metres (82ft) to avoid anti-submarine nets.

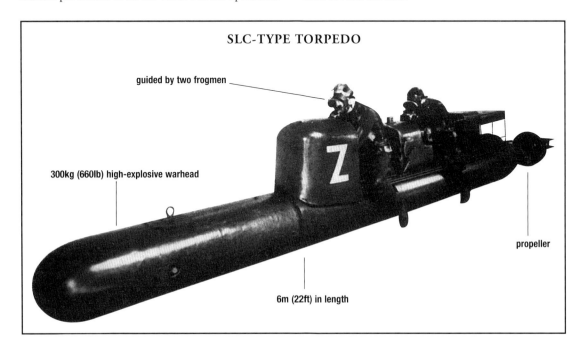

SLC-TYPE TORPEDO

guided by two frogmen

300kg (660lb) high-explosive warhead

6m (22ft) in length

propeller

SPECIAL AIR TORPEDO UNIT

- •FOUNDED: 1940
- •STRENGTH: 1500
- •THEATRE: MEDITERRANEAN

Even before World War II began, the Savoia Marchetti SM-79 bomber was considered obsolete. Constructed of a curious mixture of steel alloy, wood and canvas, the hunchback tri-motored Sparviero (Sparrowhawk) was not adequately armed to ward off enemy fighter planes. The aircraft did possess exceptional speed, however, and performed well during the Spanish Civil War of the mid-1930s, and its range of 1900km (1180 miles) was adequate for operations in the Mediterranean theatre.

Although the SM-79 was employed as a standard bomber after Italy entered World War II in June 1940, its contribution to the Axis war effort in that role was eclipsed by more modern German and Allied designs. The SM-79 did, however, become a force to be reckoned with as an anti-shipping aircraft armed with either one or two aerial torpedoes packing 198kg (440lb) warheads and slung beneath the fuselage. From 1940 to 1943 these Sparviero torpedo planes claimed 72 Allied ships and 196 merchant vessels sunk, and another 500 damaged.

Allied convoys were often subjected to severe air attack from planes of the Reparto Speciale

SM.79 SPARVIERO

The Savoia Marchotti SM.79 Sparviero is the most famous Italian combat aircraft of World War II. The bomber first saw action during the Spanish Civil War of the mid-1930s, and while it was faster than many fighters of the period its light construction, consisting mainly of canvas and wood, made it particularly vulnerable to modern Allied fighter aircraft. Eventually, the SM.79 performed well in its role as a torpedo bomber, particularly against Allied naval assets in the Mediterranean Sea. A stable platform for the launching of torpedoes, the SM.79 participated in the destruction of scores of merchant vessels and warships.

Aerosiluranti, or Special Air Torpedo Unit, the first of which was formed in August 1940. By the end of the year several squadrons, including the original 278th *Squadriglia Quattro Gatti*, 'Four Cats', had flown nearly 250 sorties and executed more than 100 attacks. The Sparviero flew from airfields in Libya, Sicily and the Italian mainland.

CAPTAIN BUSCAGLIA

The most successful of the SM-79 pilots was Captain Carlo Emanuele Buscaglia, who volunteered for service with the 240th Squadron in July 1940. Buscaglia is credited with seriously damaging the cruisers HMS *Kent* on 17 September 1940 and HMS *Glasgow* on 3 December. In October, a third Royal Navy cruiser, the HMS *Liverpool*, was hit by a Sparviero torpedo and put out of action for a year. In January 1941 Buscaglia and other Italian pilots joined German dive bombers in damaging the aircraft carrier HMS *Illustrious*.

Buscaglia rose to the rank of major and commanded both the 281st Squadron and the 132nd Torpedo Group. He was decorated with the Silver Medal for gallantry five times in 1942 and received the German Iron Cross 2nd Class. He also flew missions during the Italian Navy's defeat at the Battle of Cape Matapan. On 12 November 1942, four days after the beginning of Operation Torch, the Allied landings on the western coast of North Africa, Buscaglia was preparing to attack Allied shipping when he was shot down in flames by a British Supermarine Spitfire fighter. He was presumed dead and awarded a posthumous Golden Medal for valour. In fact, he had been seriously wounded and taken prisoner.

For nearly 10 months, Buscaglia was a captive of the United States, held at Fort Meade, Maryland. When Italy and the Allies signed a peace treaty on 8 September 1943 he was repatriated and volunteered for the air service of the new pro-Allied government of Italy. At the same time, a wing of the air force still supporting the puppet Fascist government of Benito Mussolini in northern Italy was named in his honour. After being appointed commander of the Italian 28th Bombing Wing in July 1944, Buscaglia was seriously injured during a take-off at the controls of a Martin

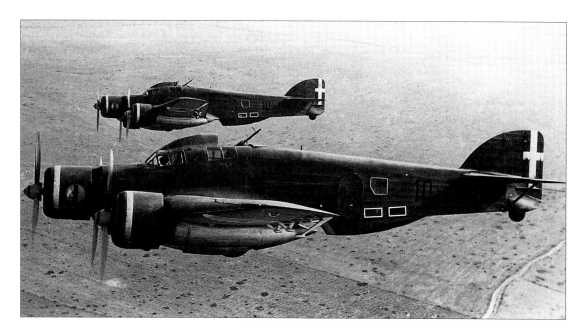

Two SM.79 Sparvieros ('Sparrowhawks') overfly the North African desert, 1941. The SM.79 was one of the best torpedo bombers of World War II.

Baltimore bomber. He died the next day in a Naples hospital.

ATTACK ON MALTA

The Reparto Speciale Aerosiluranti played a key role in Axis attempts to bomb and starve the British island of Malta into submission. Strategically located in the Mediterranean, Malta served as a base for Allied aircraft, which attacked Axis convoys bound for North Africa with supplies and reinforcements intended for the Afrika Korps of Field Marshal Erwin Rommel as it battled the British Eighth Army on the continent.

In the summer of 1942, German and Italian air and naval forces mounted a strenuous effort to prevent supply convoys from reaching Malta. In June, two convoys totaling 17 ships were ravaged. Ten were sunk, five turned back and only two reached the safety of Grand Harbour at Valletta. Malta's air defences were seriously depleted on several occasions. Food, water and ammunition continually ran low, and Axis air raids were a daily occurrence. In August a large Allied convoy,

codenamed Pedestal, was repeatedly attacked by the Sparviero, German Junkers Ju-87 dive bombers, and U-boats. Over a 72-hour period the escorting aircraft carrier HMS *Eagle* was sunk and another, HMS *Indomitable*, was heavily damaged. The cruiser HMS *Manchester* was damaged and later scuttled by its own crew.

The giant tanker *Ohio* was attacked and set ablaze, but continuous work by fire control parties kept the ship afloat, even though it had take on tonnes of water. By the time the damaged tanker and the surviving merchant ships reached Malta, nine of their number had been sunk. The Sparviero suffered 50 planes shot down and nearly 180 airmen lost during the summer.

The vital supplies and replacement fighter aircraft delivered by the Pedestal convoy caused the Axis forces to discontinue their intense bombing campaign against Malta. For their heroism under fire, the people of the island were awarded the George Cross. When King George VI addressed the Maltese, he stated: 'To honour her brave people I award the George Cross to the island fortress of Malta, to bear witness to a heroism and devotion that will long be famous in history.'

The Third Wing of the modern Italian Air Force is named in honour of Carlo Emanuele Buscaglia.

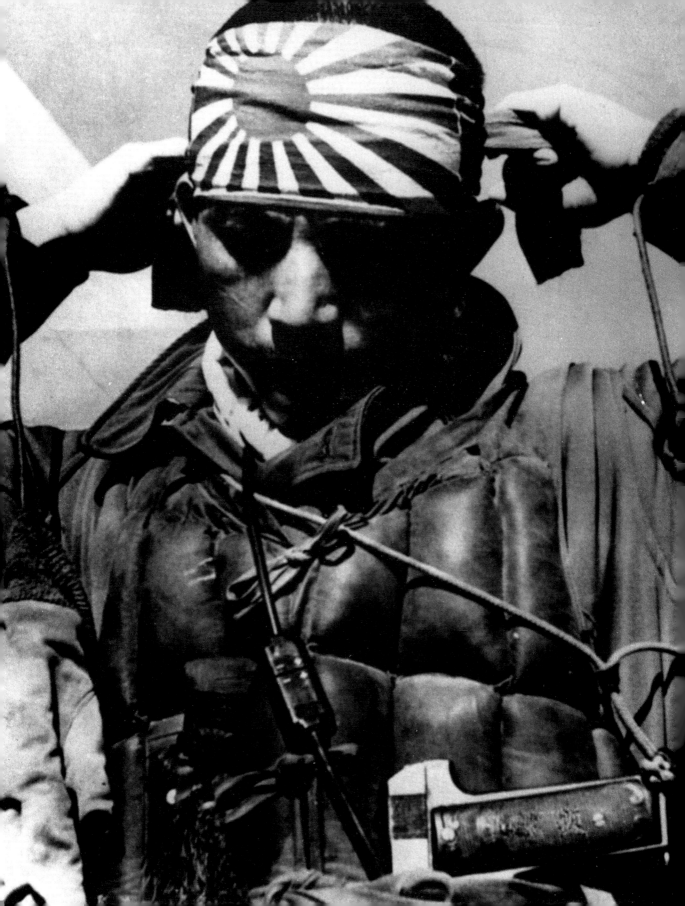

JAPAN

The code of Bushido was instilled in the armed forces of the Empire of Japan. The ancient way of the samurai dictated that death in battle was preferable to the dishonour of surrender. Therefore, the elite units of the Japanese military in World War II displayed an unwavering devotion to their country and their emperor, at times with disastrous results. Suffering horrendous casualties, Japanese forces conquered vast amounts of territory with lightning speed and subsequently fought a tenacious defensive war.

IWO JIMA AND OKINAWA – THE DEFENDERS

- •FOUNDED: 1943
- •STRENGTH: 127,700
- •THEATRE: PACIFIC

After 30 months of fighting on land, sea and air during World War II, American forces stood poised on the very doorstep of the Japanese home islands. A pair of amphibious operations was being planned simultaneously, against the island of Iwo Jima in the Volcanoes Group and Okinawa in the Ryukyus. On 19 February 1945, troops of the 4th and 5th Marine divisions, followed later by the 3rd Division, hit the beaches at Iwo Jima. On Easter

Left: A Kamikaze pilot ties the ceremonial **hakimachi** *in preparation for a death flight. In an effort to stem the American tide, suicide squadrons flew thousands of sorties against the US Navy.*

Sunday, 1 April, elements of the US Tenth Army, which included five Army and three Marine divisions, landed at Okinawa.

In both cases, the Japanese commanders chose to employ somewhat different tactics from those employed by the defenders of other islands across the vast expanse of the Pacific. At Iwo Jima, Lieutenant General Tadamichi Kuribayashi had assembled a force of 21,000 men, including the crack 145th Infantry Regiment and the 26th Tank Regiment. Kuribayashi knew that the Americans wanted possession of the island for use as a staging area for a coming invasion of Japan itself. Furthermore, from two completed airfields on Iwo Jima, just 11km sq (7 square miles) in size and 1224km (760 miles) from Tokyo, American heavy bombers could rain destruction on Japanese cities and, if damaged or low on fuel, find a haven on the long return flights to bases in the Marianas.

Kuribayashi had undergone cavalry training in the United States and had visited the country several times before the war. He respected the Americans but was determined to make them pay for every metre of Iwo Jima. To that end, he chose a pragmatic approach to defence. The prospects for reinforcement would be non-existent once the battle was joined, and sacrificing large numbers of soldiers in futile banzai charges would play into the enemy's hands. Kuribayashi chose not to place his strongest defences before the landing beaches.

LABYRINTH OF TUNNELS
Instead, he ordered the construction of a labyrinth of tunnels to fortify the island, some of them hundreds of metres long and with multiple

Shaped like a pork chop, the small island of Iwo Jima was the scene of bitter fighting in the Pacific. The 550-foot promontory of Mount Suribachi is visible at lower right.

entrances. During air attacks and naval bombardment the defenders could retreat to the safety of underground chambers. When the barrage lifted they would emerge to man concrete reinforced bunkers, some with walls more than half a metre thick, machine gun nests and artillery emplacements, some of which were located in the mouths of caves. The highest point on the island, 172m (556ft) Mount Suribachi at the southwestern tip, was itself honeycombed with a network of tunnels on seven levels connecting over 1000 chambers. Altogether, an estimated 26km (16 miles) of tunnels laced the island underground.

The Japanese soldiers, complemented by a large number of Korean conscript labourers, had worked for months moving tonnes of volcanic rock, breathing sulphur fumes and enduring temperatures which soared as high as 130 degrees Fahrenheit. Kuribayashi established his own three-room command post nearly 9m (30ft) underground in the north of the island. He urged his troops to fight to the death, taking 10 American lives each.

When the Americans came ashore, under the command of Marine Lieutenant General Holland M. 'Howlin' Mad' Smith, the Japanese did indeed allow the invasion beaches to become choked with American troops and vehicles before opening fire

with weapons already zeroed in to cover what seemed every inch of ground. Casualties began to mount quickly, but much worse was yet to come.

A SMALL AMERICAN FLAG

Four days after landing, a group of Marines fought its way to the summit of Mount Suribachi and planted a small American flag, secured to a length of pipe, on top of the extinct volcano. Within a couple of hours, a larger flag had been located, and Associated Press photographer Joe Rosenthal snapped an image which has become one of the most enduring in modern warfare. With that, he was said to have ensured the existence of the Marine Corps for the next 500 years.

Tenacious Japanese defenders clung to positions on the northern end of the island, and the Marines nicknamed some of these the Amphitheatre, the Meat Grinder, and Turkey Knob. Iwo Jima was not declared secure until 26 March, more than a month after the initial landings. Marines had assaulted individual caves and tunnels, using flamethrowers and explosive charges to burn alive or seal defenders inside, and taking only 216 prisoners. Kuribayashi was among the dead, reportedly having led a final furious attack. US casualties totalled over 5900 dead and more than 17,000 wounded. Twenty-seven men were awarded the Medal of Honour for bravery on Iwo Jima, and several of these were posthumous. Before the island was secured, crippled bombers were already touching down on it safely. By the end of the war, more than 24,000 airmen had made emergency landings. Speaking of the operation, Fleet Admiral Chester W. Nimitz, commander of American naval forces in the Pacific, said, 'On Iwo island, uncommon valour was a common virtue.'

OKINAWA – FINAL LAND BATTLE?

At Okinawa, Lieutenant Mitsuru Ushijima commanded the 77,000-man 32nd Army, which was augmented by about 20,000 Okinawans. Neither Ushijima nor Lieutenant General Simon Bolivar Buckner Jr, who opposed him, believed that this would be the final land battle of World War II. Okinawa, however, would serve as an advance staging area for American forces during an invasion of the home islands which was sure to come.

When Buckner sent two corps of American troops ashore on the western side of Okinawa the invaders encountered only token resistance. They soon crossed the island, cutting it in half. Marines headed north and the Army troops moved southward. Ushijima had placed only 2000 soldiers in the north to slow the Marines down. He counted on the hilly terrain in the southern quarter of the island and three concentric defensive rings his soldiers had spent months preparing, to take a

substantial toll in American lives. The terrain in the south included rocky ridges which stretched from one side of the island to the other, oddly shaped hills into which bunkers could be dug and machine guns positioned with interlocking fields of fire, and the ramparts of Shuri Castle, a 15th-century fortress which had once been home to Okinawa's feudal kings. Some of the ridges rose more than 50m high, and the ancient burial tombs of the Okinawans dotted their slopes. Japanese troops converted a number of these chambers into mortar and machine gun emplacements. Ushijima's soldiers had skilfully sewn minefields, dug defensive positions and sited their artillery and mortars on natural avenues of approach, which would funnel the attackers into their killing zones.

The soldiers of the 7th and 96th Infantry divisions absorbed more than 3000 casualties in nine days of fighting before the capture of such locations as Kakazu Ridge, Castle Hill, The

During mopping up operations on Iwo Jima, US Marines use a flamethrower to eradicate pockets of Japanese resistance. At least 18,000 of the island's more than 20,000 defenders died.

Pinnacle and Triangulation Hill. Buckner redirected some Marine units to the fighting in the south and committed the 27th Infantry Division to the fight for the first Japanese defence line, which was not concluded until the Japanese withdrew on 19 April. More fighting took place at Conical Hill and Kochi Ridge, and fresh American troops relieved those who had fought doggedly against the well-entrenched defenders.

JAPANESE COUNTER-ATTACK

A Japanese counter-attack launched in the first week of May failed to achieve any positive results for Ushijima, but his strategy of prolonging the battle for Okinawa was proving its worth. On 11 May Buckner sent the 6th Marine Division against the second line of Japanese defences, which included Ushijima's command post beneath Shuri Castle. One regiment, originally consisting of 200 men, numbered only 75 after hours of fighting to capture a small hill called Sugar Loaf.

The defenders of Sugar Loaf, the Horseshoe and Half Moon Ridge included the 5000 soldiers of Ushijima's 44th Brigade, which had yet to see action. The complex of hills did not fall to the Marines until 19 May, and the fight had cost them more than 2600 dead. On 29 May Marines occupied Shuri Castle after hard fighting by Army troops at Dakeshi Ridge, Wana Ridge, Wana Draw and Conical Hill.

Ushijima directed a withdrawal to his third and final defence line in the south. In the first two weeks of June, American troops continued the series of costly assaults against stubborn resistance which had characterized the horrific campaign to date. At Hill 95, the Yaeju-dake cliffs, and Kunishi Ridge, the fighting was ferocious. One Marine regiment lost 21 tanks and sustained more than 1100 casualties. Finally, with his remaining forces pushed into a small corner of the war ravaged island, Ushijima committed ritual suicide on 22 June, and organized resistance on Okinawa ended.

BUCKNER'S PLEA

Buckner also gave his life on Okinawa. The highest ranking American officer killed in action in the Pacific War had died on 18 June when a Japanese

shell fragment no larger than a dime pierced his heart. Several days earlier Buckner had sent Ushijima a plea to surrender. 'The forces under your command have fought bravely and well,' the American's letter read, 'and your infantry tactics have merited the respect of your opponents. Like myself, you are an infantry general long schooled and practiced in infantry warfare. I believe, therefore, that you understand as clearly as I that the destruction of all Japanese resistance on the island is merely a matter of days.'

While the fight for Okinawa had raged on land, the ships of the US Navy had undergone a tremendous ordeal off the coast. Wave after wave of Japanese suicide planes had attacked the fleet and sunk or damaged 120 ships. Total American casualties in the 83-day struggle for Okinawa were more than 12,000 killed and nearly 32,000 wounded. The Japanese had lost over 100,000 dead.

The end at Okinawa had always been a foregone conclusion, but the Japanese defenders had exacted a heavy price for its capture. The costliest battle of the war in the Pacific, Okinawa likely influenced the decision made by President Harry Truman to drop the atomic bomb on Hiroshima six weeks later. Historians, therefore, may only speculate as to what an invasion of Japan's home islands may have meant in lives lost, both Japanese and American.

SPECIAL NAVAL LANDING FORCE

- **FOUNDED: 1941**
- **STRENGTH: 2600**
- **THEATRE: PACIFIC**

'A million men cannot take Tarawa in a hundred years,' railed Rear Admiral Keiji Shibasaki in an address to the Japanese garrison at Tarawa Atoll in the Gilbert Islands of the Central Pacific. Shibasaki fully expected that the American enemy would be attempting to wrest Tarawa from Japanese control, particularly the islet of Betio, a spit of land only 3.2km (2 miles) long, 455m (500 yards) at its widest point, and nowhere more than 34m (110ft) above sea level. Betio was Tarawa's largest land mass, located at the edge of a lagoon which was ringed by an extensive coral reef. A seawall more than 1m (3.28ft) tall also ran much of the length of the lagoon beaches where three battalions of the 2nd Marine Division were scheduled to land on 20 November 1943.

For the Americans, the long road to Tokyo would require the capture of Betio and numerous other islands which the Japanese had fortified to preserve their territorial gains in the Pacific.

FORTRESS BETIO

Shibasaki had reason to be optimistic. Japanese and conscripted Korean workers had laboured for months to make Betio a seemingly impregnable fortress. Bunkers of steel, reinforced by concrete and coconut logs, were dug into Betio's coral. Tonnes of sand were heaped on top of the roofs to absorb the shock of naval shells and bombs. Blockhouses, some with walls 2.5m (8ft) thick and multiple firing slits, dotted the shore. Machine gun nests were scattered

across the island with interlocking fields of fire, and more than 40 artillery pieces were sighted to bombard the beaches on both the lagoon and ocean sides of Betio. Four of these guns were heavy 8-inchers (203mm), captured from the British at Singapore and transported to Tarawa. In total, more than 500 bunkers, some linked by tunnels, had been built on Betio.

Among the 5000 defenders at Tarawa were the elite troops of the Seventh Special Naval Landing Force (SNLF), numbering nearly 1500, and the attached Third Special Base Unit, with 1100 fighting men. The Seventh SNLF had been based at the Japanese port of Sasebo and formed shortly after the war began. Known to the Japanese as the Rikusentai, the Special Naval Landing Force units were ground troops of the Imperial Japanese Navy

Dead Japanese soldiers, killed almost to a man on embattled Tarawa Atoll in the Gilbert Islands, lie unburied in the tropical sun. In 76 hours, the island fell to US Marines.

which were organized in two rifle companies with either one or two heavy weapons companies to provide additional firepower.

On 7 December 1941, when Japan attacked Pearl Harbor, 12 SNLF units had been formed. Several of these participated in offensive operations in the Philippines, China and Pacific islands. At Tarawa, the Japanese garrison was prepared to fight to the death in defence of the empire.

Following a prolonged pre-invasion bombardment by warships and aircraft, the Marines hit the beaches of Betio on the morning of 20 November. They had only a handful of tracked landing vehicles, called Amtracs, which could negotiate the coral reef. A number of landing craft actually hung up on the reef, unable to deliver their troops all the way to the beach. Scores of Marines were therefore required to wade up to 1km (more than half a mile) from the reef to the beach under heavy fire. Several landing craft struck submerged obstacles or mines and began to sink. Others took fire from the Japanese, lurched to a stop, and belched flame into the lagoon.

Individual acts of bravery against the Japanese defenders prevented the landings on the first day from foundering, and as darkness fell, the

Taking aim at distant targets, US Marines move relentlessly forward against elite troops of the Japanese Special Naval Landing Force at Tarawa. The Americans learned costly lessons during the amphibious operation.

Americans held only two shallow beachheads. Lieutenant William Hawkins commanded a 34-man Marine Scout-Sniper platoon, which had come ashore on the 20th to seize a long pier jutting into the lagoon. Hawkins was awarded the Medal of Honour for knocking out several enemy bunkers before he was hit twice by bullets and died on Betio a day later.

TARAWA TIDE TURNS

Marine reinforcements arrived on the second day, still under fire from concealed Japanese machine gun and artillery positions. However, the tide of battle began to turn. Moving from bunker to bunker with explosive charges, hand grenades and flamethrowers, the Marines methodically silenced the Japanese guns. At one position a flamethrower flushed a large group of Japanese from a blockhouse through a rear entrance. Waiting Marine riflemen picked them off one by one.

Shibasaki died in his reinforced command blockhouse on 23 November after bulldozers pushed sand up to the exits and Marines poured gasoline down the ventilators and set it off. Before he died, the Japanese commander sent one final message to Tokyo. 'Our weapons have been destroyed,' he said, 'and from now on everyone is attempting a final charge … May Japan exist for 10,000 years.'

During 76 hours of tortuous combat, the 2nd Marine Division captured Betio, which was declared secure on 23 November. Only 17 Japanese soldiers and 129 Korean construction workers survived. The rest had been true to Bushido, their warrior code. More than 1000 Americans had been killed, and twice that number were wounded. Images of the dead Marines littering the beach and floating in the water of the lagoon shocked the American public, prompting some elected officials to call for an inquiry into the conduct of the operation.

US military planners applied the lessons learned at Tarawa to future landings on Pacific islands. Among those valuable lessons was the fact that naval and aerial bombardment alone would not be sufficient to reduce prepared defences. Plunging fire and the use of armour-piercing ordnance would prove to be most effective.

Communications had to be improved. Armour support and more automatic weapons and flamethrowers would increase firepower. An adequate number of tracked landing craft would be essential in future landings.

The fanatical but doomed SNLF contingent at Tarawa did usher in a new role for other elite troops of the empire. Rather than leading Japanese forces in conquest, they would be employed in a defensive role for the rest of the war.

Saluting his commander, a Kamikaze pilot stands to attention before the ranks of his comrades. Japanese suicide pilots often received minimal training and flew to their deaths in obsolete aircraft.

KAMIKAZE SQUADRONS
- **FOUNDED 1944**
- **STRENGTH: 11,600**
- **THEATRE: PACIFIC**

The Japanese pilot steered his plane, a Mitsubishi G4M Betty bomber, relentlessly toward the American warships gathered off the Philippine island of Luzon. On 15 October 1944 he led an attack group into the air. There had been other missions, but this time Rear Admiral Masafumi Arima, the 50-year-old commander of the 26th Air Flotilla based at Manila, was at the controls of the lead plane – and he intended to die.

Arima had come to the conclusion that a suicide dive into a warship of the US Navy would serve the Japanese nation best. He chose an aircraft carrier and began his final plunge only to be blasted form the sky by concentrated anti-aircraft fire. The gunners who had shot Arima down may well have been confused by his intent. However, when word of the attempt reached Admiral Takajiro Onishi, the newly appointed commander of the 1st Air Fleet, the idea resonated with him.

Japan had suffered serious losses in front line aircraft and experienced pilots. Onishi had assumed

command of only about 100 up to date planes. New pilots and obsolete aircraft would no doubt fly to their deaths anyway. It seemed logical that if this were the case the pilots should be given the opportunity to die while inflicting the greatest damage possible on the enemy.

GODS OF THE 'DIVINE WIND'

Onishi gathered 23 non-commissioned officers and asked for volunteers for his new Tekko (special attack) squadrons. All 23 pilots stepped forward and formed a squadron they called Shimpu. A second unit was quickly formed, and its pilots referred to it

*Left: A Kamikaze dives perilously close to the flight deck of the escort carrier USS **Sangamon**. The Japanese flew more than 1800 suicide sorties against the US fleet off Okinawa.*

as Kamikaze. Both names were references to a 'Divine Wind' which had blown an invading Mongol fleet into ruin as it approached the coast of Japan in 1281.

It was Onishi's hope that his volunteer suicide pilots would become a modern Divine Wind, and the nickname Kamikaze soon became a common term among sailors of the US Pacific Fleet. Ten days after the death of Arima, the young Japanese pilots headed for the American ships supporting landings on the Philippine island of Leyte. The escort carrier *Santee* was struck by a bomb-laden Mitsubishi Zero fighter. A second suicide plane struck the escort carrier *Suwanee*, and a third escort carrier, the *St. Lo*, was also hit. Wracked by internal explosions, the *St. Lo* was sunk within half an hour.

The American ships and their complements of fighter planes altered tactics to deal as well as they could with the new threat. Destroyers were placed at a distance from the main fleet, on 'picket' duty, while combat air patrols (CAP) became more diligent in their watch for enemy aircraft.

US NAVY TAKES THE BRUNT

The Kamikaze menace reached the height of its fury during the 83-day battle for the island of Okinawa, only 530km (330 miles) from the Japanese home islands. Landings by Marines and Army troops took place on 1 April 1945.

A week later, the Japanese began a concerted effort to inflict as much damage as possible on the US Navy ships offshore. Wave after wave of Kamikazes, some consisting of only a few planes while others numbered well into the hundreds, harassed the American ships incessantly. Ten major attacks took place between 6 April and 21 June, and these were called Kikisui, or Floating Chrysanthemum. During the relentless onslaught the Kamikazes sank 11 ships and damaged over 100 more.

Standard Kamikazes, inexperienced pilots on one-way missions in obsolete planes, were far more numerous. The young pilots were lauded as heroes, already gods, before taking off on their final flights. They were toasted with *sake*, Japanese rice wine, and posed for photographs with the traditional samurai sword in hand. Often they tied the ceremonial white *hachimaki*, emblazoned with the rising sun, about their heads, wrote final letters to friends and family members and left behind locks of hair, nail clippings or even a finger for loved ones to honour after their deaths.

Kamikaze attacks damaged a number of larger US ships, and some hits caused serious damage, plunging through the wooden flight decks of the aircraft carriers before exploding below.

At Okinawa, the Kamikaze were responsible for the vast majority of the almost 10,000 dead and wounded American naval personnel. The Japanese lost a staggering 11,000 men and 7800 aircraft.

In the final months of World War II it became apparent that Japan could not appreciably alter the course of the war given such attrition. Despite their bravery, the sacrifice of the Kamikaze was, in the final analysis, an exercise in futility.

REAPING THE 'DIVINE WIND'

During the battle for Okinawa no fewer than 1465 Japanese aircraft and pilots were committed to Kamikaze attacks. At times it seemed that the swarms of suicide planes might overwhelm the American defences. Many were shot down, but others seemed always to be near and ready to sacrifice themselves. The ordeal of the destroyer USS *Laffey* is indicative of the ferocity of the Kamikaze. Just before 8.30 a.m. on 16 April, the picket destroyer was set upon by multiple suicide planes and others on conventional missions during Kikisui 3, which included 165 Japanese aircraft. At one time the ship's radar picked up 50 planes closing in. During 80 minutes of continuous combat the *Laffey* withstood attacks by 22 enemy aircraft, absorbing hits from six Kamikazes and four bombs. When the hellish attacks finally subsided, only four 20mm (0.8in) guns were left capable of firing aboard the destroyer. A miraculous survivor, the *Laffey* eventually made it to Guam after losing 31 sailors killed or missing and 72 wounded.

SOVIET UNION

For months, the Soviet Union bore the brunt of the German onslaught during World War II. Relocating their production facilities east of the Ural Mountains, the Soviets held on with grim determination until the resilient Red Army compelled the Germans to retreat. The surrender of the German Sixth Army at Stalingrad proved to be the turning point of the war in Europe, while the modernized Red Air Force became more than a match for the *Luftwaffe*. Sustaining horrific casualties in the defense of their mother country, the resilient Soviet armed forces evolved into a tremendously powerful instrument of both military and political influence.

62ND ARMY

- **FOUNDED: 1942**
- **STRENGTH: 120,000**
- **THEATRE: EASTERN FRONT**

In the summer of 1942 Operation Blue, the German offensive toward the Caucasus, appeared virtually unstoppable. At first, the important manufacturing and transportation centre on the Volga River at Stalingrad to the north was not considered to be a primary objective of the offensive. However, by August it was determined

Left: General Vasily Chuikov consults staff officers during planning for operations after Stalingrad. Chuikov commanded the 62nd Army during its darkest days defending the industrial centre on the Volga River.

that the German Sixth Army, under General Friedrich von Paulus, and the Fourth Panzer Army, commanded by General Hermann Hoth, would indeed attempt to capture the city.

The defence of Stalingrad was of paramount importance to the embattled Soviet Union. The city was more than simply the namesake of Premier Josef Stalin. About a quarter of the armoured vehicles produced for the Red Army were manufactured in Stalingrad, and there were massive industrial facilities, including the Lazur chemical plant, the Red October steel works, the tractor factory, which was producing tanks, and the Barricades arms factory.

STALINGRAD'S UPHILL BATTLE

On 23 August the Germans began their push to capture the city. The Luftwaffe laid waste to vast areas, and the armoured spearheads of the *Wehrmacht* appeared on the brink of yet another stunning victory. The resurgent Red Army, however, was reorganizing in the embattled ruins of Stalingrad. The 62nd Army was constituted during this time of trial through the combining of units in the area and given primary responsibility for the defence of the city. When its original commander expressed doubts about the prospects of success, he was promptly relieved. A new leader, General Vasily Chuikov, was given the unenviable task.

Chuikov had served in the Red Army since the civil war which followed the revolution of 1917. He had spent 11 years, from 1926 to 1937, serving in the Far East as a military adviser to Chinese Generalissimo Chiang Kai-shek. When the Stalingrad battle commenced, he was the deputy commander of the 64th Army.

A Red Army soldier raises a hand grenade as comrades follow closely behind during the fierce close quarters fighting for the city of Stalingrad.

The new leader's attitude toward the city's defence was wholly different from that of his predecessor. 'We shall hold the city, or die there!' Chuikov told his superior officer, General Andrei Yeremenko. Then, taking stock, he inwardly acknowledged the grim reality of his situation. Only 55,000 men were capable of bearing arms. One armoured brigade, which would have counted 80 tanks at standard strength, could muster only one fit for service. One infantry brigade, usually at least 4000 strong, had been reduced to less than 700 men including non-combat personnel. Reinforcements and supplies would be obliged to run the gauntlet of German artillery and air attacks in the hazardous ferry crossing of the Volga.

CHUIKOV AND ZHUKOV

Some of the bitterest fighting of the war occurred in Stalingrad. During three days of fierce combat which began the day after Chuikov assumed command of

Right: The second, main assault on Stalingrad happened at the end of September. The Germans eventually captured the north of the city, making the ferry crossing – over which supplies and reinforcements were brought into Stalingrad – vulnerable to artillery fire.

the 62nd Army, a fierce fight for the Central Railway Station and the 102m (330ft) hill called Mamayev Kurgan raged. The station changed hands 15 times, and each side possessed the hill on multiple occasions only to be driven back. Fighting at Mamayev Kurgan actually lasted a total of 112 days.

Eventually, the Germans were to gain tenuous control of approximately 90 per cent of Stalingrad. Chuikov developed a severe case of eczema, no doubt brought on by the stress of the situation as the 62nd Army fought desperately to maintain a toehold in the shattered city. Every inch of territory was contested, and a battle even raged for several days over possession of a grain elevator.

Chuikov, however, was unaware of his own high command's grand strategy. The Red Army Deputy Supreme Commander, General Georgi Zhukov, had

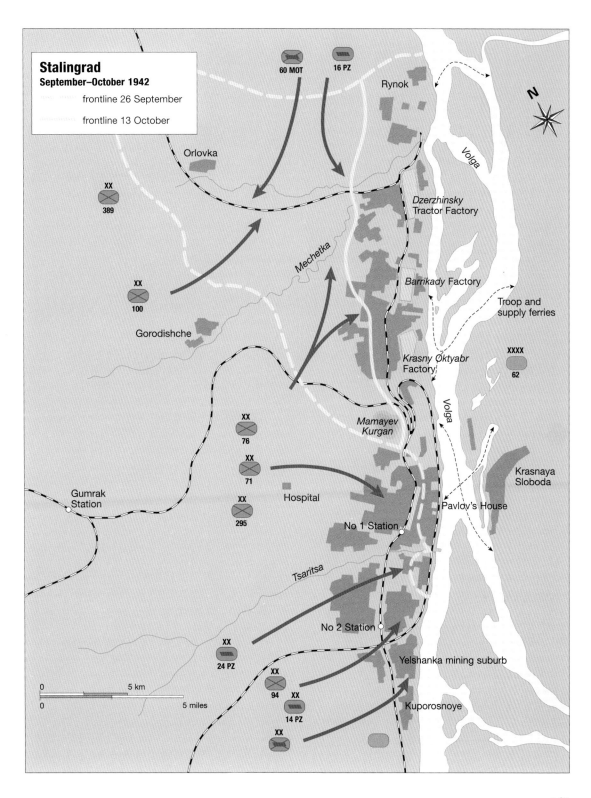

Stalingrad
September–October 1942

- - - - - - frontline 26 September

· · · · · · frontline 13 October

60 MOT

16 PZ

Rynok

Volga

Orlovka

XX
389

Dzerzhinsky
Tractor Factory

Mechetka

Barrikady Factory

XX
100

Troop and
supply ferries

Gorodishche

Krasny Oktyabr
Factory

XXXX
62

Mamayev
Kurgan

Volga

XX
76

Krasnaya
Sloboda

XX
71

Gumrak
Station

Hospital

XX
295

Pavlov's House

No 1 Station

Tsaritsa

No 2 Station

0   5 km

0   5 miles

Yelshanka mining suburb

XX
24 PZ

XX
94

XX
14 PZ

Kuporosnoye

XX

PAULUS CAPITULATES

Hours before Friedrich von Paulus surrendered the remnants of the German Sixth Army at Stalingrad, Hitler promoted the commander to the rank of field marshal. The gesture was intended to send a message to Paulus, who knew that no German field marshal had ever surrendered to an enemy force. Nevertheless, the commander was in no position to continue the fight and declined to commit suicide. One of thousands of Germans marched into captivity, Paulus became a tool of the Soviet propaganda machine. He was released from captivity in 1953 and lived in East Germany until his death in Dresden four years later.

decided that the 62nd Army would serve as the rock upon which the Red Army sledgehammer would crush von Paulus and the German Sixth Army. While Chuikov's beleaguered soldiers contested every block, street, house and even individual floors of buildings, massive Soviet reinforcements were moving into position to trap the Germans in a giant pincer movement.

For all their initial bravado and self-assurance, the Germans were being bled white amid the rubble of Stalingrad. Close quarter fighting negated much of their advantage in tanks and other heavy weapons. One German soldier wrote of his ordeal: 'We would spend the whole day clearing a street, from one end to the other. But at dawn, the Russians would start up firing from their old positions at the far end. It took us some time to discover their trick; they had knocked holes between the garrets and attics and in the night they would run back like rats in the rafters and set their machine guns up behind some upper window or broken chimney.'

Unburied corpses piled up in the streets of Stalingrad as both sides suffered horrific casualties. The major manufacturing complexes became fortresses, and repeated German attempts to capture each of them were only partially successful. In October, the *Wehrmacht* finally occupied portions of the Tank Factory, the Barricades arms plant and the Red October steel works, but at tremendous cost. By mid-November Chuikov had reached breaking

point. On the 19th, however, the thunder of Red Army guns meant that Zhukov's great counter-offensive was under way.

TURNING POINT IN THE WAR

The destruction of the German Sixth Army at Stalingrad proved to be one of the turning points of World War II. When von Paulus surrendered his shattered army, more than 750,000 casualties had been sustained on both sides. Over 100,000 Germans were taken prisoner, and only a small fraction of these ever returned home.

Moulded in the crucible of Stalingrad, the 62nd Army was later renamed the Eighth Guards Army, a fitting tribute to its heroic sacrifice during the stand at the Volga. Chuikov led his troops during the fighting in the Ukraine and Poland in 1944. In the spring of 1945 the Eighth Guards Army was the spearhead of Zhukov's 1st Belorussian Front during the capture of Berlin, the German capital. After the war, Chuikov served as supreme commander of Red Army troops in Germany and as the highest ranking inspector general in the ministry of defence. He died in 1982 and is buried on Mamayev Kurgan.

Today, on top of the hill, a massive figure of Mother Russia completed in 1967 towers 53m (171.6ft). She faces westward and holds aloft a stainless steel sword weighing 14 tonnes.

RED ARMY SNIPERS

- •**FOUNDED: 1942**
- •**STRENGTH: 50,000**
- •**THEATRE: EASTERN FRONT**

In September 1941 elements of the German 465th Infantry Regiment were ordered to advance against Red Army positions to their front. As they moved forward through a thickly wooded area the Germans came under fire from an unseen enemy, and in a matter of hours 75 were dead and 25 wounded. The cause of the calamity, according to German sources, was the accurate fire and effective camouflage of 'tree snipers'. As early as the 1920s the high command of the Soviet military had recognized the value of snipers, not only as a means of inflicting casualties on the enemy, but also in their role as intelligence gatherers. In 1924 the Red Army established several sniper training schools, and the graduates were eventually deployed throughout the ranks.

At the beginning of the Great Patriotic War, as the Russians have remembered World War II, squads of snipers were assigned to Red Army divisions. However, during the course of the war their numbers grew to as many as 18 snipers per battalion, or about two in each infantry platoon.

The Soviets themselves had felt the sting of effective sniper operations during the brief Winter War with Finland (1939-40). Finnish snipers took a heavy toll, and one of these, Simo Hayha, may well be the highest scoring sniper of all time with 505 kills. Another Finn, Suko Kolkka, had claimed more than 400 Soviet soldiers.

In the autumn of 1942 the battle for Stalingrad, a centre of Soviet war production and transportation on the west bank of the broad Volga River, was raging. The war-torn city, buildings

demolished and streets strewn with rubble, proved to be an ideal killing ground for Red Army snipers.

ZAITSEV'S KEEN EYE

The most famous of the Soviet snipers at Stalingrad was Senior Sergeant Vassili Zaitsev, called Vasha by those who knew him well. When the Nazi war machine rolled across the Russian frontier on 22 June 1941 Zaitsev was far away, serving as a bookkeeper with the Soviet Pacific Fleet at Vladivostok. One of many who requested reassignment to fight the Germans, he reached Stalingrad on 20 September 1942 with the 284th Rifle Division. Over a brief 10-day period he was said to have dispatched 40 enemy soldiers with his sniper rifle.

Dependence upon a reliable weapon and a keen eye were nothing new to Zaitsev, who had been raised as a shepherd and hunter near the village of

Clad in warm winter camouflage, Vassili Zaitsev (left) and two sniper comrades observe German positions at Stalingrad, January 1943.

Elininski in the Ural Mountains of Central Russia. As word of his exploits spread, Zaitsev became a national hero in the Soviet Union. He also established a sniper school in Stalingrad amid the ruins of the Lazur chemical plant. Eventually, he finished the war with a reported 242 kills before being blinded by a land mine.

Soviet propagandists seized upon the successes of the Red Army snipers and spread the news of their exploits throughout the embattled land. Some of the high scores of the sniper heroes were exaggerated; however, there is no question that they accounted for a fearful number of enemy soldiers. The most successful included Ivan Sidorenko, 500; Nikolai Ilyin, 496; (unknown first name) Kulbertinov, 487; Mikhail Budenkov, 437; Fyodor Okhlopkov, 429; and Fyodor Djachenko, 425. Approximately 2000 women were trained as snipers, and 500 of these died in combat. Ludmilla Pavlichenko was credited by some sources with as many as 309 kills.

SNIPER VERSUS SNIPER

Perhaps the greatest story of sniper versus sniper in military history, most likely a blended version of fact and fiction, occurred during the fighting at Stalingrad. Zaitsev's notoriety had extended beyond the Soviet Union, and the Germans were determined to exact revenge on this prolific killer. To that end, the chief of the SS sniper school at Zossen, near Berlin, a shadowy figure known by several different names but most often referred to as Colonel Heinz Thorwald, was sent to Stalingrad to hunt Zaitsev down.

As casualties among his comrades began to mount, Zaitsev remembered an admonition from his grandfather: 'The man of the forest is without fear.' He became convinced that rumours of the arrival of a German super sniper in Stalingrad were true. Years later he remembered their confrontation.

'The arrival of the Nazi sniper set us a new task: We had to find him, study his habits and methods, and patiently await the moment for one, and only one, well-aimed shot.

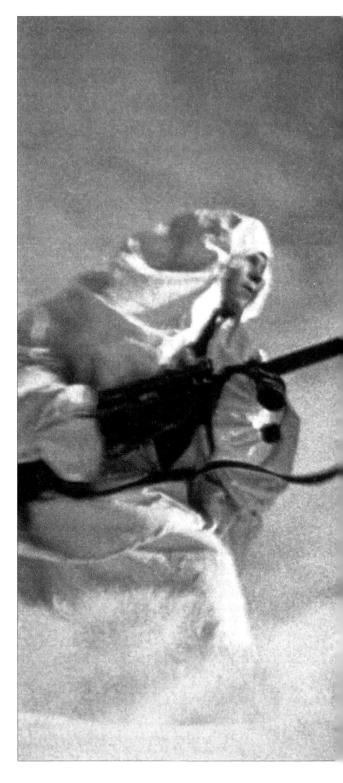

Armed with Mosin Nagant rifles, a Soviet sniper team struggles through a winter blizzard on the Leningrad Front, December 1943.

'I knew the style of the Nazi snipers by their fire and camouflage. But the character of the head of the school was still a mystery for me. Our day-by-day observations told us nothing definite. It was difficult to decide in which sector he was operating. He presumably altered his position frequently and was looking for me as carefully as I for him …

'At dawn I went out with Nikolai Kulikov to the same positions as our comrades had occupied the previous day. Inspecting the enemy's forward positions, I found nothing new. The day was drawing to a close. Then above a German entrenchment unexpectedly appeared a helmet, moving slowly along a trench. Should I shoot? No! It was a trick: The helmet somehow or other moved unevenly and was presumably being held up by someone helping the sniper, while he waited for me to fire.

A Soviet sniper prepares to fire on a distant target. By 1945, the number of snipers in the Red Army rose to 18 per battalion. Reportedly, they killed as many as 40,000 Germans.

'WHOSE NERVES WOULD BE STRONGER?'

'A second day passed. Whose nerves would be stronger? Who would outwit whom?

'On the third day, the political instructor, Danilov, also came with us to the ambush. The day dawned as usual: The light increased and minute by minute the enemy's positions could be distinguished more clearly. Battle started close by, shells hissed over us, but, glued to our telescopic sights, we kept our eyes on what was happening ahead of us.

'"There he is! I'll point him out to you," said the political instructor, excitedly. He barely – literally for one second – but carelessly, raised himself above the parapet, but that was enough for the German to hit and wound him.

'For a long time I examined the enemy positions, but could not detect his hiding place. To the left was a tank, out of action, and on the right was a pillbox. Where was he? In the tank? No, an experienced sniper would not take up position there. In the pillbox, perhaps? Not there, either – the embrasure was closed. Between the tank and the pillbox, on a stretch of level ground, lay a sheet of iron and a small

pile of broken bricks. It had been lying there a long time and we had grown accustomed to it being there. I put myself in the enemy's position and thought – where better for a sniper? One had only to make a firing slit under the sheet of metal, and then creep up to it during the night.

'Yes, he was certainly there, under the sheet of metal in no-man's-land. I thought I would make sure. I put a mitten on the end of a small plank and raised it. The Nazi fell for it. I carefully let the plank down in the same position as I had raised it and examined the bullet hole. It had gone straight through from the front; that meant that the Nazi was under the sheet of metal.

'"There's our viper!" came the quiet voice of Nikolai Kulikov from his hide-out next to mine.

'Now came the question of luring even a part of his head into my sights. It was useless trying to do this straightaway. Time was needed. But I had been able to study the German's temperament. He was not going to leave the successful position he had found. We were therefore going to have to change our position.

'We worked by night. We were in position by dawn. The Germans were firing on the Volga ferries. It grew light quickly and with daybreak the battle developed with new intensity. But neither the rumble of guns nor the bursting of shells and bombs nor anything else could distract us from the job in hand.

'The sun rose. We had decided to spend the morning waiting, as we might have been given away by the sun on our telescopic sights. After lunch our rifles were in the shade and the sun was shining directly on the German's position. At the edge of the sheet of metal something was glittering: an odd bit of glass – or telescopic sights?

'THE GERMAN'S HEAD FELL BACK'

'Kulikov carefully, as only the most experienced can do, began to raise his helmet. The German fired. For a fraction of a second Kulikov rose and screamed. The German believed that he had finally got the Soviet sniper he had been hunting for four days, and half raised his head from beneath the sheet of metal. That was what I had been counting on.'

'I took careful aim. The German's head fell back, and the telescopic sights of his rifle lay motionless, glistening in the sun until night fell.'

The supposed encounter between Zaitsev and Colonel Thorwald served as the inspiration for the feature film *Enemy At The Gates* (2001). The skill and resourcefulness of the Red Army snipers, whether embellished or not, remains a phenomenon which must be acknowledged. Those who achieved 40 kills were decorated for bravery and awarded the title 'noble sniper.'

One incident, perhaps better than any other, illustrates the level of dedication of the Red Army sniper to his or her craft. A German panzer unit, which had been pulled out of combat to rest and refit, reported being harassed by a sniper and sustaining casualties for five straight days. Finally, on a cold, clear morning a German sentry noticed what appeared to be smoke curling from the turret of a Soviet T-34 tank, which had been silenced for some time.

The smoke turned out to be the breath of the sniper, who had positioned himself inside the tank among the corpses of the crewmen, for at least a week. Surviving on the crew's frozen rations and thawing their water bottles beneath his clothing and against his body, this determined soldier had never intended to surrender.

ILYUSHIN IL-2 SHTURMOVIK SQUADRONS

- **FOUNDED: 1939**
- **STRENGTH 36,000 AIRCRAFT**
- **THEATRE: EASTERN FRONT**

The Ilyushin Il-2 Shturmovik was arguably the most successful ground attack aircraft of World War II. Certainly, the fact that more than 36,000 of the Il-2, its variants and the next generation Il-10 were produced between 1939 and 1945 bears testimony to the success of the aircraft in its specialized role.

The Germans came to respect and fear the Il-2, nicknaming it 'Black Death' and 'Iron Gustav'. It was known to *Luftwaffe* pilots by the rather unflattering sobriquet 'Concrete Aircraft'. Many Allied pilots who observed the plane fittingly called it the 'Flying Tank'. Not only was the heavily armed Il-2 effective against enemy tanks and armoured vehicles, transportation infrastructure and personnel, it was also very difficult to shoot down. Frequently, the Il-2 absorbed incredible punishment and safely returned to base. Much of the aircraft's vital engine and cockpit were reinforced with steel up to 13mm (0.5in) thick, which was a key factor in its survivability.

The pilots who flew the Il-2 were combat aviators with nerves which seemed every bit as steel-reinforced as the aircraft itself. Often, the planes were required to fly low and slow to deliver effective attacks against ground targets. Multiple passes were the standard order, requiring the pilot to subject his plane to concentrated ground fire.

Then there were the ever present *Luftwaffe* fighters, which took their toll, many times with attacks from the rear. Later versions of the Il-2 were improved to add a rear-facing gunner armed with a machine gun. The improved Il-2 was capable of defending itself in air-to-air combat, and it was not unusual for a Shturmovik pilot or rear gunner to shoot down a German Messerschmitt Me-109

The Il-2 was one of the most effective ground attack aircraft ever devised. At the battle of Kursk in July 1943, IL-2s accounted for hundreds of German tanks and AFVs.

fighter. The Il-2 was designed by Sergey Ilyushin in 1938 and first appeared in combat with the 4th Ground Attack Regiment days after the German invasion of the Soviet Union on 22 June 1941. Initially, Red Air Force losses were tremendous as the unit lost 55 of its original 65 operational aircraft. However, tactics were refined and soon the Il-2 was becoming a deadly adversary in the hands of a skilled pilot. Armed with either eight 82mm (3.3in) rockets and four 99kg (220lb) bombs, or 594kg (1320lb) of bombs alone, cannon ranging from 20mm (0.8in) to 37mm (1.48in), and its defensive machine gun, the Il-2 was capable of taking on the thick armour of German Panther and Tiger tanks and winning.

DRACHENKO'S GLORY

The most successful Il-2 pilot of the war was Junior Lieutenant Ivan Grigorevich Drachenko, who was one of only four men in World War II to receive the Order of Glory three times and be proclaimed a Hero of the Soviet Union. Drachenko joined the Red Army in 1941 and became a pilot two years later. His first combat took place during the epic armoured battle at Kursk. Seriously wounded in the summer of 1944, he escaped from a German prison camp and once again flew the Il-2 with the 140th Guards Ground Attack Regiment even though he had lost an eye.

Drachenko received the three Orders of Glory for actions during the summer and autumn of 1944. On one occasion he managed to return to

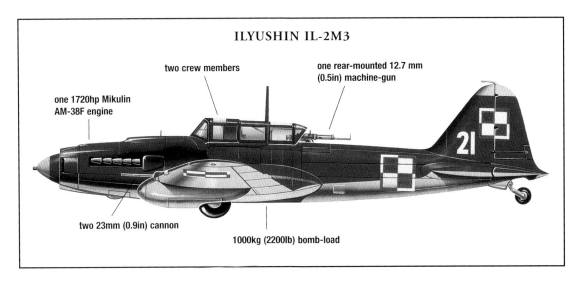

ILYUSHIN IL-2M3

two crew members

one rear-mounted 12.7 mm
(0.5in) machine-gun

one 1720hp Mikulin
AM-38F engine

two 23mm (0.9in) cannon

1000kg (2200lb) bomb-load

The IL-2 was built in greater numbers than any other military aircraft in aviation history. In 1944 alone, more than 16,000 were built.

base in his heavily damaged Il-2 after fighting off an attack by at least nine German fighters. In the same month he shot down an enemy plane and blew up a train on the same mission. Later, at the head of a flight of six Il-2s, he led an attack which destroyed three Tiger tanks and cleared the way for a Red Army advance on the ground.

Having flown more than 150 missions, Drachenko was credited with destroying at least 76 German tanks and armoured vehicles, six trains and more than 600 automobiles. He shot down five German aircraft to become an ace, destroyed four bridges and killed more than 1600 enemy soldiers.

Talgat Yakubekovich Begeldinov joined the Red Army in 1940 and graduated from aviation school in 1942. He rose to command a ground attack regiment, flew more than 300 combat missions and was awarded the Hero of the Soviet Union twice before ending the war with the rank of colonel. Lieutenant Anna Timofyeyevna Yegorova, Hero of the Soviet Union, was reported to have flown 260 missions with the 305th Ground Attack Regiment before being shot down. Decorated for bravery three times, the last of these was supposedly posthumous. However, after the war she emerged from a prison camp very much alive.

The Il-2 became a key component in the defence of the Soviet Union against the Nazi juggernaut and then during the long offensive toward the Nazi capital of Berlin. At a time of critical shortages of frontline aircraft, Soviet Premier Josef Stalin wrote to those responsible for their manufacture: 'You have let down our country and our Red Army. You have not manufactured Il-2s until now. The Il-2 aircraft are necessary for our Red Army now, like air, like bread. Shenkman produces one Il-2 a day and Tretiakov builds one or two MiG-3s daily. It is a mockery of our country and the Red Army. I ask you not to try the government's patience and demand that you manufacture more Il-2s. I warn you for the last time. Stalin.'

Soviet reports of the Il-2 squadrons in combat are remarkable at times. One relates the destruction of 34 German tanks by three waves of up to 30 Shturmoviks, compelling the attackers to withdraw. Another states that during the Battle of Kursk no fewer than 70 tanks of the 9th Panzer Division were destroyed by marauding Shturmoviks in less than half an hour.

The concept of the heavily armed and armoured ground attack aircraft, which was born with the Ilyushin Il-2 and the German Henschel Hs-129, survives in today's most modern close support aircraft. As does the pilot with nerves of steel who is willing to fly low and slow to ensure the destruction of the enemy.

UNITED STATES

When the United States entered World War II on 7 December 1941, its armed forces had been undergoing a period of urgent growth and modernization. This was born of necessity since the nation's standing army had been allowed to dwindle to 100,000 during the isolationist period of the 1930s. By the end of the war, however, the US emerged as a military superpower. On land, sea, and air, elite American units distinguished themselves in combat. Several of these, such as the US Army Rangers, owed much of their skill and development to the British soldiers who trained them.

1ST INFANTRY DIVISION

- •FOUNDED: 1917
- •STRENGTH: 15,514
- •THEATRES: NORTH AFRICA, WESTERN EUROPE

The oldest continuously serving division in the US Army, the 1st Infantry Division – known as the 'Big Red One' for its distinctive insignia – was formed on 24 May 1917, weeks after the United States entered World War I. The division was composed of troops serving in the army throughout

Left: During training exercises in preparation for D-Day, a paratrooper of the 101st Airborne Division boards his transport aircraft. He carries a bazooka anti-tank weapon and has strapped a knife to his leg.

the country, particularly along the border between the US and Mexico.

As war clouds gathered over Europe once again in the autumn of 1939, the 1st Infantry Division trained at Fort Benning, Georgia, and subsequently participated in a series of manoeuvres. When the Japanese attacked Pearl Harbor on 7 December 1941, the division was stationed at Fort Devins, Massachusetts. Following relocation to Florida, the 1st Infantry Division participated in Operation Torch, the invasion of North Africa. The 8 November 1942 landing at the port of Oran, Algeria, was part of the first offensive land action by the United States in the war against Nazi Germany.

After an embarrassing defeat at the hands of seasoned German veterans of Field Marshal Erwin Rommel's Afrika Korps at Kasserine Pass, the fighting ability of the American soldier seemed questionable to many. The 1st Infantry Division was thrown into the breach at Kasserine and ordered to hold the line in Tunisia. On 23 February 1943, when the Germans renewed their attacks in an attempt to exploit their initial gains, the Big Red One halted the veteran 10th Panzer Division in its tracks on two separate occasions.

BIG RED ONE GROWS

A month later, Major General Terry Allen led the division as part of a coordinated offensive across the Algerian frontier into western Tunisia, through the crossroads town of Gafsa and eventually reaching El Guettar, 32km (20 miles) to the southeast. The 1st Division raced to its objective but three days of

bitter fighting followed. Accurate artillery fire and armoured support held the Germans off, accounting for 32 enemy tanks. This was a defining moment for the Big Red One. From this point forward its reputation as a tough, battle-hardened unit continued to grow.

On 10 July 1943 the 1st Division landed at Gela, on the island of Sicily, in the vanguard of Operation Husky. At first, the Italians manning the coastal defences put up little resistance. A powerful German counter-attack the following day was turned back with heavy losses. Moving across the centre of the island the division captured the town of Troina on 29 July. At the conclusion of the campaign in Sicily, the division was withdrawn to England to rest and refit for the upcoming invasion of Normandy, Operation Overlord.

OMAHA BEACH

On 6 June 1944 the 16th Regimental Combat Team (RCT) of the 1st Infantry Division landed at Omaha Beach between the villages of Saint-Laurent and Colleville, to the left of the 29th Infantry Division's 116th RCT, which came ashore between Vierville and Saint-Laurent. The epic fighting at Omaha Beach was the most difficult on D-Day and the most costly. On beaches codenamed Easy Red

In this photo taken in Tunisia in 1943, soldiers of the 1st Infantry Division, combat veterans of Operation Torch, march to their barracks.

and Fox Green, the men of the 16th RCT were greeted by a withering fire and pinned down.

Colonel George Taylor, commander of the 16th Regiment, recognized the futility of remaining in the killing zone and shouted: 'Two kinds of people are staying on this beach! The dead and those who are going to die! Now, let's get the hell out of here!'

The 16th RCT was finally rallied by junior and non-commissioned officers who gathered small groups of soldiers and led them against the German positions guarding the exits from Omaha Beach. One of these officers was 1st Lieutenant Jimmie W. Monteith, Jr, who received a posthumous Medal of Honour for his actions.

'…1st Lieutenant Monteith landed with the initial assault waves on the coast of France under heavy enemy fire,' his citation reads. 'Without regard to his own personal safety he continually moved up and down the beach reorganizing men for further assault. He then led the assault over a narrow protective ledge and across the flat, exposed terrain to the comparative safety of a cliff. Retracing his steps across the field to the beach, he moved over to where two tanks were buttoned up and blind under violent enemy artillery and machine gun fire. Completely exposed to the intense fire, 1st Lt. Monteith led the tanks on foot through a minefield and into firing positions. Under his direction several enemy positions were destroyed. He then rejoined his company and under his leadership his men captured an advantageous position on the hill. Supervising the defence of his newly won position against repeated vicious counter-attacks, he continued to ignore his own personal safety, repeatedly crossing the 180-270m (200-300 yards) of open terrain under heavy fire to strengthen links in his defensive chain. When the enemy succeeded in completely surrounding 1st Lt. Monteith and his unit and while leading the fight out of the situation, 1st Lt. Monteith was killed by enemy fire. The courage, gallantry, and intrepid leadership displayed by 1st Lt. Monteith is worthy of emulation.'

By the evening of 6 June, reinforcements from the 1st Division's 18th Regiment had joined the 16th, which was conducting a house-to-house

Under heavy fire, American troops wade ashore in waist-high surf toward Omaha Beach on 6 June 1944. Elements of the 1st Infantry Division landed in the first wave on D-Day.

assault against Germans holed up in the town of Colleville. Eventually, these elements of the Big Red One had succeeded in penetrating the German defences at Omaha Beach with a lodgment about 2.4km (1.5 miles) deep. Heavy casualties had been suffered, some units losing up to 30 per cent of their fighting strength during the first hour. The towns of Formigny and Caumont were also secured.

AACHEN TAKEN

Six months of almost continuous combat followed D-Day. The 1st Infantry Division, commanded by Major General Clarence R. Huebner since July 1943, took part in Operation Cobra, the breakout from the hedgerow country of Normandy. The division captured the city of Aachen, the one-time capital of Charlemagne and the Holy Roman Empire, on 21 October 1944. Aachen was the first major German city to fall to the Allies. The 1st Division continued its eastward advance through the Hurtgen Forest to the Roer River, halting early in December for a much needed rest.

On 16 November 1944, near the town of Hamich, Germany, Technical Sergeant Jake W. Lindsey advanced ahead of his hotly engaged platoon, destroyed two German machine gun nests, forced two tanks to retire, and pushed back enemy

attempts to outflank his unit. He fought hand to hand with eight German soldiers, killing three, taking three prisoner and causing two others to run for their lives. For this action, he received the Medal of Honour. The division's December respite was short-lived. The German offensive in the Ardennes Forest, which became known as the Battle of the Bulge, required the Big Red One to take up arms again. In a tremendous test of endurance under the command of Major General Clift Andrus, the division was engaged for six weeks, from 17 December 1944 to 28 January 1945, in reducing the German penetration.

By the end of the war, the 1st Infantry Division had crossed the Rhine River at Remagen, participated in the encirclement of German forces in the Ruhr Pocket, and advanced into Czechoslovakia. Sixteen of the division's soldiers had received the Medal of Honour during World War II, while about 4300 had died and over 15,000 had been wounded. All told, the soldiers of the Big Red One had killed thousands of enemy personnel, captured more than 100,000 prisoners, and received more than 20,000 medals. The 1st Division remained in Germany as occupation troops for a decade.

MERRILL'S MARAUDERS

- **FOUNDED: 1943**
- **STRENGTH: 963**
- **THEATRES: BURMA–CHINA**

The 5307th Composite Unit (Provisional) is hardly a name which resonates through history. However, Mcrrill's Marauders is one which is instantly recognized by those who recall the exploits of Allied arms against the Japanese in the steaming, inhospitable climate of the Burmese jungle. Formed in August 1943 after the conference of Allied

Cleaning their weapons during a short break, soldiers of Merrill's Marauders operate behind Japanese lines in the Burmese jungle. The Marauders sustained heavy casualties during months of fighting.

Brigadier-General Frank Merrill, commander of the famous jungle fighting Marauders, cooks a meal during a stop along a trail. Merrill suffered a heart attack while in the field and was evacuated.

Members of the press dubbed the 5307th Merrill's Marauders, and the name stuck. In February 1944 the Marauders embarked on their first mission against the Japanese. On 1 March they began a five-day battle with the veteran Japanese 18th Division at the southern end of the Hukawng Valley, inflicting more than 800 casualties on the enemy. By the end of May they had marched more than 1200km (750 miles) and fought five major engagements while coordinating efforts with the Chinese in the capture of the vital airfield at Myitkyina.

The Marauders paid a heavy price for their success, however, taking 700 casualties. These losses, incurred by a unit which never numbered more than 3000, were crippling. Among them was Merrill himself, who suffered the second heart attack of his military career on 31 March prior to the Marauders' defeat of Japanese reinforcements at Nhpum Ga, which had been intended for the 18th Division. Merrill was replaced by the Marauders' executive officer, Lieutenant Colonel Charles Hunter.

OPERATION END RUN

Ravaged by malaria and thoroughly spent after more than three months of jungle fighting and the capture of Myitkyina airfield, Merrill's Marauders had expected to be withdrawn to recuperate. Stilwell, however, had other plans. With only about 1500 of their original complement fit for duty the

leaders at Quebec, the 5307th came into being as a long-range penetration force which would operate in similar fashion to the famed Chindits of the British Army commanded by charismatic Brigadier Orde Wingate. The 5307th actually trained with the Chindits for a time, and General Joseph Stilwell personally chose the new unit's leader. Frank Merrill, who had risen remarkably from the rank of major to brigadier general in a matter of months, was Stilwell's choice. Merrill had accompanied Stilwell on the retreat from Burma in 1942, and though his experience with infantry units was limited, he proved to be an excellent choice.

BRIGADIER-GENERAL FRANK MERRILL

After recovering from a heart attack, Merrill was promoted to major general and appointed chief of staff to General Simon Bolivar Buckner, Jr., commander of the US Tenth Army. Buckner was killed in action on Okinawa, and Merrill took command for five months He returned to the United States in the autumn of 1945 and held staff positions before retiring from the military in 1948. In civilian life, Merrill was named commissioner of roads and public highways for the state of New Hampshire. He died in 1955 at the age of 52.

Marauders were hurled against the Japanese defenders of the town of Myitkyina, moving eastward in a sweeping offensive codenamed Operation End Run. Along with three Chinese divisions, the Marauders repeatedly assaulted the 3500-man garrison at Myitkyina, but to no avail. Stilwell was unaware that the Japanese in the city were continuing to receive supplies and reinforcements.

By June 1944 a mere 200 of the original Marauder force remained. Before they were eligible for evacuation soldiers were required to run a fever of 102 degrees Fahrenheit for three straight days and then pass a review by a committee of doctors. Some of the men simply went mad. Eighty per cent of them suffered from dysentery, and typhus had become a serious problem.

Morale among the Marauders was so poor that their ability to function as a cohesive unit appeared to have been completely eroded. In May Lieutenant Colonel Hunter had petitioned Stilwell to disband the unit.

Finally, in August 1944, when their supply lines were finally cut, the Japanese surrendered after a siege of several weeks. During the fighting, 570 Marauders were put out of action by disease, while Allied forces lost a total of 1244 dead and 4140 wounded.

PRESIDENTIAL CITATION

The exhausted remnants of Merrill's Marauders were withdrawn, but not before their effort was formally recognized for the tremendous feat of arms that it was. Every soldier in the Marauders' ranks was awarded the Bronze Star, and in June the Marauders received a Presidential Unit Citation.

In mid-August 1944, Merrill's Marauders were absorbed into the 475th Infantry Regiment. In the 1950s the 475th was re-designated the 75th Infantry Regiment, and later the 75th Ranger Regiment. Thus, the Rangers of the modern US Army trace their lineage back to the gritty, tough, long-suffering soldiers of Merrill's Marauders.

Merrill survived with his weak heart and was transferred to a staff position with Southwest Asia Command. He was promoted to major general in September 1944, becoming chief of staff of the US Tenth Army and then its commander following the death of General Simon Bolivar Buckner, Jr, at Okinawa. He later served again under Stilwell with the Sixth Army and in the Philippines. In 1948 he was appointed commissioner of roads and public highways for the state of New Hampshire. Merrill died in 1955 at the age of 52.

US ARMY RANGERS

- **FOUNDED: 1942**
- **STRENGTH: 3400**
- **THEATRES: NORTH AFRICA, WESTERN EUROPE**

Just after 7 a.m. on 6 June 1944, a contingent of 225 men of the US Army 2nd Ranger Battalion landed on the coast of Normandy before the 30m (100ft) cliffs of Pointe du Hoc. Their mission, deemed one of the most important of D-Day, was to scale the cliffs and silence a battery of 155mm cannon which the Germans had reportedly placed there. If left alone, these heavy weapons could pound both American invasion beaches, Omaha to the west and Utah to the east.

Some of the Ranger landing craft veered off course, causing a delay of more than half an hour in reaching the sliver of beach, barely 10m (33ft) wide, at the foot of the cliffs. Allied destroyers raced into the shallow water just off the beach to pound German positions with 127mm (5in) shells in order to allow the Rangers to gain a foothold.

Immediately coming under enemy fire from the cliff top, the Rangers, commanded by Colonel James E. Rudder, fired rockets with grappling hooks attached and began the perilous climb. They also used 25m extension ladders which had been loaned to them by the London Fire Department. Many were hit and fell to their deaths below, but the Rangers kept coming. Finally, they reached the summit and scattered the remaining defenders. Then, to their shock, they discovered that the guns had been removed.

A pair of Rangers, Sergeant Len Lomell and Sergeant Jack Kuhn, observed some tracks in the mud, which had apparently been made by the towing of something heavy. Guessing that the guns might have been moved, the two men ventured inland across a landscape so pocked with bomb and shell craters that it resembled the surface of the moon. Soon they came across the cannon, hidden from aerial view by the canopy of an orchard.

Although a group of 100 or more German soldiers was nearby, the guns, pointing in the direction of Utah Beach, were neither being serviced nor guarded. The two Rangers set to work. They demolished the sights of one gun with a rifle butt and dropped thermite grenades down the barrels of the other two to disable them. In little more than 90 minutes the guns were put permanently out of action.

'RANGERS LEAD THE WAY!'
The Rangers' D-Day mission was accomplished, but in a very different way from the one envisaged. The cost had been high: after three German counter-attacks had been repulsed back at the cliffs, only 90 of the original

A US Army Ranger sergeant sharpens his knife. Among other exploits, Rangers scaled the cliffs of Pointe du Hoc on D-Day and rescued prisoners at Cabanatuan in the Philippines.

complement of Rangers was fit to fight. Still, they held their ground until relieved two days later.

Troops of the 5th Ranger Battalion also landed at Dog White Sector on Omaha Beach on D-Day. The Ranger motto 'Rangers Lead the Way!' was reportedly coined on the embattled beach that day when General Norman Cota of the 29th Infantry Division met Major Max Schneider, commander of the 5th Rangers. 'What outfit is this?' Cota asked as machine gun bullets kicked up sand all around him. When the response came that it was the Ranger unit, Cota blurted, 'Well,… it then, Rangers, lead the way!'

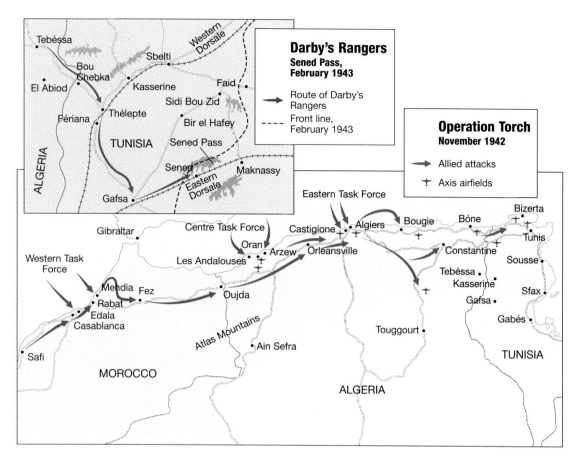

Darby's Rangers played a crucial role in routing Axis forces in North Africa with a hit-and-run attack on Italian forces at Sened Pass. For the loss of just one man killed and 18 wounded, the Rangers killed or captured more than 100 Italians and destroyed six heavy cannon.

The story of Pointe du Hoc is memorable for the heroism displayed by the Rangers, but it is only one of several chapters in the history of the elite unit, formed in the midst of World War II on 19 June 1942. The 1st Ranger Battalion had been authorized that spring, recruited from troops stationed with regular US Army units in Northern Ireland, and trained in Scotland under the direction of the British Commandos. Colonel William O. Darby was named their commander, and eventually several more Ranger battalions were to be formed before the end of the war.

Prior to his selection to organize the Rangers, Darby had served in the field artillery and in staff positions. He accepted the challenge with zeal and soon led the 1st, 3rd and 4th Ranger Battalions into action in North Africa and Sicily. A small force of about 50 Rangers had also previously accompanied Allied troops during the ill-fated Dieppe Raid on the coast of France in August 1942.

During the Allied landings at Salerno on the Italian mainland in September 1943, the Rangers earned acclaim for their swift capture of the Chiunzi Pass, 1240m (4000ft) high and overlooking the route to Naples, 19km (12 miles) west of the main invasion beaches. Once Allied forces had secured their foothold at Salerno and begun their drive toward the major Italian port city, control of the pass would prevent German reinforcements from reaching the front and facilitate the advance of the Fifth Army. The Rangers fought continuously for

three weeks, hurling back repeated German attempts to force them from the heights.

ANZIO LANDING

At Anzio the following January, General John P. Lucas, commander of the US Sixth Corps, ordered the Rangers to spearhead a two-pronged offensive against German positions. Operation Shingle, as the Anzio landing was known, had been designed to outflank the formidable German defences at the Gustav Line in central Italy and open the way for the swift capture of Rome. At first Lucas hesitated, and eight days after a virtually unopposed landing he ordered the 1st and 3rd Ranger Battalions along with members of the 3rd Infantry Division forward to seize the town of Cisterna.

The Rangers set out in the pre-dawn darkness of 30 January 1944, using the cover of a large irrigation ditch. All apparently was going according to plan, and no alarm was raised among the Germans. However, when the Rangers rushed from cover they were immediately caught in a hail of machine gun and mortar fire. German troops of the Hermann Goering Division and the 715th Infantry Division had sprung a trap, from which only six Rangers of the original 767 would return. Four months of difficult fighting lay ahead before Allied troops entered Rome.

Rangers were also active in the Pacific, where the 6th Battalion, supported by Filipino guerrillas, rescued more than 500 American prisoners held in deplorable conditions by the Japanese at the Cabanatuan prison camp on the Philippine island of Luzon. On the night of 30 January 1945, the Rangers and guerrillas surprised the prison guards and liberated British and American prisoners, some of whom had been in captivity for three years. Many of these were survivors of the infamous Bataan Death March, which followed the capitulation of American forces on the island of Corregidor in Manila Bay.

After the disastrous defeat at Cisterna, Darby

Left: Equipped with an anti-tank Rocket Launcher M1A1 (popularly known as a 'Bazooka'), grinning US Rangers look out their landing craft prior to the D-Day landings.

briefly commanded the 179th Infantry Regiment. He then assumed a staff position in Washington DC and returned to action as the assistant commander of the US 10th Mountain Division in Italy. On 30 April 1945 he was killed by a shell fragment. Posthumously Darby was promoted to brigadier general.

After World War II the Rangers were briefly disbanded, but with the outbreak of the Korean Conflict Ranger companies were quickly reconstituted. Throughout their history, the Rangers have been recognized as one of the world's elite combat units, having participated in numerous military actions around the world. Today, the 75th Ranger Regiment functions as an elite unit of the United States Army.

OSS DETACHMENT 101

- **FOUNDED: 1942**
- **STRENGTH: 1000**
- **THEATRES: BURMA–CHINA**

The first US unit created to operate for extended periods behind enemy lines during World War II, OSS Detachment 101 was formed on 14 April 1942. Its purpose was gathering intelligence, conducting sabotage, disrupting supply lines, and organizing the Kachin tribesmen of northern Burma into an effective guerrilla force against the Japanese.

The clandestine Office of Strategic Services (OSS) was the forerunner of the modern Central Intelligence Agency (CIA), which conducted various covert operations around the globe during the war. Detachment 101 came into being upon the recommendation of a report by members of the staff of General Joseph W. Stilwell, who was appointed commander of US forces in the China-Burma-India theatre and leader of Chinese troops under Generalissimo Chiang Kai-shek.

The organizing commander of Detachment 101 was Captain Carl Eifler, who was allowed to hand-pick the original members of his team. He, in turn, appointed Captain John Coughlin and Captain William Peers to leadership roles in the organization.

The original group of Americans numbered only 21, and there were never more than 120 US personnel in the field with Detachment 101 at any given time. The Americans trained the Kachins in the use of small arms, explosives, radio communications and evasion tactics, while the Americans were taught jungle survival techniques by their hosts.

BEHIND JAPANESE LINES

From their training camp in northern Assam, India, Detachment 101 infiltrated Japanese-held territory in attempts to destroy bridges and raid supply lines around the enemy airfield at Myitkyina, near the frontier with India. Japanese aircraft flying from the area were active in harassing the Allied airlift across the Himalayas to China, the dangerous 'Hump' route, which was necessitated when the invaders cut the Burma Road.

The first Detachment 101 operation was against a rail line and bridge along the route to Myitkyina in late 1942. A small group of 10 men, designated A-Group, parachuted into the Kaukkee Valley of Burma, blew up the

CHANGING SIDES

After a group of Burmese nationalists known as the "30 Comrades" assisted the Japanese in taking control of their country, members of the group became disappointed to discover that the conquerors had no intention of granting their country independent rule. When the decision was made to change sides, contact was established with an operative of Detachment 101, and a representative of the group was flown to meet General William Slim, commander of the British 14th Army. Negotiations were concluded successfully, and on March 26, 1945, the Burma National Army joined the Allied effort against its one-time benefactors.

rail line in 30 places, and dropped the bridge into the river below.

During the following year, a number of Detachment 101 bases were effectively operating in occupied Burma, while radio communications teams gathered intelligence on Japanese troop movements and provided information for targeting by Allied air power. Eifler was seriously wounded during a rescue operation to recover the crew of a

US forces from the OOS Detachment 101 and Kachin tribespeople move along a trail along the Burma–China border, 1945.

downed American bomber, and Peers was elevated to command Detachment 101. By the end of 1943, the unit's successes had resulted in authorization to expand the Kachin guerrilla force to 3000 men, and then eventually to more than 10,000. The unit was also provided with its own air transport planes for the insertion of covert forces.

BURMA SUPPPORT

During 1944 and 1945, Detachment 101 provided crucial support for conventional Allied operations in Burma, protecting the flanks of advancing units such as Merrill's Marauders and British and Chinese army units. The force also completed a more conventional operation in clearing the enemy from a long stretch of the Burma Road, an effort for which it received the Presidential Unit Citation.

Detachment 101 personnel participated in some of the most hazardous covert missions of the war, often parachuting into enemy territory and sustaining operations for an extended period of time. From 1942 to 1945, the unit killed or wounded more than 15,000 Japanese troops, captured 78 prisoners, rescued at least 230 downed Allied airmen, destroyed 272 trucks, 57 bridges, and nine trains, and provided vast amounts of intelligence to assist Allied air targeting and ground operations in Burma. A total of 27 Americans and 338 Kachin guerrillas were killed in action.

After the war, President Dwight D. Eisenhower recognized Detachment 101 as one of the most effective forces of its kind in military history.

1ST SPECIAL SERVICE FORCE

- •FOUNDED: 1942
- •STRENGTH: 1600
- •THEATRES: WESTERN EUROPE, MEDITERRANEAN

'The black devils are all around us every time we come into the line,' wrote a German soldier whose diary was found on his dead body after the 1st Special Service Force had moved on. With a reputation for fighting skill and daring which was unsurpassed during World War II, this 1800-man unit composed of troops from the United States and Canada was never defeated on the battlefield.

Formed in July 1942, the 1st Special Service Force, which the Germans nicknamed the 'Devil's Brigade', consisted of American and Canadian soldiers who were, for the most part, already experienced outdoorsmen. Through months of rigorous training at Fort Harrison near Helena, Montana, and other locations, the soldiers honed their skills in hand-to-hand combat, mountain climbing, skiing and amphibious warfare. Canadian soldiers accounted for approximately a third of the force's overall strength, which consisted of three regiments of two battalions each.

The men of the 1st Special Service Force held rank designations of the US Army, and their commander was American Lieutenant Colonel Robert T. Frederick, who, ironically, had once opposed the formation of a unit combining American and Canadian troops. Frederick, a graduate of the US Military Academy at West Point, had served in the army since 1928. He commanded the force into 1944, while a Canadian typically served as its executive officer.

'DEVIL'S BRIGADE' OPERATIONS

In the autumn of 1942, the first deployment of the force was called off with the cancellation of a commando-style mission to destroy hydroelectric facilities and installations in the mountainous terrain of Norway, called Operation Plough. The following summer, frustration once again occurred during operations to recapture the Aleutian island of Kiska from the Japanese. When the troops landed, it was discovered that the enemy had previously evacuated the island. Finally, the 1st Special Service Force was assigned to the Fifth Army and sent to Italy.

Fighting at the Mignano Gap in the rugged terrain south of Cassino, the force engaged in combat for the first time in December 1943. At Monte la Difensa, 600 troops scaled the final third of the 900m (3000ft) mountain in a remarkable feat. At times, the rocky outcroppings were virtually perpendicular to the ground. Under cover of darkness the attackers moved into position to assault

Standing up and hooking up, soldiers of the First Special Service Force prepare for a training jump. The rigorous exercises the soldiers endured paid off during combat deployment in Italy.

a German force occupying the summit. With first light a fierce battle erupted, and casualties were high on both sides.

'When we first got to the top and were pinned down I ran a little way and lay down beside a soldier and talked to him for a long time before I found out that he was dead,' one member of the force related. 'I recall borrowing Captain Border's rifle when I came across him in a kneeling position observing the enemy through binoculars on the opposite ridge. When I returned with his rifle, some 30 minutes later, he was dead with a sniper's bullet in the head.'

One Allied officer was killed when he stepped forward to accept the surrender of a group of Germans waving a white flag. As he approached the enemy soldiers one of them raised a weapon and shot the officer in the face. The entire group of Germans was mowed down, and from the on the men of the 1st Special Service Force rarely took prisoners unless specifically instructed to do so. The mountain was captured, and the men of the Devil's Brigade held off German counter-attacks for three days, suffering 511 casualties.

Other actions followed in the mountainous terrain of the Camino Hills, including the capture of Monte la Remetanea in early December, Monte Sammucro on Christmas Day and Monte Vischiataro on 8 January 1944. Casualties in some formations ran as high as 77 per cent during weeks of continuous fighting, and without respite the force was redeployed to the Anzio beachhead on 1 February.

Operation Shingle, as the Allied landing at Anzio was called, had been intended as a lightning strike beyond the flank of the German forces ensconced in the mountains of central Italy at the Gustav Line. The bold offensive was to brush aside enemy resistance and open the road to Rome. Instead, it became a costly and protracted affair. During the difficult fighting at Anzio, the 1st Special Service Force earned its Devil's Brigade nickname, operating against the Germans for a stretch of 99 continuous days.

'THE WORST IS YET TO COME'

Often conducting raids and ambushes under the cover of darkness, the men of the force, their faces blackened with boot polish, stealthily approached German positions and slit the throats of enemy soldiers with their familiar V-42 fighting knives. They often left demoralizing calling cards which read in German: 'The Worst Is Yet To Come'.

In the spring of 1944 the Devil's Brigade attacked German positions on the route to Rome and secured several vital bridges to facilitate the drive to capture the Italian capital. Elements of the force entered Rome in the pre-dawn hours of 4 June 1944, the vanguard of the Allied army which captured the Eternal City.

In August the Devil's Brigade landed on the coast of southern France during Operation Dragoon, contributing to the advance of Allied forces in the mountainous country along the border between France and Italy. By December, however, the tired unit had suffered casualties in its multiple engagements which amounted to a staggering 60 per cent of strength. The lack of available replacements precipitated the decision to disband the force. Many of the soldiers were reassigned to airborne units, while some fought with the 474th Infantry Regiment of the US Third Army.

Frederick rose to the rank of major general and went on to command the

The distinctive badge of the First Special Service Force, or the Devil's Brigade as it came to be known, honors its soldiers from both Canada and the United States.

1st Airborne Task Force and the 4th, 6th and 45th Infantry Divisions. He received an astounding eight Purple Hearts and was wounded more than any other American officer of the war holding the rank of general. He was also decorated with two Distinguished Service Crosses, two Distinguished Service Medals, the Silver Star, the Bronze Star, two Legion of Merit awards and the British Distinguished Service Order. He retired from the army in 1952.

The 1st Special Service Force is estimated to have inflicted more than 12,000 casualties on the enemy and taken 7000 prisoners. It is also credited with giving rise to the modern special forces of the US military, including the Green Berets, Delta Force, the Navy SEALs, and Canada's covert JTF2.

DOOLITTLE'S RAIDERS

- **FOUNDED: 1942**
- **STRENGTH: 79**
- **THEATRE: PACIFIC**

Five months after the attack on Pearl Harbor plunged the United States into war on 7 December 1941, the Japanese military and political hierarchy was stunned by reports that American aircraft had dropped bombs on Tokyo, their nation's capital, and four other major industrial cities in the home islands.

Indeed, on 18 April 1942 Lieutenant Colonel James H. Doolittle led a force of North American B-25 Mitchell medium bombers in the attack which shook the Japanese leadership to its very foundations. The Japanese leaders had considered the threat of aerial attack by American forces remote at best. They had also fostered a sense of invincibility among their people and their armed forces. Now, they were gripped by a sense of urgency to extend their defensive perimeter across the expanse of the Pacific Ocean.

That urgency led to an accelerated

operational timetable, which contributed to the disastrous defeat of the Imperial Japanese Navy at the Battle of Midway six weeks later. When asked by reporters about the location from which Doolittle's Raiders had flown, a beaming President Franklin D. Roosevelt responded that the planes had taken off from a secret base at 'Shangri-La'. The morale of the American people soared with the news of the attack, which had followed a series of major military setbacks, and Doolittle became a national hero.

ATTACK ON TOKYO

American military planners had begun seriously considering an air raid on Tokyo just three months before the mission occurred. They concluded that the only available option for staging such a raid would be to fly the planes from the deck of a US Navy aircraft carrier. At that time, the range of most carrier-based aircraft was 480km (300 miles) or less, and it would be virtually impossible for an American naval task force to approach so near to the Japanese coastline. Larger Army Air Corps bombers did have the range, but operating these from the pitching deck of a carrier had not been attempted before.

When the mission was approved, General Henry 'Hap' Arnold, commander of the Army Air Corps, selected Doolittle to command the squadron of 16 bombers and 79 pilots and air crewmen who were accepted as volunteers from the 17th Bombardment Group. The 17th had been chosen for one very good reason – it had enough planes. Doolittle was an Air Corps veteran who had served as a flight instructor in World War I.

Between the wars Doolittle gained notoriety as a racing pilot, winning the Harmon and Bendix cups in 1930 and 1931 respectively and setting a world speed record in 1932. He was also the first aviator to fly successfully the outside loop manoeuvre and to execute a take-off and landing with the use of instruments only. With the outbreak of war,

On the flight deck of the carrier USS **Hornet,** *Lieutenant Colonel Jimmy Doolittle prepares to affix a medal given to him by the Chinese government to a bomb destined for Tokyo.*

Doolittle left his position with Shell Oil Company as an aviation manager working on the development of high-octane fuels, and returned to the Air Corps with the rank of major.

Doolittle's squadron assembled at Eglin Field near Pensacola, Florida, and trained incessantly for the Tokyo Raid. Lines were painted on a concrete landing strip to match the length of an aircraft carrier's flight deck, and the crews were instructed to bomb their targets and fly on to friendly airfields in China. Time was limited and the take-off training was so important to the success of the mission that the crews were not given instructions on how to bail out should their bombers sustain damage.

Leaving the port of San Francisco on 2 April 1942, Doolittle's squadron was aboard the carrier USS *Hornet*, its planes lashed to the ship's deck. The *Hornet* was accompanied by the carrier USS *Enterprise*, whose planes would provide protective air cover for the task force, which also included three heavy cruisers, one light cruiser, eight destroyers and a pair of fleet oilers. Admiral William F. 'Bull' Halsey was in command.

B-25 BOMBARDMENT

As the flotilla neared a distance of 966km (600 miles) from the Japanese shore, the carefully laid plan, which had called for a nocturnal mission, began to unravel. Several contacts with Japanese

early warning vessels convinced Halsey that his ships had been discovered. There appeared to be no alternative but to launch Doolittle's bombers at the critical limit of their range. At approximately 8.20 a.m. Doolittle nosed his B-25 forward, raced down the *Hornet's* flight deck, lifted, dropped toward the windswept wave tops, and then gained altitude. One by one, the planes took to the air without incident.

Only two of the bombers managed to stay with the original flight plan. The others were scattered over many kilometres but pressed home their attacks. Doolittle dropped his incendiary bombs at 12.15 p.m. These were originally intended to ignite fires to guide the other attacking planes during the planned night attack.

One B-25 was reported to have dropped bombs on the Tokyo Gas and Electric Engineering Company, while another hit the Japanese Special Steel Company. Several of the American pilots flew directly over the Imperial Palace, and the confusion of the Japanese was compounded by an air-raid drill which was coming to an end when the bombers appeared. No message of alarm had actually been received from the early warning vessels.

Named for General Billy Mitchell, a tireless airpower advocate during the inter-war years, the B-25 proved to be a capable medium bomber in use throughout World War II.

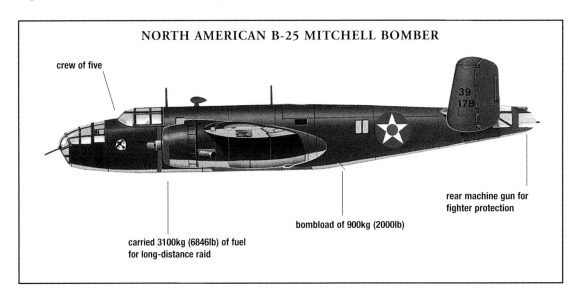

NORTH AMERICAN B-25 MITCHELL BOMBER

crew of five

39
17B

rear machine gun for
fighter protection

bombload of 900kg (2000lb)

carried 3100kg (6846lb) of fuel
for long-distance raid

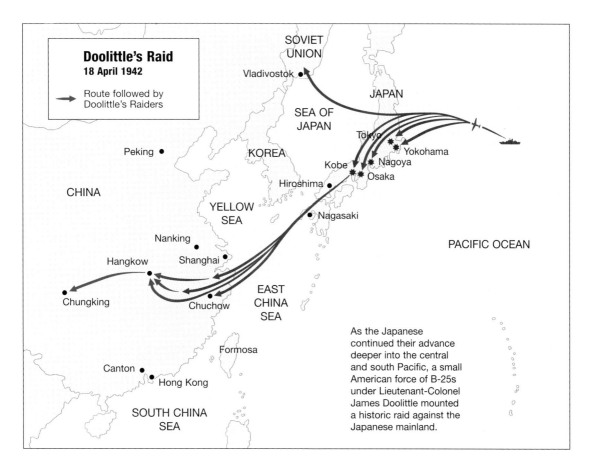

Doolittle's Raid
18 April 1942

→ Route followed by Doolittle's Raiders

SOVIET UNION

Vladivostok ●

JAPAN

SEA OF JAPAN

KOREA

Peking ●

Tokyo
Yokohama
Kobe Nagoya
Hiroshima ● Osaka

CHINA

YELLOW SEA

Nagasaki

Nanking ●

Hangkow ●
Shanghai ●

Chungking ●
Chuchow ●

EAST CHINA SEA

PACIFIC OCEAN

Formosa

Canton ●
Hong Kong ●

SOUTH CHINA SEA

As the Japanese continued their advance deeper into the central and south Pacific, a small American force of B-25s under Lieutenant-Colonel James Doolittle mounted a historic raid against the Japanese mainland.

On 18 April 1942 carrier-borne B-25s mounted an historic raid aganst the Japanese mainland, before landing successfully in Allied China.

As darkness gathered, all but one of the B-25s flew on toward China. A single bomber had consumed fuel at an extremely high rate, and the pilot elected to fly on to Vladivostok, where the crew was interned by the Soviets. The other planes either ditched, crash landed or stayed airborne long enough for their crews to bail out. Eight airmen were captured in Japanese-occupied China. Three of these were executed, and a fourth died in a prison camp. With the aid of friendly Chinese, the surviving airmen were hidden from enemy patrols, the injured received medical attention and the fliers were repatriated.

Although the Doolittle Raid did not cause extensive damage to Japanese industrial targets, its impact on the course of the war was tremendous. Doolittle received the Medal of Honour for leading the attack and eventually rose to the rank of lieutenant general. He commanded the 12th Air Force in North Africa, the 15th Air Force in Italy, and the Eighth Air Force in England. His order which altered American fighter tactics, sending them in pursuit of German fighters rather than remaining in defensive positions around bomber formations, inflicted heavy losses on the *Luftwaffe* and hastened Allied control of the skies over Western Europe. World War II ended as he was transferring the Eighth Air Force to the Pacific.

After the war, Doolittle returned to an executive position with Shell Oil and remained in the Reserves until retiring from both in 1959.

In 1985, President Ronald Reagan promoted him to four-star rank (retired). The general died in 1993 at the age of 96.

UNDERWATER DEMOLITION TEAMS

- **FOUNDED: 1942**
- **STRENGTH: 3500**
- **THEATRES: WESTERN EUROPE, PACIFIC**

The Underwater Demolition Teams (UDT) of the United States Navy came into being due to the need for reconnaissance and demolition on the shores of enemy-held islands and coastlines. The forerunners of today's elite Navy Sea-Air-Land teams (SEAL), the UDTs were an outgrowth of the Navy Bomb Disposal School, which was founded in the autumn of 1942, in Washington DC.

In early 1943, the organizer of the Navy Bomb Disposal School, Lieutenant Commander Draper Kauffman, had also assisted in the organization of a similar US Army school at Aberdeen, Maryland. By June of that year he had gained enough support to establish the UDT School in Fort Pierce, Florida, and attracted 500 initial recruits, most of whom were from the Navy Construction Battalions, popularly known as the Seabees. Some British Commandos and US Army Rangers were also among the original students and instructors at the school.

Preparing demolition charges, a shirtless member of an Underwater Demolition Team gathers his gear for the next mission.

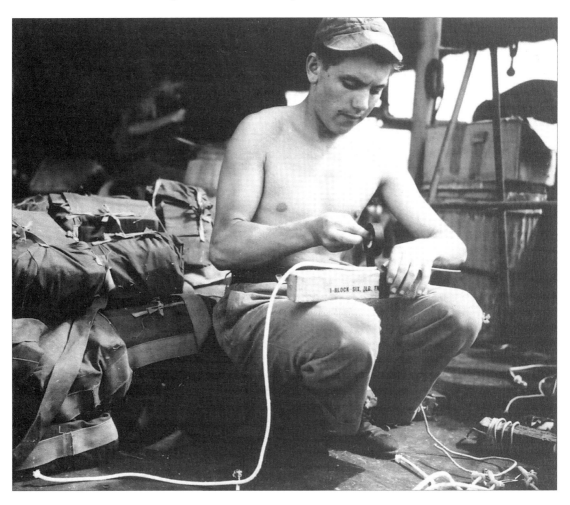

Those recruits who completed a rigorous eight-week training programme were originally intended for operations against the coastline of Nazi-occupied France. The UDT teams did perform heroic work on D-Day and during the invasion of southern France; however, they were also deployed for much more extensive operations in the Pacific theatre.

In Europe, UDT teams were deployed in darkness with the first wave of assault troops and cleared beach obstacles, while in the Pacific the UDTs hit the beach typically in daylight. In company with naval gunfire support personnel, they cleared beach obstacles and performed reconnaissance. A total of 31 UDT teams were constituted during World War II, and their organizational structure differed in the theatres as well. The need for effective demolition of beach obstacles, whether natural or man-made, became painfully obvious with the landing of US Marines at Tarawa in the Gilbert Islands in November 1943. Many of the landing craft carrying the assault troops became hung up on an extensive coral reef, forcing the Marines to wade the final metres to the beach under withering Japanese fire. Had UDT teams been available to blast passages through the reef, casualties at Tarawa might have been substantially lower.

KWAJALEIN INVASION

The first UDT deployment occurred during the American landings on the Pacific island of Kwajalein in the Marshalls in February, 1944. Despite difficulties with drone boats, which were steered by remote control, the UDT men reported that the invasion beach at Kwajalein was essentially clear of obstacles and that no barrier reef existed to interfere with the landing craft.

On 14 June, the eve of the invasion of the island of Saipan in the Marianas, Kauffman received his second Navy Cross for leading one of two 96-man UDT teams during a daylight reconnaissance of the invasion beach. The other team, commanded by Lieutenant Richard F. Burke, was brought with Kauffman's UDT 5 to the area aboard destroyer transports. The teams arrived on the invasion beach at dawn, dropping a pair of swimmers with a marker buoy. One swimmer went straight for the

LESSON APPLIED

When US Marines attempted to land at Tarawa Atoll in the Gilbert Islands in November 1943, they encountered an unforeseen obstacle. A substantial coral reef barred the approach to the beaches for many of the Marine landing craft, and the occupants were obliged to wade across a lagoon under withering Japanese fire. One solution to the problem was the formation of the Underwater Demolition Teams which could blast openings in the coral with high explosives and allow landing craft to disgorge assault troops directly onto the beach. The UDTs also dealt effectively with manmade obstacles intended to hamper landings.

beach to measure the distance from the buoy, while the other sounded the depths for accurate measurements. The following day, the UDT teams returned with explosives to blast paths through the island's reef.

A barrage of naval gunfire offered some protection for the swimmers, but Japanese mortar fire killed four and wounded five. Following the successful landings at Saipan, Admiral Richmond Kelly Turner, commander of the amphibious force, said of the UDTs: 'Their skill, determination and courage are deserving of the highest praise.'

UDT HELP ON D-DAY

At Omaha and Utah beaches in Normandy, the UDT teams performed significant work on D-Day, using 1kg (2lb) explosive charges to clear a variety of German obstacles, such as concrete and steel tetrahedra, Belgian Gates and teller mines. The UDT teams at both beaches consisted of seven Navy men and five Army engineers. The ordeal at Omaha was greater than that at Utah due to a heavier concentration of obstacles, stronger German defensive fire, and the rising tide. Casualties among the 16 UDT teams at Omaha were 31 killed and 60 wounded, just over 50 per cent, while six were killed and 11 wounded among the 11 UDT teams deployed at Utah Beach.

At Omaha, just as it approached the beach, one entire team was killed by a direct hit on its landing craft. The intrepid men of another team had set

Left: Paddling their dinghy toward the shore, the four-man Underwater Demolition Team became expert in various methods of clearing beach obstacles.

their charges but were unable to get clear before a German shell exploded and detonated all of the charges simultaneously, killing every man but one. Nevertheless, five large gaps and three smaller ones were successfully blown among the beach obstacles.

The participants in the Omaha Beach operation earned the Presidential Unit Citation, while those at Utah Beach were awarded the Navy Unit Commendation. Seven Navy Crosses were awarded for bravery.

Kauffman continued to serve in the Pacific, leading a reconnaissance of the landing beach at Tinian in the Marianas, and participating in the assaults on Iwo Jima and Okinawa. A career Navy man, he rose to the rank of rear admiral and held various staff positions, including that of Chief of the Strategic Plans and Policy Division. In 1965 he became the 44th Superintendent of the US Naval Academy at Annapolis. Kauffman retired in 1973 and died in 1979 at the age of 68.

101ST AIRBORNE DIVISION

- •FOUNDED: 1942
- •STRENGTH: 8200
- •THEATRE: WESTERN EUROPE

The stakes could not have been higher for a military unit entering combat for the first time. The troopers of the 101st Airborne Division had trained for nearly two years, and their baptism of fire was to be a crucial role in the invasion of Normandy, 6 June 1944.

Elements of the 101st were to parachute behind German lines on Utah Beach and secure four narrow causeways which traversed the marshy ground just off the exits from the beach. Key bridges across the Douve River were also to be seized or destroyed as the situation dictated. The 101st was to hold its positions until relieved by the 4th Infantry Division advancing from Utah Beach.

BATTLE FOR UTAH BEACH

In the pre-dawn hours of D-Day, however, the combat debut appeared to get off to an inauspicious start. Buffeted by high winds and scattered by anti-aircraft fire, the transport planes disgorged their human cargoes across a wide area. As many as 1500 of the division's 6600 men came down outside their assigned operating zone. One battalion was so scattered that it was unable to participate in any action on D-Day as a cohesive unit. One transport dropped an entire stick of paratroopers over the English Channel, where they drowned to a man.

Nevertheless, ad hoc groups of troopers, some consisting of men of both the 101st and another airborne division, the 82nd, took action. Lieutenant Colonel Robert G. Cole, for example, assembled a mixed force of 75 soldiers, seized one of the vital causeways, and decimated a German unit retreating across it from Utah Beach. By 1 p.m., troops of the 8th Infantry Regiment had completed the successful link-up.

EASY COMPANY

Apart from the capture of the causeways, another major reason for the success of the landings at Utah Beach was the decisive action of 101st troopers from Company E, 2nd Battalion, 506th Parachute Infantry Regiment, under the command of Lieutenant Richard Winters. Decades later, this unit would receive acclaim as the subject of the landmark history *Band of Brothers* by the late Stephen Ambrose. Winters and a dozen troopers attacked a heavily defended battery of four 105mm guns positioned at a large farmhouse named Brecourt Manor, which were firing on Utah Beach and had been unnoticed during pre-invasion reconnaissance. Over a three-hour period, Winters and his men methodically and in textbook fashion disabled three of the guns, which had been pre-sighted to fire directly down one of the causeways. In the process, they killed 15 enemy soldiers and captured 12. The fourth gun was silenced by a detachment from Company D. Four paratroopers were killed and two wounded. The assault on Brecourt Manor is still taught today at the United States Military Academy as a classic implementation of the tactic of fire and manoeuvre.

THE FARMHOUSE CHARGE

By 10 June, units of the 101st were heavily engaged in the fight for control of the Norman town of Carentan. Lieutenant Colonel Cole and his 3rd Battalion, 502nd Parachute Infantry Regiment, were forced to advance single file across yet another causeway, marked at intervals by small bridges, across the flooded plain of the Douve. The move met heavy resistance from the vicinity of a farmhouse at the opposite end of the causeway, and under cover of darkness a few small groups of soldiers were able to reach the western side.

Annoyed by the delay, the next morning Cole ordered a bayonet charge against the German troops concentrated around the farmhouse. Cole personally led the charge as his 250 men ran the gauntlet. Firing their weapons and throwing hand grenades as they went, the paratroopers silenced enemy machine gun nests. The remnants of the German defenders were killed in hand-to-hand fighting. For his bravery, Cole was awarded the Medal of Honour. However, he did not live to receive the medal personally. He died during Operation Market-Garden in Holland three months later.

After three weeks of continuous combat, the 101st Airborne Division was relieved and marched to Utah Beach where ships were waiting to return the paratroopers

This private from the 101st Airborne Division is wearing the M1943 combat uniform. This newly issued kit relied on a layering principle that combined waterproof and windproof elements with additional layers of warm clothing – ideal for the cold winter of 1944–45.

to England. Rest and the absorption of replacements consumed the coming weeks, and preparations were made for Market-Garden, an ambitious effort to secure bridges over several rivers in Holland and facilitate a drive into the Ruhr, the industrial heart of Germany.

The journey thus far had been long and arduous for the 101st Airborne Division, which was activated on 15 August 1942 at Camp Claiborne, Louisiana. Although the US Army had maintained smaller airborne units for some time, the successes of early German airborne and glider operations, along with the emphasis placed on such capabilities by the Soviet Red Army, had convinced American military planners that airborne units could perform the role of vertical envelopment, seizing key positions and disrupting enemy communications and reinforcement efforts. With this in mind, the 101st and 82nd Airborne divisions were created; however, the great majority of the time both units spent in combat was as conventional infantry.

Originally commanded by Major General William C. Lee, the 101st was led for most of World War II by Major General Maxwell Taylor, who took over when Lee suffered a debilitating heart attack in February 1944. Training took place at several locations, the most memorable of which were the jump school at Fort Benning in western Georgia and Camp Toccoa in the northeast corner of the state, near the South Carolina border where the 506th Parachute Infantry Regiment received its basic and infantry training as a cohesive unit.

Unlike their deployment on D-Day, the jump into Holland took place during daylight hours and was executed flawlessly. The 101st, the 82nd and the British 1st Airborne divisions each were assigned bridges to capture to facilitate the ground advance of the 30th Corps eventually across the Rhine River as the vanguard

'HELL'S HIGHWAY'

The Germans, however, were by no means defeated. Intense counter-attacks took place for several days, the Germans cutting the road only to be pushed back by the determined paratroopers. The fighting was so intense and the casualties so high that the stretch of road came to be known as 'Hell's Highway'. At the end of September, the exhausted troops of the 101st and the 82nd expected to be relieved. However, they were transferred northward to an area known as 'The Island' and occupied trench lines reminiscent of the static warfare of World War I. On 5 October, Winters, now a captain, led 35 troopers of E Company against German SS troops attempting to infiltrate American lines. Winters killed a German scarcely 10m (3ft) away and, with support from F Company, his men decimated the Germans along a road adjacent to a dyke near the banks of the Neder Rijn River. Finally, in late November, after 72 days in the line, the 101st was withdrawn to France.

General Maxwell Taylor, commander of the 101st Airborne, salutes prior to entering a transport aircraft. Taylor took command of the unit when General William C. Lee suffered a heart attack.

of a larger thrust into Germany. The 101st was to capture bridges over the Wilhelmina Canal, the Dommel River and the Aar River, while also securing the town of Eindhoven and holding a stretch of road 24km (15 miles) long for the use of the 30th Corps.

Within hours the 101st held its objectives. The most vicious fighting had taken place at Son near the bridge over the Wilhelmina Canal. Jubilant Dutch civilians welcomed the 101st as liberators.

'NUTS!' TO SURRENDER

On 16 December 1944 Adolf Hitler launched his final ground offensive in the West through the Ardennes Forest. The initial German advance created a great bulge in the Allied line. The only available troops to stem the German tide were the depleted airborne divisions. General Taylor had been called away to a meeting in Washington DC, and the 101st artillery chief, Brigadier General Anthony McAuliffe, was in temporary command of the division. The troopers of the 101st boarded trucks for deployment to the vital Belgian crossroads town of Bastogne.

During their sternest test of the war, the 101st was pounded by heavy infantry supported by tanks and artillery. At the height of the Battle of the Bulge,

Dragging much needed supplies which have been airdropped to them, troopers of the 101st Airborne Division continue to resist German efforts to capture Bastogne during the Battle of the Bulge.

Bastogne became an island in a sea of enemy occupied territory. Still, the stubborn defenders refused to crack. On several occasions German units penetrated the defensive perimeter only to be cut off or thrown back with heavy losses. When McAuliffe was presented with an opportunity to surrender the surrounded garrison at Bastogne, his one-word reply resonated around the world. 'Nuts!' he responded to the Germans.

Eventually, on the day after Christmas, 1944, a spearhead of the 4th Armoured Division broke through the German cordon and lifted the siege of Bastogne. Still, there was no rest as the 101st fought to reduce the bulge in the Allied line. Not until 18 January 1945 was the division relieved.

By the end of the war, the 101st Airborne Division had fought its way through southern Germany, occupied Hitler's Berchtesgaden retreat, and entered Austria. In November 1945 the 101st was deactivated and its remaining members absorbed into the 82nd Airborne. During 10 months of operations the 101st received two Presidential Unit Citations and suffered more than 2000 killed and 6400 wounded. During the Korean Conflict the 101st was reactivated, and it has continued to the present day as an active division in the United States Army. Although it retains the 'Airborne' designation, the division no longer participates in parachute operations, deploying its troops primarily from helicopters as air assault formations.

BLACK SHEEP SQUADRON
•Founded: 1943
•Strength: 27
•Theatre: Pacific

A curious blend of fact and fiction, the story of United States Marine Corps Fighter Squadron VMF-214, the fabled Black Sheep Squadron, is one of the more colourful chapters of World War II in the Pacific. The fighter ace who led the squadron during four months of intense aerial operations from 12 September 1943 to 3 January 1944 was also an enduring, controversial personality.

Major Gregory 'Pappy' Boyington, a former Flying Tiger with the American Volunteer Group who had claimed six aerial victories in China and would end the war as the highest scoring fighter pilot in the Marine Corps with 28 victories, came to VMF-214 more than a year after the squadron's formation, on 1 June 1942 at the Ewa Marine Corps Air Station on the Hawaiian island of Oahu. The original pilots of VMF-214, known as the Swashbucklers, had flown one tour of duty from Henderson Field on the island of Guadalcanal in the Solomons and subsequently disbanded. In August 1942 the VMF-214 designation was resurrected on the island of Espiritu Santo in the New Hebrides with 27 pilots and Boyington as their commander.

The pilots chose the nickname 'Black Sheep'

Later shot down and captured, Major Gregory 'Pappy' Boyington led the original Black Sheep Squadron. Boyington was the highest scoring US Marine Corps ace of World War II.

because of the way the squadron had come together. A number of the pilots had flying experience, some of them with aerial victories, while others had only recently arrived from the United States and had never seen combat. Training time was limited before the squadron had to be operationally ready, but during their first two weeks of action from an advanced base the Black Sheep shot down 23 Japanese planes and claimed another 11 probables in more than 600 sorties. Five of their own pilots were killed, wounded or missing. It had been an impressive beginning.

BOYINGTON AND BASEBALL CAPS
During the course of two combat tours which included 84 days of flying, the Black Sheep claimed nearly 100 enemy aircraft shot down and about the same number destroyed on the ground, while eight pilots accounted for five or more victories to become aces. When the squadron ran low on baseball caps in October 1943, Boyington and company offered to shoot down one Japanese aircraft for every cap sent to them by a major league

Chance Vought F4U Corsair fighter aircraft of VMF-214 prepare to take off on a mission. The notoriety of the Black Sheep and their distinctive gull wings contributed to the Corsair's fame.

baseball team. When the St Louis Cardinals promptly forwarded 20 caps to the squadron, they received 20 stickers representing 20 downed enemy planes. In reality, the Black Sheep had done far better. They had shot down 48 planes, and 14 of them belonged to Boyington.

The fourth of October 1943 was a particularly memorable day for Boyington in the skies above the island of Bougainville in the Solomons. Escorting a flight of Douglas SBD Dauntless dive bombers, the Black Sheep pilots, flying the famed Vought F4U Corsair fighter, located Japanese Mitsubishi Zero fighter planes rising to do battle. Boyington attacked from behind, his stream of machine gun bullets shredding the tail section of the nearest enemy aircraft. He banked and took a second Zero under fire from above, then watched as the pilot bailed out of the stricken plane. A third Zero quickly fell to his guns, a ribbon of flame streaking from its right wing. Boyington had dispatched all three Japanese fighters in less than one minute.

Throughout his life, Boyington was a hard drinking risk taker who had sometimes fallen foul of his superiors in the military. Some of that reputation undoubtedly rubbed off on the Black Sheep Squadron; however, much of the reputation of the pilots as misfits or discipline problems seems to have been exaggerated. A popular television show of the 1970s also kept the bad boy image alive. One thing is certain: the pilots of VMF-214 proved themselves worthy adversaries of the Japanese during their short tenure in the Central Solomons.

TAUNTING

Boyington and the Black Sheep reportedly taunted the Japanese from time to time with Boyington occasionally bantering back and forth with English-speaking Japanese pilots or airfield personnel. One particular incident resulted in the Major receiving the Medal of Honour. His citation reads in part: '…Resolute in his efforts to inflict crippling damage on the enemy, Major Boyington led a formation of 24 fighters over Kahili on 17 October [1943] and, persistently circling the airdrome where 60 hostile aircraft were grounded, boldly challenged the Japanese to send up planes. Under his brilliant command, our fighters shot down 20 enemy craft in the ensuing action without the loss of a single ship …'

At first, Boyington's award of the Medal of Honour was thought to be posthumous. The Major had just shot down his 28th enemy plane on 3 January 1944 when he was shot down in turn, picked up by a Japanese submarine, and spent the last 20 months of the war in a prison camp. Five days after Boyington was listed as missing, the second combat tour of the Black Sheep ended and the pilots were placed in other squadrons.

On 29 January 1944, VMF-214 was formed for a third time at Marine Corps Air Station Goleta in Southern California. The squadron deployed to the Pacific aboard the aircraft carrier USS *Franklin*. When a pair of Japanese bombs hit the *Franklin* on 18 March nearly 800 men were killed, including 32 VMF-214 pilots.

Boyington received his Medal of Honour from President Harry S. Truman on 5 October 1945, was promoted to lieutenant colonel and then full colonel, and retired from the Marine Corps on 1 August 1947. He had also been awarded the Navy Cross for heroism in combat. Boyington struggled with alcoholism for the remainder of his life, wrote his autobiography, *Baa Baa Black Sheep*, and died on 11 January 1988 at the age of 75.

Today, the Black Sheep survive as Marine Attack Squadron VMA-214, flying the AV-8B Harrier V/STOL jet. The squadron has been deployed twice in support of Operation Iraqi Freedom.

FLYING TIGERS

- •FOUNDED: 1941
- •STRENGTH: 300
- •THEATRE: CHINA

Flying obsolete aircraft against overwhelming odds, the fighter pilots of the American Volunteer Group (AVG) made the most of their opportunity to become the stuff of legend. When the United States entered World War II on 7 December 1941, war had already been raging on the Asian mainland for a decade. Japanese aggression in China had killed hundreds of thousands of people and conquered large portions of the vast country.

In contrast to their Japanese counterparts, the Chinese armed forces were often ill-trained and ill-equipped. The sheer size of China may have been its greatest defence, since the Japanese could not hope to bring the entire country under occupation. The Government of Nationalist China, led by Generalissimo Chiang Kai-shek, appealed for humanitarian assistance from the United States, both publicly and privately.

Chiang knew that one of the greatest weaknesses of his military was the lack of an effective air force, particularly fighter defences. Japanese bombers roamed China's skies at will. Unescorted, they rained destruction on Chinese cities and inflicted terrible casualties on military and civilian targets

A Curtiss P-40 fighter of the Flying Tigers prepares for takeoff from a dirt airstrip. The pilots of the AVG inflicted considerable damage on the enemy despite long odds.

CURTISS P-40 WARHAWK

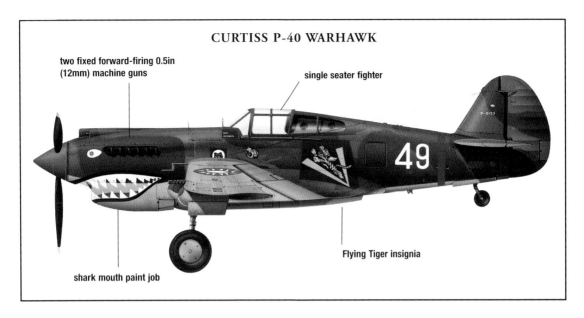

two fixed forward-firing 0.5in
(12mm) machine guns

single seater fighter

Flying Tiger insignia

shark mouth paint job

This Warhawk 81-A2 was assigned to the 3rd Pursuit Squadron, American Volunteer Group, stationed at Kunming, China in 1942.

alike. Something had to be done. In the spring of 1937, Claire L. Chennault, a retired US Army Air Corps captain, arrived in China at the request of Madame Chiang, whose husband had placed her in charge of developing a viable Chinese Air Force. Chennault had been asked to advise the Chinese Government in this endeavour due to his experience with fighter aircraft and tactics. However, at the age of 47, Chennault was partially deaf and suffered from chronic bronchitis. He held only junior rank in the military at the time of his retirement mainly due to his outspoken advocacy of air power. Unlike his famous contemporary, General Billy Mitchell, Chennault was not court martialed for his opinions. His career, though, had suffered what appeared to be irreparable harm.

Although Chennault set about his task with vigour and introduced discipline and improved tactics, the Chinese air defences remained inadequate to fend off the marauding Japanese. By 1940 it was determined that an all-out effort to recruit American pilots and obtain American aircraft for the defence of China were the only options left open.

TOMAHAWKS OVER CHINA

In response to the entreaties of Madame Chiang's brother, T.V. Soong, President Franklin D. Roosevelt was persuaded to allow American pilots to join with Chennault. In the winter of 1940 Chennault worked to finalize the purchase of 100 Curtiss P-40 Tomahawk fighter planes, which had been originally earmarked for Great Britain through the Lend-Lease programme but which the British had deemed obsolete and refused. He also recruited pilots from the Army Air Corps, the Navy and the Marine Corps with the promise of aerial action against the Japanese, base pay of at least $600 per month, and a bounty of $500 for every enemy plane shot down.

In the summer of 1941 more than 100 of these hired pilots sailed for China to become 'employees' of the fictitious Central Aircraft Manufacturing Company. These original pilots were organized into three squadrons, the Adam and Eves, the Panda Bears and the Hell's Angels. Having seen photographs of British P-40s in North Africa whose pilots had painted gaping, razor-toothed sharks' mouths on their noses, the fliers of the AVG decided to do the same. They went a step further and nicknamed themselves the Flying Tigers. An artist at Walt Disney Studios in California offered them a striking emblem, a winged tiger flying through a V for victory.

General Claire Chennault, commander of the Flying Tigers, talks tactics with a group of pilots. In the summer of 1942, the AVG was incorporated into the US 14th Air Force.

Two of the Flying Tiger squadrons were based at Kunming in China, while the third was stationed near the Burmese capital of Rangoon. The AVG met the Japanese enemy in combat for the first time on 20 December 1941, in an engagement near Kunming. As 10 unescorted bombers neared their target they were jumped by a number of P-40s emblazoned with the Flying Tiger and Nationalist Chinese emblems. Varied accounts state that at least four and as many as nine of the enemy bombers were destroyed.

Protecting the vital overland supply route, the Burma Road from Lashio to Kunming, was an initial task. When the Japanese overran Burma in March 1942 the Flying Tigers continued to mount

an aerial defence, withdrawing their remaining planes to China after conducting a fighting retreat. Always undersupplied and short of everything from aviation fuel to spare parts, the AVG could never claim more than 100 serviceable aircraft at any one time. However, the pilots employed tactics taught them by Chennault to take full advantage of the best attributes of the P-40.

SYNCHRONISED DIVING

The light, nimble Japanese Zero fighter was a deadly adversary, but Chennault knew that the P-40 was a rugged, heavy aircraft which could achieve a speed of more than 640km per hour (400mph) in a dive. The Tomahawk could not hope to outclimb or out-turn the Zero. Therefore, Chennault instructed his pilots to attack in pairs or groups, never alone, not to dogfight with the Zeros, and to initiate attacks from higher altitudes than enemy aircraft wherever possible. The Flying Tiger pilots

TIGER KILLS

Accounts of the Flying Tigers' fighting record vary; however, most estimates state that they accounted for approximately 300 confirmed kills and more than 100 probable enemy planes destroyed. Thirteen AVG pilots were killed, captured or missing in action during this period, and 10 more were lost to accidents.

also did their part in deceiving the Japanese, repainting the numbers on their planes to give the appearance of a much larger force of fighters engaged and often calling out to phantom formations during contact with the enemy to offer the illusion of greater numbers.

In July 1942 the Flying Tigers were incorporated into the United States Army Air Forces (USAAF) and designated the 23rd Fighter Group of the 14th Air Force. During this transition period, some Flying Tiger pilots remained with the fighter formation while others transferred to different air units or returned to the United States. The 23rd Fighter Group continued to carry the Flying Tigers moniker through the remainder of the war, and its appeal widened to include many more units than the original three squadrons.

Although the tenure of the original Flying Tiger squadrons was remarkably short at about seven months, their impact on the war cannot be discounted. At a time when the Japanese military machine seemed everywhere victorious, this relative handful of American pilots did its part to dispel the myth of the enemy's invincibility. The Chinese people learned of the fierce Flying Tigers, and their exploits were celebrated in the newspapers in the United States.

TOP PILOTS

The AVG was reported to have produced a total of 38 aces with five or more confirmed kills. Among these were former Navy dive bomber pilot Robert H. Neale with 16, David 'Tex' Hill with 12 and later six more with the USAAF, and Charles H. Older with 10 AVG kills and eight more with the USAAF. One of the Flying Tiger pilots, Marine Lieutenant Colonel Gregory 'Pappy' Boyington,

claimed six Japanese planes with the AVG and 22 more as a Marine Corps pilot. Boyington, the leading Marine ace of the war, also founded the legendary Black Sheep Squadron. He was eventually shot down and spent months in a Japanese prison camp.

Chennault returned to active duty with the USAAF, was promoted to colonel, and assumed command of the 23rd Fighter Group. Later, he led US Army Air Forces in China, and with the rank of major general was elevated to command of the 14th Air Force. When his former commander and rival, General Joseph Stilwell, was relieved of command in the China-Burma-India Theatre in October 1944, Chennault briefly served as theatre commander. After the war he continued to work with the Chinese Nationalist forces. Chennault died in 1958 at the age of 68.

MEMPHIS BELLE CREW

- •FOUNDED: 1942
- •STRENGTH: 14
- •THEATRE: WESTERN EUROPE

Nearly 160,000 Allied airmen lost their lives during the coordinated bombing offensive by the United States Army Air Forces (USAAF) and Royal Air Force (RAF) Bomber Command against Nazi-occupied Europe. At times the rate of losses among aircraft and crews was dangerously high, threatening the continuation of the effort to cripple Germany's industrial capacity and the morale of the German people.

Originally, in order to complete a standard tour of duty, American air crews were required to complete a total of 25 missions. However, in the spring of 1943 General Ira C. Eaker, commander of the US Eighth Air Force, raised the number to 30 missions due to a critical shortage of crews. During that period the number of bombers available to Eaker was rarely more than 100. In April 1943 a raid against aircraft factories in the German city of Bremen had resulted in losses of nearly 14 per cent, as 16 of 115 attacking bombers failed to return to base. If losses continued at such a rate the US daylight bombing offensive would grind to a halt.

TWENTY-FIVE MISSIONS

That spring, however, just as Eaker's necessary revision was being implemented, a Boeing B-17 Flying Fortress heavy bomber, christened *Memphis Belle* by its pilot, Captain Robert K. Morgan, made history. On 19 May 1943 the Memphis Belle touched down at its permanent base at Bassingbourne, England, following a raid on the German port city of Kiel, becoming the first American bomber to complete 25 missions.

A B-17F with the serial number 41 24485, the Memphis Belle began its service with the 91st Bombardment Group in September 1942, deploying to England from Bangor, Maine, at the end of the month. The bomber's first mission took place on 7 November, against the German submarine base at Brest, France. Morgan had named the Memphis Belle for his girlfriend,

Margaret Polk, who was a resident of the city in West Tennessee. The pilot and his crew were also the first to complete 25 missions, and all but four of these were aboard the *Memphis Belle*. The crew's 25th mission was completed on 17 May 1943, against the German submarine pens at Lorient, France.

Miraculously, though the *Memphis Belle* sustained some damage the plane remained airworthy, and none of those crewmen who manned it were seriously injured. The bomber was the subject of what has become a classic documentary film produced during the war and a rather fanciful feature film released in 1990. After World War II the *Memphis Belle* was rescued from the scrapyard when the city of Memphis paid $350 for the plane. For decades, the historic bomber was displayed in

The Boeing B-17 Flying Fortress **Memphis Belle** *looms behind two of the bomber's crewmen. One of the aircraft's 12.5mm (0.50 cal) machine guns may be seen protruding from the plexiglass nose.*

various locations around the city. Years of exposure to the elements, however, took their toll, and in 2005 the *Memphis Belle* was delivered to the National Museum of the United States Air Force for restoration.

Captain Morgan went on to command the 869th Squadron of the 479th Bombardment Group in the Pacific, flying the Boeing B-29 Superfortress. After the war he remained in the Air Force Reserve, retiring in 1965 with the rank of colonel. Morgan worked in real estate and died in 2004 at the age of 85. The bombardier, Captain Vincent B. Evans, stayed with Morgan for a second tour in the Pacific and died in 1980. The *Memphis Belle*'s co-pilot, Captain James Verinis, later piloted his own B-17. He retired with the rank of lieutenant colonel, was active in the furniture business, and died in 2003.

Other crew members included Captain Charles B. Leighton, the navigator, Technical Sergeant Harold P. Loch, the engineer and top turret gunner, Technical Sergeant Robert P. Hanson, the radio operator, Staff Sergeant Cecil Scott, the ball turret gunner, Staff Sergeant Clarence Winchell, the left waist gunner, Staff Sergeant Casimir Nastal, the right waist gunner, and Staff Sergeant John P.

Flying in formation, a squadron of B-17s plasters a target in Nazi occupied Europe. The B-17 and the Consolidated B-24 Liberator were heavy bomber workhorses of the US Eighth Air Force.

Quinlan, the tail gunner. Three other men flew aboard the *Memphis Belle* but did not complete 25 missions with the crew or participate in the war bond tour which followed in the summer of 1943.

During their historic seven-month combat tour the crewmen of the *Memphis Belle* were credited with flying nearly 149 combat hours over more than 32,200km (20,000 miles), dropping more than 60 tonnes of bombs on Nazi-occupied Europe and shooting down eight German fighter planes.

Ultimately, American industrial capacity began producing larger numbers of bombers, and more crews were trained to replace those which were lost. Allied long-range fighter escorts took on the Luftwaffe and protected bomber formations all the way to and from their targets. German cities and industrial centres sustained heavy damage, but the debate concerning the overall effectiveness of the round-the-clock bombing effort by the USAAF and the RAF is conducted to this day.

INDEX

Page numbers in *italics* refer to illustrations

PICTURE CREDITS

TRH: 6,7, 8, 13, 15, 16/7, 19, 20, 22, 25, 28, 31, 32, 34, 38, 39, 40/41, 42, 48, 51, 52, 53, 56, 57, 59, 60/61, 63, 64, 65, 67, 69, 71, 81, 82, 85, 88, 89, 90, 91, 92, 96/7, 101, 103, 106, 108, 109, 111, 112, 114, 116, 117, 120, 122, 124, 126, 132, 133, 136, 137, 138, 140, 145, 148, 152, 154, 155, 156/7, 158, 160, 162, 164, 172, 174, 177, 178, 179, 180/1, 182, 186, 187

Amber: 10, 29, 37, 47, 49, 73, 99, 127, 160, 166, 167

DeAgostini/Art-Tech: 23, 36, 50, 62, 78, 84, 95, 118, 123, 176

Corbis: 24, 135

Art-Tech/Aerospace: 27, 35, 44, 45, 46, 74, 75, 76/7, 100, 104, 119, 129, 150, 151, 168/9 170, 183, 184,

Getty: 33, 68, 130, 146/7

Popperfoto: 55

Will Fowler: 86

Süddeutscher Verlag: 94

Alcaniz Freson's S.A: 105

RIA Novosti Photo Library: 142